Por los desaparecidos y las desaparecidas

. . . for the disappeared and disappearing voices of the past and present, in affirmation of our commitment to them. The presence of their words among us amplifies the prospects of rhetoric, and fosters an understanding of what future rhetorics—and our study of them—may be able to accomplish.

"I observe that you do not hear with equal favor the speakers who address you, but that, while you give your attention to some, in the case of others you do not even suffer their voice to be heard. And it is not surprising that you do this; for in the past you have formed the habit of driving all the orators from the platform except those who support your desires. . . ."

Isocrates, *On the Peace*

The Rhetoric Society of America — Organized in 1968 for the advancement of the study of rhetoric, "The purpose of this Society shall be to gather from all relevant fields of study, and to disseminate among its members, current knowledge of rhetoric, broadly construed; to identify new areas within the subject of rhetoric in which research is especially needed, and to stimulate such research; to encourage experimentation in the teaching of rhetoric; to facilitate professional cooperation among its members; to organize meetings at which members may exchange findings and ideas; and to sponsor the publication of newsletters and reports concerning all aspects of rhetoric."

—RSA Constitution

Rhetoric, the Polis, and the Global Village

Selected Papers from the 1998 Thirtieth Anniversary Rhetoric Society of America Conference

Editor

C. Jan Swearingen
Texas A&M University

Associate Editor

Dave Pruett
Texas A&M University

LONDON AND NEW YORK

First published 1999 by Lawrence Erlbaum Associates, Inc.

Published 2020 by Routledge
2 Park Square, Milton Park, Abingdon, Oxon OX14 4RN
52 Vanderbilt Avenue, New York, NY 10017

Routledge is an imprint of the Taylor & Francis Group, an informa business

Copyright © 1999 by Taylor & Francis

All rights reserved. No part of this book may be reprinted or reproduced or utilised in any form or by any electronic, mechanical, or other means, now known or hereafter invented, including photocopying and recording, or in any information storage or retrieval system, without permission in writing from the publishers.

Notice:
Product or corporate names may be trademarks or registered trademarks, and are used only for identification and explanation without intent to infringe.

Interior Design by Susan M. Hagan

Cover design by Kathryn Houghtaling Lacey

Library of Congress Cataloging-in-Publication Data
Rhetoric Society of America. Conference (30th : 1998: Carnegie
  Mellon University)
    Rhetoric, the polis, and the global village : selected papers from
  the 1998 Thirtieth Anniversary Rhetoric Society of America
  Conference / edited by C. Jan Swearingen : associate editor, Dave
  Pruett.
         p.   cm.
    Includes bibliographical references and index.
    ISBN 0-8058-3294-7 (hb : alk. Paper) . -- ISBN 0-8058-3295-5 (pb :
  alk. Paper)
    1. Rhetoric—Congresses.   I. Swearingen, C. Jan.   II. Pruett,
  Dave.   III. Title.
  P301.R4714   1998
  808-dc21   98-56276
                                                                  CIP

ISBN 13: 978-0-8058-3295-2 (pbk)

Contents

Preface ix

Introductions 1

    Rhetoric, the Polis, and the Global Village:
    Now and Then 3
        C. Jan Swearingen

    Inclusive Rhetorics and Lost Voices 9
        Shirley Wilson Logan

    Race and Rhetoric: An Unlikely Tandem? 11
        Kermit E. Campbell

    Latina and Latino Rhetorical Issues 15
        Jaime Armin Mejía

    Redefining an 800-Pound Godzilla 19
        Jacqueline Lambiase

    Cybercommunities and McLuhan: A Retrospect 23
        Collin Gifford Brooke

    Seven Ways of Looking at Religion and Rhetoric 27
        Grant Boswell

    Rhetoric, Religion, and Social Practices 31
        Cheryl Glenn

Keynote Address 37

    Sarah's Story: Making a Place for
    Historical Ethnography in Rhetorical Studies 39
        Jacqueline Jones Royster

Selections from the Charles Kneupper Memorial Lecture ... 53

Rhetoric and Culture/Rhetoric and Technology ... 55
George A. Kennedy

I. Classical Roots ... 63

Pity and the *Polis* ... 65
Shawn Smith

The Global Village, Multiculturalism, and the Functions of Sophistic Rhetoric ... 75
Bruce McComiskey

Orality, Literacy, and Isocrates' Political Aesthetics ... 83
Ekaterina Haskins

Pudentilla's Anger: The Indirect Discourse of a Roman Matron ... 93
Margaret Imber

Advertising as Epideictic Rhetoric ... 103
Stephen McKenna

II. Rhetorics of Culture/Recovering Rhetorical Cultures ... 111

Unstifling the Rhetorical Impulse: Style and Invention in Thomas De Quincey's Rhetoric ... 113
Lois Agnew

Performing Conversion: Washingtonian (In)Temperance Rhetorics ... 121
Jill Swiencicki

Brave New World: How Alexander Bain's Educational Reforms Addressed Student Needs During the Industrial Age ... 129
Shelley Aley

**Facing the Audience: Reconsidering "Audience"
Through the Chinese Concept of "Face"**   139
   Pegeen Reichert Powell

**The Incorporation of the Indian Body:
Peyotism and the Pan-Indian Public, 1911-23**   147
   Scott Richard Lyons

**Hannah More, Lydia Sigourney, and the Creation
of a Women's Tradition of Rhetoric**   155
   Jane Donawerth

**Reconstructing Home in Early Feminist Rhetorics:
The Religious Discourses of Protestantism and
Transcendentalism as Sites of Production for
Sarah Grimké and Margaret Fuller**   163
   Melissa J. Fiesta

III. Rhetoric Tech: Defining Rhetorics in Modern Media and Electronic Discourses   173

**Are the Barbarians of Technology
Knocking at the Gate? Vico and Scientism
in Twentieth-Century Culture**   175
   Susan Giesemann North

**It's a Great Place to Visit, but I Wouldn't
Want to Live There: Virtual American Landscapes
of the Nineteenth Century**   183
   S. Michael Halloran and Gregory Clark

CyberEthos: *Ethos* as a Cybernetic System   191
   Kristie S. Fleckenstein

**And Now a Word About Our Sponsors:
Advertising and Ethos in the
Age of the Global Village**   199
   Sally Gill

**Dialectic of Technology: Critical Affinities between
Kenneth Burke and the Frankfurt School**   209
   Ed Cutler

IV. Rhetorics of Ethics and Agency   219

   Rhetoric, Democracy, and the Deliberative Horizon   221
      Alan Bilansky

   **When Language Is Just Another Commodity:
Enlightenment Theories, Erasure of Agency,
and the End of the Political**   231
      Doug Sweet

   **Nourishing Equality, Converting Difference:
Matthew Arnold and the Rhetoric of
Popular Education**   239
      David C. Plotkin

   The Rhetoric of Civility and the Fate of Argument   247
      Rolf Norgaard

Index   255

Preface

Formulating the topic for the Thirtieth Anniversary Rhetoric Society of America (RSA) Conference, "Rhetoric, the Polis, and the Global Village," was helped along by a number of conversations. Michael Halloran, Cheryl Glenn, Gregory Clark, Ross Winterowd, Carolyn Miller, Rex Veeder, Kathleen Welch, Robert Gaines, Fred Reynolds, Carol Poster, and Beth Kolko, among others, provided numerous helpful suggestions. The idea of a thirty-year reprise, revisiting key points in RSA's history, and addressing the question of the polis in ancient and modern times, gradually converged with the thirty-year span between the decade of the global village and today's rhetorical rehearsals for a political global economy. The 1996 RSA conference theme, "Making and Unmaking the Prospects of Rhetoric," found ample and well-received extensions in the 1998 conference's reprise of thirty years of scholarship and growth. Looking to the future, I invited colleagues to define key issues in new, just-emerging areas of rhetorical studies: Shirley Wilson Logan, Kermit Campbell, Jaime Mejía, Grant Boswell, Cheryl Glenn, Collin Brooke, and Jacqueline Lambiase. My special thanks to them for providing sketches of our future directions, and for their willingness to revise their comments as part of the proceedings introduction.

Carnegie Mellon University, the host of the 1998 conference, merits our ongoing thanks for local arrangements and shared labor in corresponding with participants. In particular, I thank David Kaufer, chair of Carnegie Mellon's English department, and Danny Josephs, the business manager and site coordinator. Their patience, help, and support—before, during, and after the conference—were essential to its success and to my sanity. CMU's Susan Hagan designed and produced our camera-ready copy.

Without the voluntary assistance of RSA colleagues, the expeditious review of the program and proceedings would not have been possible. More than 380 program proposals and 79 proceedings proposals each received evaluations from at least three readers. Many thanks to the members of the Program Committee and the Proceedings Review Committee for insuring that all program proposals and all proceedings proposals received attentive peer review: Collin Brooke, Kermit Campbell, Gregory Clark, Beth Daniell, Linda Ferreira-Buckley, Robert Gaines, Cheryl Glenn, Larry Green, Michael Halloran, Nan Johnson, Beth Kolko, Jaime Mejía, Jacqueline Lambiase, John McMillan, Carolyn Miller, Fred Reynolds, Jack Selzer, Ryan Stark, Jeffrey Walker, Hui Wu.

The final preparation of the proceedings manuscript would not have been possible without the expertise of the associate editor, Dave Pruett, of Texas

A&M University. Thanks to the Texas A&M English department for this generous support, and particularly to J. Lawrence Mitchell, head, for subsidizing my time at the Centre for Rhetoric Studies, University of Cape Town, where I completed the revisions and copyediting for the volume. I remain indebted to Philippe Joseph Salazar, director of the Centre for Rhetoric Studies, for the four-week fellowship and residency that provided research time alongside the lectures I presented there.

Linda Bathgate, RSA's editor at Lawrence Erlbaum Associates, has contributed to this volume an unusually up-to-date and wide-ranging knowledge of the field of rhetoric, attentive comments at each stage of the planning process, and efficiency. My thanks to her and to her staff for making the editing process pleasantly untroubled at each stage.

> C. Jan Swearingen
> RSA President and Proceedings Editor
> Texas A&M University

Introductions

C. JAN SWEARINGEN
Texas A&M University

Rhetoric, the Polis, and the Global Village: Now and Then

When I became president of the Rhetoric Society of America (RSA) I had no premonition that proofreading the 1998 proceedings manuscript would be completed while I was a fellow at the Centre for Rhetoric Studies at the University of Cape Town, South Africa. During August and September 1998, I observed firsthand an emerging democracy that only eight years ago was still disentangling itself from the habits and bureaucracies of the apartheid regime that had for so long silenced a multitude of voices. An entire generation of intellectuals, and hosts of ordinary citizens of conscience simply disappeared, and with them any public trace of the many antiapartheid rhetorics that quietly persisted within universities and among international political and academic colleagues. It was a privilege to be invited to witness many of the themes comprised in *Rhetoric, the Polis, and the Global Village*. The goals even now being formulated within the new South African Parliament include a number of projects discussed at the 1998 Pittsburgh RSA conference: language policy, educational reform and diversity, linguistic and rhetorical pluralism, and retaining national identity and coherence amidst rhetorics of globalization. The new South Africa seeks to create a unified society not defined in terms of racial, ethnic, or linguistic polarities. At the same time, it is forging a state and a culture that can recognize as equal—in Parliament, in education, and in print and broadcast media—over twelve linguistic and cultural groups. The European colonial languages, English and Afrikaans, are now joined by indigenous African languages—some written, most still largely oral. Television news broadcasts alternate among nine languages. Television and radio broadcasts of routine arts and news programs are transmitted in at least two and usually more spoken languages. Each of the languages now visible and audible in South Africa is also a rhetorical tradition, a set of practices that must be learned, understood, and honored by interlocutors and auditors. Among the current projects of the University of Cape Town's Centre for Rhetoric Studies is the creation of materials that will assist multirhetorical exchanges in government, classroom, and media.

What better examples than these could there be of the intersections among rhetoric, the polis, and the global village? The United States is a large space, demographically and geographically, yet we struggle with far fewer rhetorical, linguistic, and cultural diversities than South Africa. Or do we? Reflections on the current South African scene provided instructive counterpoints to contributors' discussions of the global and the local, diverging media and differences among rhetorical communities. In our retreat from Affirmative Action and related civil rights policies are we regressing into an unofficial, unstated apartheid? How much curricular and literary attention to African American and Hispanic cultures is being pushed aside in the wake of antimulticultural rhetorics? In many curricula, all that remains is a remedial program, and the often cruel partnership between remediation and assimilation. Belying the recently revived official story—that

> people of color and the poor don't read or can't read, ... thousands streamed into the Los Angeles Convention Center in late August to attend the Latino Book and Family Festival; books were being sold by the thousands—in English and in Spanish. ... Blatant censorship is a problem. Luis Rodriguez and Carlos Jiminez have fought celebrated battles in Illinois and California, where school administrators are alleging that those authors' books are inappropriate reading material for students. (Gonzales and Rodriguez)

Censorship cases now include successful elimination of Maya Angelou's *I Know Why the Caged Bird Sings*, alongside other works of African American and Latino literature. Many controversies have been provoked by revised American history textbooks that recount the details of slavery and early Southwestern territorial annexations.

Here rhetoric should step in to join what may seem broadly literary and cultural questions. For it is the rhetoric—real and imagined—of the literature in each case, the rhetoric of revisionist histories and in defense of multiculturalism and diversity that draws the fire. The rhetoric cuts both ways:

> Latinos do support Latino authors when they know about their works and get notice of their readings, says Helena Maria Viramontes. At an Arizona Barnes and Noble that was promoting her book, *Under the Feet of Jesus*, the store manager was amazed that grandmothers came, as did professionals and farmworker families as a result of an interview and book review. They wanted to see someone, "who worked in the fields and succeeded because she studied." But a thousand Latino bookstores cannot replace the need to make Chicano/Latino literature an integral part of mainstream literature. The titles have to be accessible to all, lest Latino literature continues to be "barrioized"—or nonexistent as far as most Americans are concerned. ... We've often wondered where it is that people get their ideas about reading and about their "right"

to censor. Perhaps they are vestiges of uncivilized societies that prohibited Indians and Africans from reading. To this day it is said that the indigenous people of the Americas are an oral people, with oral traditions. True. However, these societies also had great written traditions, which produced tens of thousands of books or codices before the arrival of Europeans. (Gonzales and Rodriguez)

Rhetoric about oral traditions, about ethnic populations, and about the literatures of minority cultures has sometimes suggested deficiency, second-class status, and only recently claimed voices. Among African-American and Hispanic populations in the United States are emerging rich literatures, diversified histories of rhetorical traditions, renewed commitments to more recovery of lost written and oral traditions, and reassessments of how we have analyzed what is already there. In addition to heralding new literary and rhetorical traditions, we are now providing reclaimed accounts, and reassessments, of what has been there all along.

Rhetorical scholars have become painfully conscious of the dangers inherent in contrastive studies of orality and literacy. The contrast can suggest the superiority of literate to oral, and, if only implicitly, the superiority of European to all other literate traditions. Contrastive studies of orality and literacy can simultaneously romanticize and degrade oral cultures and traditions. Such studies rightly are rebuked. Yet, abandoning the effort to seek improved understanding of local and global oralities, including the comparative study of rhetorical traditions across cultures, will obstruct an improved understanding of literate traditions as well. A complex blend of oral and literate traditions shapes the teaching of rhetoric in formal education and its extracurricular counterpart: the cultural transmission of knowledge and identity. Among Southwestern borderlands Mexican Americans, "women prize their tamale recipes but even more so pride themselves on handing down 'un-Americanized' versions to their children" (Mejía 9). "Clustered extended families, with women at the very heart of their control, push against" the foreign push of American educational ideals. For aspiring, middle-class borderlands Hispanics, "the Americanized push for achievement, competitiveness, profit, and mobility, . . . creates a struggle over cultural relevance, . . . a resistance against the loss of children to consumptive and self-absorbed attitudes, an ethnic situation of cultural conflict, self-doubt, and uncritical acceptance of destructive ethnic stereotypes" (Vélez-Ibáñez 138, 180). Studying the rhetoric of family cultures helps define formal education's objectives to teachers and students alike. The absence of such knowledge can lead to educational misfires on a grand scale: the overeducated who cannot read; worshippers of orality who cannot hear. Overly literate, literal readers of Frederick Douglass's *Narrative* miss the rich double voice, the ironies, and the sermonic rhythms. Studies of genre and performance in contemporary oral and literate rhetorics now extend globally. The range of historical and cultural appraisals undertaken by our keynote speakers and by the authors of the chapters included here provide a thirty-year benchmark. Our infancy, perhaps, is over.

Initial discussions of possible topics for the 1998 conference took many of us back to the 1960s, and in particular to 1968, the first year of RSA. Ross Winterowd remembers that the concept of RSA began in a hotel room in St. Louis, in a conversation with Nelson Smith. "After Nelson started a newsletter, Dick Larson picked it up, and George Yoos took over" (Winterowd). The year 1968 was not only the first year of RSA but also of student demonstrations in Chicago and Paris, harbingers of the darker sides of the great reforms witnessed within the sixties: Marshall McLuhan and Buckminster Fuller—among the members of the "Toronto school" of literacy and media studies; civil rights movements and finally legislation, the fruits of political and pulpit oratory at which still we marvel; the turn to process, problem solving, and classical rhetorical pedagogies that reunited rhetoric and writing instruction, if not speech communication and English departments. Where have we come on these topics and themes in thirty years? The voices of conference panelists and contributors to the proceedings volume begin to provide an answer.

How are rhetoricians thinking about literacy and orality, media, race, and civil rights today? Is Internet technology the latest stage in a happy utopian continuum, the next logical step in an ever-evolving Ewok global village? Or, this time around, is globalization a darker force? It may take more than a village to overcome the perils of the present global economy. As I flew toward Pittsburgh in June of 1998, these questions seemed to receive the gold seal of approval as bona fide commonplaces in articles appearing in airline magazines. "Breaking the Waves" proclaimed that "new digitally driven technologies are spurring a communications revolution that goes beyond Web sites and e-mail" (Fandray 14). Of particular interest to rhetorical studies, this article announced that "as the shift takes place, it will become increasingly difficult to draw a distinction between voice and data communications" and that the division between the public and private spheres will undergo total renovation (63). "Great Hype" included a subtitle: "this essay will (almost without a doubt) change civilization as we know it" (14). The proclamation that new technologies will end war, bring total global understanding, and foster unprecedented prosperity has accompanied every introduction of new media in the twentieth century. Historians of rhetoric and literacy know of some counterparts in earlier eras as well: the centrality of scripture and scriptural exegesis to religious movements, the Gutenberg galaxy, the cognitive consequences of literacy.

The Pittsburgh conference papers speak to one another not only of, but across these issues: of the rhetoric of student rebellions and other political protest movements; of the rhetorics of radio, television, and visual design in architecture and print graphics; of the voices of marginalized groups, genders, cultures, and religions who have forged their way into the collective public sphere, nearly always with great difficulty and inspiring persistence. We are reminded of the ongoing tenuousness of their inclusion. Our much celebrated multicultural world is necessarily a world of divisions, a world in which we must relearn the cultural, political, and spiritual value of common places as constructs, as difficult, hard won achievements that we covenant and contract *ad bellum purificandum*—toward the purification of war (Burke i).

We review more than seventy years' of attitudes toward new technological media. Radio, then television, computers, and now the Internet have each in turn been hailed as transforming humanity and even establishing world peace through improved understanding. David Sarnoff's predictions about radio in the 1930s echo I. A. Richards's definition of the purpose of rhetoric in the same era: to minimize misunderstanding. NBC founder Sarnoff put it this way: "Wars result from misunderstanding: when people understand one another they are likely to become friends" ("Great Hype" 16). Alas, this hopeful prediction, like Buckminster Fuller's hearty prophecies concerning the global village that would be created by television, and Marshall McLuhan's warm embrace of the Mechanical Bride, was followed by the darker side of each of these technological forces: Hitler's use of radio rhetoric, news-byte news, and the revealing-all narrative narcissism of contemporary television talk shows. Is advertising, which many conference papers addressed, an art, a capitalist evil, or the jewel in the crown of rhetoric? Should we be glad, or sad, when we read ads for the latest version of the *ars dictaminis*? Now available on CD-ROM through Model Office: "2001 letters that work—letters that guarantee that neither you nor your staff will ever again have to go through that awkward process of composing from scratch."

Yet that is where it all began, is it not? With the speechwriters and state historians composing from scratch, and being paid to do so, at least allegedly. The first rhetors brazenly borrowed from the poets, and from their religious counterparts, pieces of speeches and styles of speeches—time-honored ways with words that formed the headwaters of ancient Near Eastern and classical rhetorics. At least that is one version of where it all began. As we excavate and redefine ethnographies for rhetoric and culture, for rhetorics in cultures, and cultures within rhetoric, we "put our stories down" beside one another (Morrison 273). Together they form a more whole story, a more whole individual, a more whole culture, a more true story." Unfortunately, many forces today espouse dogmatically exclusive stories, and rhetorics of division. In June 1998, the vote against bilingual education in California provided the latest in a series of reactionary votes *against* affirmative action and bilingual education, and in some cases against the very words "multicultural," "tolerance," "pluralism," and "diversity." Colleagues in "the rainbow nation," Mandela's new South Africa, are astonished to hear of these recent developments in the United States, whose civil rights legislation has been a model and an inspiration to the long South African struggle against apartheid. This contrast takes me back again to the sixties and to the Headstart programs that were among the first fruits of civil rights legislation.

Seems like only yesterday I left my mind behind, lost on a gypsy highway near Corpus Christi, Texas, where in 1966, the summer after my first year in college, I taught as a volunteer aide in a new Headstart program. Veteran public school teachers formed the bulk of the teaching staff; South Texas English teachers used what was then the standard issue "ESL" method: lock Hector Garcia, age five, in a closet to punish him for speaking Spanish. We now seem to have come full circle with many parents and school districts refusing the insights that thirty years of pedagogical scholarship in rhetoric have brought to composing processes, second-language acquisition, and cultural rhetorical traditions that shape student learning. The demographics of conference paper proposals, and areas within rhetorical studies today, suggest how much that remains to be done. We received quite a few proposals dealing with Hispanic and Latino/a issues in South America, Mexico, Chiapas, Chicago, and New York City, but none on Southwestern Hispanic and Chicano/a topics. What about the rich and growing indigenous Chicano literary traditions that readers are flocking to find? Where are the studies we need of their rhetorical cousins and counterparts?

Alongside the reappraisals of technology and rhetoric in the global village today, the 1998 Pittsburgh conference addressed questions of variation and values across and within the rhetorics of many cultures. The keynote lectures and select conference proceedings papers celebrate the universality of rhetoric across cultures, including those cultures, oral and literate, which have no name for rhetoric. The introduction to this volume now continues with contributions from colleagues who characterize present and future directions for the specially featured themes of the 1998 RSA conference: race and rhetoric, rhetoric and religion, and rhetoric and technology.

Works Cited

Burke, Kenneth. *A Grammar of Motives*. 1945. Berkeley: U of California P, 1968.
Douglass, Frederick. *Narrative of the Life of Frederick Douglass, Written by Himself*. New York: Penguin, 1968.
The Editors of US Airways *Attaché*. "Great Hype." *US Airways Attaché* (June 1998): 14-16.
Gonzales, Patrisia, and Roberto Rodriguez. "Latino Writers Abound—If You Know Where to Look." *Column of the Americas*. Universal Press Syndicate. For Release Week of September 4. XColumn@aol.com (Friday Sept. 4, 1998. 9:20 EDT).
Fandray, Dayton. "Breaking the Waves." *Midwest Express Magazine* May-June 1998: 14-16, 63-64.
Mejía, Jaime Armin. "Tejano Rhetorical Issues: A Proposal." Panel Presentation. Rhetoric Society of America Conference. Pittsburgh, PA, 3-7 June 1998.
Morrison, Toni. Beloved. New York: Signet, 1987.
Vélez-Ibáñez, Carlos. *Border Visions: Mexican Cultures of the Southwest United States*. Tucson: U of Arizona P, 1996.
Winterowd, Ross. Letter to the author. Mar. 1997.

SHIRLEY WILSON LOGAN
University of Maryland

Inclusive Rhetorics and Lost Voices

Where do we start when we start to talk about rhetoric? And with whom do we start? And from whose cultural perspective do we discuss it? The 1998 Rhetoric Society of America (RSA) conference has served as catalyst for such questions in the historical context of ongoing multiple discourses in which rhetors have always used symbols to effect persuasion. The conference suggests to me that we need to continue to peel back the layers of assumptions we hold with respect to starting points, with respect to origins, with respect to motives, and with respect to agency. We need to develop new approaches to answering a number of questions about the nature of rhetoric. As we develop these approaches, let us remember that whereas the call for multiple cultural perspectives may be new, multiple cultures are not. Further, the catchy phrase "race and rhetoric" should be used in full awareness of the slippery meaning of the term "race." It almost always applies to those who have been labeled other, who are non-white and therefore considered different. I propose to use the phrase "race and rhetoric" here to call attention to the extent to which all peoples are raced and to call attention to the silent, unmarked category of whiteness; thus, when we speak of race, we reference all people. We also need to ask ourselves what constitutes African American, Asian American, Anglo-American, or Chicano American rhetoric. Does the classification depend on the racialized identification of the rhetor? If so, what are the distinguishing features of such rhetorics aside from this identification? Will such distinguishing features, if identifiable, remain consistent across rhetorical situations? These questions, too large to tackle here, are nonetheless too important to ignore. One of the skills we have honed in this current environment of politeness is silence. We need to be careful that the rhetoric of silence does not result in the erasure of whole rhetorical cultures. That is, simply not talking about certain issues and certain peoples can help to make them invisible. Many of the "race and rhetoric" issues discussed during the conference should continue to capture our attention, and engage our most careful thought.

What does it mean from a rhetorical perspective to presume the existence of a global community? As we broaden our understanding of this community, what will be the languages of public discourse? In the context of bilingual education debates, the English-only movement carries with it the assumption that public discourse in the United States must be conducted in the language of the dominant culture. The recent White House memorandum requiring the use of plain language, not plain English, in all government documents is an encouraging sign. Surely, the RSA can no longer concern itself solely with contemporary discourse conducted in English, given the country's rapidly changing demographics. The challenge is not to teach everyone the "proper" use of English; the challenge is to acknowledge the ways in which English is already multicultural. Even English-language discourse must be reexamined to take into account—not just tolerate or submit to—a broad range of American Englishes used by those who have not participated in the public sphere of policymakers. Those denied access to public debates have developed their own counterpublics with their accompanying Englishes.

As we move toward a more inclusive rhetoric, we need to be clear about who is being included into what already existing discursive community. In the effort to diffuse dissent and to compromise, power must be distributed equally. As we broaden our understanding of rhetoric to encompass non-Western traditions, we can begin to understand theory as a product of culture and as specific to given civilizations. We can further the notion of rhetoric as multicultural, developing out of mutual exchange and participation rather than sustaining a unidirectional study of rhetoric as an investigation of the influence of Western culture on othered cultures.

Finally, we need to pay attention to the intersections and parallels between rhetorical studies of gender and race. We should consider how notions of a "feminine style," or a "feminine voice" shift with changes in cultural perspective. In some Chinese cultures, for example, nonadversarial rhetoric, often associated with women and submissiveness, is common across genders. We must be careful not to import our assumptions about gendered discourse into non-Western contexts. How do different cultural rhetorics frequently reinforce the marginalization they seek to overcome by developing their discourses on Western models? Often the role of rhetor who claims to represent an oppressed constituency shifts. Such representation potentially endangers the rhetor's membership in the represented group, whether that group is defined by class, race, or gender.

If we approach with care these critical issues about the nature and significance of a range of "available means of persuasion," then we may be able to overcome the problems presented by prematurely silencing (once again) the voices of the marginalized in our rush to multicultural inclusiveness. If we can learn once again to teach audiences as well as speakers how to study the available means of persuasion, the potential value of greater inclusion will not be paid for in the hard cash of lost voices and identities surrendered.

KERMIT E. CAMPBELL
University of Texas at Austin

Race and Rhetoric: An Unlikely Tandem?

To some—perhaps many—of us, the terms *race* and *rhetoric* are an unlikely tandem. After all, except in a few now obscure scholarly publications like James Golden and Richard Rieke's *The Rhetoric of Black Americans* or Arthur Smith's *Rhetoric of Black Revolution* (published in 1971 and 1969, respectively, and by authors who, at that time, were more likely to be members of the Speech Communication Association, not the Rhetoric Society of America), the terms have rarely appeared together in our scholarship or professional discourse. In fact, race and rhetoric probably would not have been one of the themes of this thirtieth biennial meeting of RSA had it not been for the foresight and fortitude of RSA president C. Jan Swearingen to go with this innovative and risky concept, even though it was, at least for me, still in the formative stages of development.

This concept began for me last fall as I was trying to put together portions of a book on rap, race, and rhetoric. What I proposed to do in the section on rhetoric was to critique current rhetoric historiographies for their failure to take into account issues of race and racism. Given Martin Bernal's assertions about classical civilization and modern historiography in *Black Athena*, I reasoned that our canons and historiographies might not be telling the whole story about rhetoric. Further, I conjectured that if race, class, and gender analyses could appropriately apply to history and literature, then they could apply to rhetoric as well. And thankfully they have applied to rhetoric (well, they have insofar as gender is concerned). In the last decade or more, we have witnessed some groundbreaking work on gender and rhetoric, much of it by members of this very organization. Yet, to my knowledge, we have no comparable work on race and rhetoric or, for that matter, rhetoric and class.

Perhaps, though, such an undertaking is imminent. Featured in these proceedings are several papers and a keynote address on the rhetorics of racialized others (e.g., ancient Egyptians, Chinese, Latinos, Arabs, and African Americans, among others). There are the recently published works by some among us here—Shirley Wilson Logan's (1995) critical anthology on African American women orators of the nineteenth century and George Kennedy's (1998) text on comparative rhetoric. And there are some recent and fairly comprehensive anthologies of African American orators and oratory (e.g., Foner and Branham, *Lift Every Voice: African American Oratory 1787-1900* and Leeman, *African American Orators: A Bio-Critical Sourcebook*).

Our field appears to be poised for a monumental turn to what Jacqueline Jones Royster (1996) has called the "rhetorical others." Yet, for reasons that should not be too difficult for anyone to discern, I fear that this turn to the other might, ultimately, skirt the issue of race. Kennedy's *Comparative Rhetoric: An Historical and Cross-Cultural Introduction*, for instance, is a remarkable study of cultural rhetorics as unique and varied as the aboriginal Australians, the Limba of Sierra Leone, and the ancient Mesopotamians, Indians, and Greeks, but one will not find there a critical examination of race and rhetorical history or theory—not even, if I am not mistaken, in the author's account of the contacts between the North American natives and Europeans during the era of European exploration and colonization. What I mean to suggest is that the topic of race and rhetoric should not be limited to, say, studies of African American oratory or Native American rhetorical practices (though we surely must have these), but should include as well canons and histories that take into account, where appropriate, racist and antiracist discourses; patterns of linguistic and cultural displacement and reassertion; essentialist representations of rhetoric and nation; hybrid racial/ethnic identities and discursive practices; the conspicuous absence of the other in treatises or theories that purport universal application; the assumption of raceless or race neutral theories and theorists; and the inexplicable silences about struggles for literacy, humanity, sovereignty, civil rights, and the right to speak.

These are some of the ways I see race and rhetoric intersecting. But, practically speaking, what might such scholarship look like? Well, for one, it could be looking for instances where rhetoric is deployed during periods of intense racial debate or racial fragmentation. I was surprised to discover recently from the Steven Spielberg movie *Amistad* that John Quincy Adams, first holder of the Nicholas Boylston chair of rhetoric at Harvard and author of *Lectures on Rhetoric and Oratory*, defended before the U.S. Supreme Court the Africans who rebelled against their Spanish enslavers aboard the schooner *La Amistad*. Although, admittedly, Adams's *Lectures* do not deal with the slave question or with the abolition of slavery, one could make the case that his lengthy speech before the court in 1841 is a perfect example of the judicial oratory he describes in the *Lectures*. No doubt there are other stories, other experiences worth recounting in the *Amistad* case, as Jacqueline Jones Royster has made clear in the keynote address.

Having recently visited the Mexican Fine Arts Museum in Chicago and having attended a rhetoric conference in Mexico City, I was also surprised to discover that Mexico has in its history not only traces of Aztec rhetoric, as Kennedy points out, and Renaissance Spanish missionary rhetorics, as Don Abbott reveals in *Rhetoric in the New World*, but also traces of Afro-mestizo culture and rhetoric. Such observations, however, seem to elude us in our otherwise laudable attempts to recount rhetoric's history and to reinstate rhetoric among the disciplines. Hopefully, the proceedings from this conference will underscore so many new observations about rhetoric and will begin the noble work of inscribing them into our professional discourse.

Works Cited

Abbott, D. P. *Rhetoric in the New World: Rhetorical Theory and Practice in Colonial Spanish America*. Columbia: U of South Carolina P, 1996.

Adams, J. Q. *Lectures on Rhetoric and Oratory*. 2 vols. New York: Russell and Russell, 1962.

Bernal, M. *The Fabrication of Ancient Greece, 1785-1985*. New Brunswick: Rutgers UP, 1987. Vol. 1 of *Black Athena: The Afroasiatic Roots of Classical Civilization*. 2 vols.

Foner, Philip, and Robert Branham. *Lift Every Voice: African American Oratory 1787-1900*. Tuscaloosa: U of Alabama P, 1998.

Golden, James, and Richard Rieke. *The Rhetoric of Black Americans*. Columbus: Merrill, 1971.

Kennedy, George A. *Comparative Rhetoric: An Historical and Cross-Cultural Introduction*. New York: Oxford UP, 1998.

Leeman, Richard. *African-American Orators: A Bio-Critical Sourcebook*. Westport, CT: Greenwood, 1996.

Logan, Shirley W. *With Pen and Voice: A Critical Anthology of Nineteenth-Century African-American Women*. Carbondale: Southern Illinois UP, 1995.

Royster, J. J. "New Histories of Rhetoric." Rev. of *Oratorical Culture in Nineteenth-Century America*, by Gregory Clark and S. Michael Halloran; *Eighteenth-Century British and American Rhetorics and Rhetoricians*, by Michael G. Moran; *Things, Thoughts, Words, and Actions*, by H. Lewis Ulman. *College English* 58 (1996): 219-24.

Smith, A. *Rhetoric of Black Revolution*. Boston: Allyn and Bacon, 1969.

JAIME ARMIN MEJÍA
Southwest Texas State University

Latina and Latino Rhetorical Issues

Among U.S. Latinos and Latinas over the last three decades, the study of rhetoric has taken a different trajectory compared to the study of rhetoric in the mainstream. Rhetorical issues for Latinas/os can be and are of a different kind than rhetorical issues for mainstream rhetoricians, because our rhetorical issues can often necessitate differing understandings and analyses that other rhetorics based on different cultures may not require in the United States. A primary concern has been the conducting of rhetorical studies in tandem with composition studies to further the critical literacy of Latino/a groups at all levels of our educational careers, as well as outside of our educational settings. What distinguishes Latino/a rhetorical issues for many Latino/a groups is a difference in language codes, specifically Spanish-language codes originating from cultural backgrounds often marginalized by the mainstream. For no matter which Latino/a group one refers to, the use of some form of Spanish is perhaps the one overlapping commonality among all U.S. Latino/a groups. This commonality, however, varies considerably as the numerous cultures among Latinas/os are situated at the interstices of cultures where rhetorical situations and cultural contexts are often problematized by the unfair and unequal distribution of power seldom favoring many Latino/a groups. Reducing "rhetoric" to a generic "literacy and empowerment" issue in Latino/a rhetorical studies should be replaced by a more careful study of differences among a variety of Latino/a rhetorical situations and cultural contexts. The study of the richness of these traditions and their current cominglings is an inviting and as yet largely unexplored area.

The Rhetoric Society of America (RSA) Proceedings illustrate a use of the term *America* in a manner that often fails to acknowledge what this term means for Latin Americans and U.S. Latinas/os, that is, for the majority of peoples and nations living in the Western hemisphere. The unwitting pejorative assumption here is that America means and only means the United States—that is, the English-speaking, Anglo-centered United States. The opening remarks to these RSA proceedings stand as a case in point: the year "1968 was not only the first year of RSA but also of student demonstrations in Chicago and Paris, harbingers of the darker sides of the great reforms witnessed within the decade of the sixties . . ." (see page 6 in this volume). During 1968, however, government troops in Mexico City massacred, by some estimates, as many as 300 student demonstrators in this city's centuries-old Plaza de las Tres Culturas at Tlatelolco. It is certainly no wonder that these students' deaths are often forgotten in the United States. Current rhetorical studies continue to follow a west-east trajectory instead of a south-north one—dark harbingers, indeed.

Over the past three decades, rhetoric—and composition—studies for Latino/a scholars and educators have reflected a continuing and increasing resistance to forgetting our mixed and multifarious cultural heritage(s). Papers presented by Latinas/os at rhetoric and composition conferences, for instance, continue to raise concerns over the complexities involved in rhetorical analyses of our literatures and cultural contexts. We have also been raising our concerns over the pedagogical strategies best suited for Latinas/os in our rhetoric and composition classrooms. And, finally, we have been finely attuned to the problematics involved with our rhetorical stances—as Latinas/os—within the profession of English studies, where our ethnic stances and identities are often unnecessarily compromised: lumped together as generic, and located in a hastily compiled array of remedial bilingual pedagogical issues, and confused definitions of literary and cultural rhetorical origins.

At this year's RSA conference, these rhetorical concerns were raised in a Latino/a panel (Cecelia Rodríguez Milanés, Raúl Sánchez, Beatrice Mendez Newman, and myself) once again. Had we not been invited to present these concerns, it is highly doubtful these issues would have been raised at all. Our presence in the field of rhetoric and composition, however, is growing and changing, and as it does, Latino/a issues will become even more important and relevant in a global village that is increasingly becoming interconnected. But let us not forget the hemispheric scope of American rhetorical studies that still awaits definition. Within that, specifically U.S. Latino/a issues remain conspicuously unrepresented in our field. The absence of proposals in this area led to the invitation to convene a panel on the subject, and to address the issue in these opening remarks.

As we all move forward in time, we will continue to face the changing interethnic trajectory in this country that will compel us to engage rhetorical situations where Latinas/os will play even larger roles. Hopefully, the RSA can become "American" in the broader sense. In the future, this change should mean that the unequal distribution of power, grounded in language(s), will shift to allow more of us to acknowledge that before English rhetorical issues and contexts, there were Spanish ones in many places. And before Spanish-based issues and contexts, there were many other languages, cultures, and peoples in our long-suffering American pueblos within the United States and to our south. Rhetorical issues for U.S. Latinas/os live, have not died, and will not be forgotten as long as our vision—our rhetorical vision of "Our America" to invoke José Martí's words—encompasses them to integrate what the mainstream has often been reluctant to embrace.

Integrating Latino/a issues into the mainstream will require recognizing more of what inevitably happens when cultures encounter each other:

transculturation. In a transnational global village, the inevitable transcultural consequence requires more than the limited taco-counting studies now found in mainstream rhetorical and cultural studies. Understanding overlapping rhetorical contexts and cultural tropes, bringing people together rather than segregating them along language, ethnic, or cultural lines—Latinas/os will continue to pursue these objectives as we move forward in time.

JACQUELINE LAMBIASE
University of North Texas

Redefining an 800-Pound Godzilla

A recent cover of *Wired* magazine features Godzilla and the headline: "Forget the Dow: Here Comes the New Economy" (June 1998). The article suggests that gonzo, globalized companies are building an exciting übereconomy with intelligent use of technology and strategic vision. Through media reporting of this sort, Internet and computer technology have indeed been made into an 800-pound Godzilla, weighed only in terms of economics. We Americans have become so self-conscious about what cyberspace means to our economy that it has become just about capitalism and .com. At least that is what I think when I am feeling gloomy.

On the other hand, some tout the Internet as a democratic sphere where our wildest utopian dreams of egalitarianism come true, and we know that, too, is not exactly what the Internet is coming to be. It is more than that limited scenario, despite our global village inclinations toward neo-McLuhanism. Too much of the Internet is mired in discord or in enclave mentalities to believe otherwise.

The Rhetoric Society of America's (RSA) thirtieth anniversary conference began to fill in the excluded middle of such polarized, good and evil, Internet characterizations so prevalent in our mass media. Many papers addressed rhetoric and computer-mediated communication. The single most important part of our ethnographic work may be in definition, in describing the Internet and its rhetorical possibilities, so that definitions about economics and capitalism do not stick too tenaciously. There is a copious variety of definitions to which these papers add more rhetorically informed shadings.

Cyberspace, the Internet, and computer-mediated communication are seen:
1. by George Landow as a hypertextual "democratic or multicentered system" (179);
2. by Richard Lanham as an "electronic invasion" causing "democratic movement from big to small, impersonal to personal, citadel to coat pocket" (200);
3. by Jay David Bolter as a "network culture" that is "in the final stages of the transition from a hierarchical social order" (232);
4. by Nicholas Negroponte as a "totally new, global social fabric" (183) that is no longer about computing, but "about living" (6);
5. by former Well owner Bruce Katz as "one of the bright hopes that we have in reinvigorating a civil dialogue that is the foundation of a free democratic society" (qtd. in Hafner 134);

6. by Robert Markley as a "metaphysical construct" (57), a "myth" (73), and a "dynamic and complex idealization—one that offers the alluring fiction of limitless possibilities and connections—rather than a stale recasting of oppositional logic" (69);
7. by M. Kadi as an agent of change since "ownership slips away," but "I do not think, as so many do, that a great democracy of thought is upon us" (606);
8. by Elizabeth Weise as an "adjunct, a backyard fence, a coffee shop, a favorite hangout, a weekly support group" that is "not a social revolution, but at times . . . a revelation" (xv);
9. by Stephanie Brail as the "Wild, Wild West," where "relative freedom and a lack of government control made it one of the coolest places to be," but "it's easy to romanticize these pioneer days of the Internet" (148);
10. by Ester Dyson as "not a new form of life. It is just a new activity" (qtd. in Dreifus 19); and
11. by David Shenk "as if internet information is a renewable fuel, and all we need to do is simply plug our computers and our brain stems into the global network in order to be supplied with everything we need to live happy, healthy, wealthy lives. What kind of techno-sap would fall for such a preposterous notion?" (72).

These definitions may signify an encouraging diversity of opinion or little more than academic one-upsmanship.

John Fiske offers a note of caution to consider alongside these definitions:

> Postmodern culture is often characterized as one of extreme multiplicity—a multiplicity of commodities, of images, of knowledges, and of information technologies. . . . Multiplicity is to be applauded only when it brings diversity, and the two are not necessarily the same, though they are closely related. Multiplicity is a prerequisite of diversity, but it does not necessarily entail it—more can all too often be more of the same. (239)

Electronic discussions oftentimes contain the same hierarchy that is found offline; modernism lurks not just in cyberspace but persists in noncyberspace as well. Disrupting the master narrative about Internet discourse and its definitions can help us to reconfigure online opportunities and to craft new ones, thereby creating rhetorical situations and narratives of our own. This important work will enable alternative discursive settings and styles that are egalitarian, multiethnic, nonmodernist, and not reliant on stereotypes and misconceptions.

Works Cited

Bolter, J. D. *Writing Space: The Computer, Hypertext, and the History of Writing.* Hillsdale, NJ: Erlbaum, 1991.
Brail, S. "The Price of Admission: Harassment and Free Speech in the Wild, Wild West." *Wired Women: Gender and New Realities in Cyberspace.* Ed. L. Cherny and E. R. Weise. Seattle: Seal, 1996. 141-57.
Dreifus, C. "The Cyber-Maxims of Ester Dyson." *The New York Times Magazine* 7 July 1996: 16-19.
Fiske, J. *Media Matters: Race and Gender in U.S. Politics.* Minneapolis: U of Minnesota P, 1996.
Hafner, K. "The World's Most Influential Online Community." *Wired* May 1997: 98-143.
Kadi, M. "The Internet Is Four Inches Tall." *The Press of Ideas: Readings for Writers on Print Culture and the Information Age.* Ed. J. B. Dock. Boston: Bedford/St. Martin's, 1996. 598-607.
Landow, G. *Hypertext: The Convergence of Contemporary Critical Theory and Technology.* Baltimore: Johns Hopkins UP, 1993.
Lanham, R. *The Electronic Word: Democracy, Technology, and the Arts.* Chicago: U of Chicago P, 1993.
Markley, R. *Virtual Realities and Their Discontents.* Baltimore: Johns Hopkins UP, 1996.
Negroponte, N. *Being Digital.* New York: Knopf, 1995.
Shenk, D. *Data Smog: Surviving the Information Glut.* San Francisco: HarperEdge, 1997.
Weise, E. Introduction. *Wired Women: Gender and New Realities in Cyberspace.* Ed. L. Cherny and E. R. Weise. Seattle: Seal, 1996. xv.

COLLIN GIFFORD BROOKE
Old Dominion University

Cybercommunities and McLuhan: A Retrospect

One of the themes for the 1998 Rhetoric Society of America (RSA) conference was "rhetoric and technology." The relation between them is as yet not well defined. There has been a tendency, particularly with new computer technology, to spend money first and ask questions later. As Cynthia Selfe's 1998 chair's address at the Conference on College Composition and Communication (CCCC) revealed, that pattern has continued with the rise of computers in education. President Clinton's call for national standards for computer literacy only accelerates this tendency. It is becoming increasingly important for us to ask questions of the machines that we are being asked to incorporate into our pedagogical practices.

I want to introduce three different threads, ideas that I perceive as central to the concerns of rhetoric and technology. The title of this year's conference, *Rhetoric, the Polis, and the Global Village*, alludes to the work of Marshall McLuhan, one of the most outspoken supporters of technological change. I will review some of his ideas to see how much of what he wrote thirty years ago is of relevance to us today. Each of these three threads will begin with a quote from McLuhan's (1996) *The Medium Is the Massage*, to which I will juxtapose contemporary counterparts.

I. Present Needs Versus Future Possibilities

> *When faced with a totally new situation, we tend always to attach ourselves to the objects, to the flavor of the most recent past. We look at the present through a rear-view mirror. We march backwards into the future.*

Marshall McLuhan (74-75)

It is comforting and tempting to search for analogies that might serve to make technology less intimidating—the Web is like television you can read, Usenet groups are like electronic salons, and so forth. At some point, though, we should worry less about analogies and more about possibilities. McLuhan routinely criticized our culture for forcing new media into doing the work of the old. We might find one example of this in the state of most of our online journals, which have retained many of the features of print journals, such as infrequency of publication, a pass/fail referee process, and so on, features necessitated by publication costs that do not exist online. We can contrast that model (print documents transferred to the screen) with models for online scholarship and document production that consciously make use of the medium to produce new possibilities. I am thinking here of the collaborative review process of the journal *Kairos* (Doherty 1995), or the work done by the participants on the e-mail lists RhetNet and the PreText Conversations, for example. Although a few of us are beginning to invent goals for new media, there are still too many who would march backward.

II. Community

> *Print technology created the public. Electric technology created the mass. The public consists of separate individuals walking around with separate, fixed points of view. The new technology demands that we abandon the luxury of this posture, this fragmentary outlook.*
>
> Marshall McLuhan (68-69)

There is a tendency on the part of those who celebrate the Internet to argue that it will make a more participatory democracy possible, and that therefore the Internet and its various platforms are inherently democratic. Nothing could be further from the truth. Once again, it is a case of asking new media to accomplish the political goals of the old. We need to consider what sorts of communities might be possible thanks to the Internet, and to pay close attention to arguments like Esther Dyson's distinction between democracy and decentralization. Too often, hopes and anxieties replace analysis in our descriptions of cyberspace, and we end up assuming that we can simply wish all of the nastiness of the real world away by entering cyberspace. It is far easier to take the path of least resistance, to invest cyberspace with either dreams of democratic utopias or fears of cyberstalking and pornography. Reality is somewhere in the middle.

III. Ecology

> *All media work us over completely. They are so pervasive in their personal, political, economic, aesthetic, psychological, moral, ethical, and social consequences that they leave no part of us untouched, unaffected, unaltered. The medium is the massage. Any under-*

> *standing of social and cultural change is impossible without a knowledge of the way media work as environments.*
>
> Marshall McLuhan (26)

There is still a prevailing view that would have computers simply be tools, to be used or ignored as each of us chooses. It is no longer that simple. We have already been affected by issues of access, speed, and availability that computers have helped to introduce. That does not mean that we are determined solely by the machines around us. But McLuhan is right to think of media as an environment, as an ecology, one that has profound effects on us whether or not we accept technology. We do not have to like technology, but we must accept it, because that is the only way that we can shape the environment that we find ourselves in.

All three of these themes merge fairly easily, and there are more that could be added. They all fall under the umbrella of "paying attention to technology," which was the overriding theme of Selfe's CCCC address. It is no less important to pay attention to technology than it is to pay attention to rhetoric, because both, as forms of interface, have the potential to change us at least as much as we change them. Most important, perhaps, is that we begin to ask the kinds of questions, as a discipline, that some of our colleagues will be asking over the next few days. As important as technological innovation was to McLuhan's thought, equally necessary was the social maturity to interrogate technology: "There is absolutely no inevitability as long as there is a willingness to contemplate what is happening" (25).

Works Cited

Doherty, M. (1996). "Editorial Process." *Kairos: A Journal for Teachers of Writing in Webbed Environments.* 31 May 1998. <http://english.ttu.edu/kairos/edprocess.html>

Dyson, E. *Release 2.0: A Design for Living in the Digital Age.* New York: Broadway Books, 1997.

McLuhan, M., and Q. Fiore. *The Medium Is the Massage: An Inventory of Effects.* San Francisco: HardWired, 1996.

Selfe, C. "Technology and Literacy: A Story About the Perils of Not Paying Attention." 1998 CCCC Keynote Address. 7 Apr. 1998. <http://www.ncte.org/forums/selfe/index.html>

GRANT BOSWELL
Brigham Young University

Seven Ways of Looking at Religion and Rhetoric

For anyone familiar with the history of our discipline, the relation of rhetoric to religion is not a new topic. In recent years, several of the members of the Rhetoric Society of America have made important contributions to the study of rhetoric and religion. Two examples come readily to mind. James L. Kinneavy's *Greek Rhetorical Origins of Christian Faith: An Inquiry* is an important study of the concept of faith in Christianity as it developed in part from the notion of *pistis* from classical rhetoric. And George A. Kennedy's *New Testament Interpretation through Rhetorical Criticism*, although not receiving as much recognition among historians of rhetoric perhaps as it deserved, has been influential among New Testament scholars. Both of these members of the society participated in the 1998 conference.

As a representative anecdote of my discussion of rhetoric and religion, I would like to paraphrase an exchange held on H-Rhetor during the fall 1997 on the topic of Christian rhetoric. As one might imagine, the discussion soon turned to the semantic potential of the label "Christian rhetoric." That discussion is instructive for how we might explore the topic of rhetoric and religion as it is developing today. As I recall, there were at least seven possible directions for study that ensued from that discussion.

The first is rhetorical theory by persons with religious purposes. An example from the tradition would be St. Augustine's *De Doctrina Christiana*. More recently is David Cunningham's *Faithful Persuasion: In Aid of a Rhetoric of Christian Theology*.

A second sense in which the topic of rhetoric and religion might be pursued is in rhetorical analysis of avowedly religious rhetorical practices. These would include sermons, prayers, hymns, spirituals, homilies, meditations, polemic, and other religious genres. A good example is Oliver Shaw Rankin's *Jewish Religious Polemic of Early and Later Centuries*.

Another way in which this topic might be explored is through rhetorical analysis of practices by persons who are avowedly religious to determine how their religious orientation affects their seemingly secular speeches or writings. For example, someone might analyze Karl Jaspers's philosophical writings with a focus on his communications philosophy in light of Jaspers's religious beliefs.

A fourth sense in which this topic might be considered is the rhetorical analysis of religious texts. In recent years this kind of rhetorical analysis has greatly enlivened biblical studies, especially New Testament scholarship, as Duane Watson's bibliography attests. From Amos Wilder's lectures on the rhetoric of the New Testament in the early 1960s to the present day, rhetorical studies in New Testament scholarship have burgeoned into a very lively discipline. This energy has informed Old Testament studies and is beginning to influence Vedic studies as well. Certainly, similar analyses could and should be made of the texts of the world's other religions.

A fifth direction implied by the topic is the recovery of lost or marginalized texts, voices, and speeches from religious material through rhetorical analysis. Examples of this kind of work include Vernon Robbins's attempts to recover all the voices from the first century of Christianity through what he has called sociorhetorical criticism in his *The Tapestry of Early Christian Discourse: Rhetoric, Society, and Ideology*, Brian Blount's attempts to include marginalized interpretations of the New Testament text from minority sermonic and spiritual traditions in *Cultural Interpretation: Reorienting New Testament Criticism*, and Phyllis Trible's attempts to restore feminine voices to Old Testament texts in *God and the Rhetoric of Sexuality*.

A sixth direction in which scholarship on rhetoric and religion may find fertile ground is the impact of a particular religious orientation on rhetoric in its broadest sense. Such a study would investigate how religious worldviews might affect rhetorical theory or practice. Examples of this kind of rhetorical investigation include George Kalamaras's *Reclaiming the Tacit Dimension: Symbolic Form in the Rhetoric of Silence* and Stephen O'Leary's *Arguing the Apocalypse: A Theory of Millennial Rhetoric*.

Finally a seventh possible direction this study might take is the relation of rhetoric and religion in an era of discontinuity, past or present. This study would investigate how rhetorical theory and practice adapt to social and ideological circumstances in eras of perceived unrest and change. In this sense, two examples come to mind, the theses of which I will summarize for your consideration and scrutiny. The first is David Jasper's *Rhetoric, Power and Community*, which argues that theology in the Western tradition has always been preoccupied with power and has constituted itself rhetorically through texts. Rhetorical self-consciousness, Jasper argues, will foster a more just implementation of authority. The second example is a recent book by Catherine Pickstock, entitled *After Writing: On the Liturgical Consummation of Philosophy* (1998), already in a second printing. Pickstock advances the remarkable thesis that there is no meaning outside of liturgy, and although the word "rhetoric" is not in her title, her book is entirely about language and its effects. Moreover, Pickstock's argument derives from her reading of texts that figure prominently in the rhetorical tradition, specifically Plato's *Phaedrus*, but also Peter Ramus's works. She also specifically takes up the subject of language and the formation of a sacred *polis*, which should be of interest to rhetoricians.

The subject of rhetoric and religion is an area of scholarly interest and lively debate that the 1998 Rhetoric Society of America conference papers amply represented in several of these seven categories. In concert with one another, they suggested how far we have come in defining this area of investigation, and how much farther we yet have to go in defining the cross-cultural comparative study of rhetoric and religion.

Works Cited

Blount, Brian K. *Cultural Interpretation: Reorienting New Testament Criticism.* Minneapolis: Fortress, 1995.

Cunningham, David S. *Faithful Persuasion: In Aid of a Christian Theology.* Notre Dame: U of Notre Dame P, 1991.

Jasper, David. *Rhetoric, Power and Community.* Louisville: Westminster/John Knox, 1993.

Jaspers, Karl. *Philosophy.* Trans. E. B. Ashton. Vol. 2. Chicago: U of Chicago P, 1970.

Kalamaras, George. *Reclaiming the Tacit Dimension: Symbolic Form in the Rhetoric of Silence.* Albany: State U of New York P, 1994.

Kennedy, George A. *New Testament Interpretation through Rhetorical Criticism.* Chapel Hill: U of North Carolina P, 1984.

Kinneavy, James L. *Greek Rhetorical Origins of Christian Faith: An Inquiry.* Oxford: Oxford UP, 1987.

O'Leary, Stephen D. *Arguing the Apocalypse: A Theory of Millennial Rhetoric.* Oxford: Oxford UP, 1994.

Pickstock, Catherine. *After Writing: On the Liturgical Consummation of Philosophy.* Oxford: Blackwell, 1998.

Plato. *Phaedrus.* Trans. R. Hackforth. Cambridge: Cambridge UP, 1987.

Ramus, Peter. *The Logike.* 1574. Leeds: Scholar, 1966.

Rankin, Oliver Shaw. *Jewish Religious Polemic of Early and Later Centuries: A Study of Documents Here Rendered in English.* Edinburgh: Edinburgh UP, 1956.

Robbins, Vernon K. *The Tapestry of Early Christian Discourse: Rhetoric, Society and Ideology.* London: Routledge, 1996.

Trible, Phyllis. *God and the Rhetoric of Sexuality.* Philadelphia: Fortress, 1978.

Watson, Duane. *Rhetorical Criticism of the Bible: A Comprehensive Bibliography with Notes on History and Method.* Leiden: E. J. Brill, 1994.

Wilder, Amos. *Early Christian Rhetoric: The Language of the Gospel.* Cambridge: Harvard UP, 1971.

CHERYL GLENN
Pennsylvania State University

Rhetoric, Religion, and Social Practices

I would like to build on Grant Boswell's informative piece (previous chapter) by expanding the topic to include the notion of "social practices." The topic is broad, so I will turn to that axis we all refer to as "history" and stake out a few moments that represent where we have come from, where we are, and where we are heading in terms of rhetoric, religion, and social practices.

Any general overview that connects rhetoric and religion must feature social practices that constitute belief: those speeches, deeds, and actions of persuasive mortals and gods. Even though rhetoric and religion can each be separated, neither of them can separate from belief. In *Greek Rhetorical Origins of Christian Faith*, James Kinneavy tells us that "many of the major features of the concept of persuasion, as embodied in Greek rhetoric of the Hellenistic period, are semantically quite close to the Christian notion of faith" (4). In other words, *pistis*, or belief, the cornerstone of early persuasive political and social practices, became the cornerstone of Hebraic-Christian piety. Plato makes clear that mere faith plays no part in the construction or establishment of knowledge, yet belief and truth do. Faith and belief are mighty close in meaning.

Rhetoricized belief systems, both secular and religious, spanned the historical constructs of Greco-Roman antiquity and the early Judeo-Christian period. Politics, state religions, mystery cults, Judaism, and Christianity all manifested the interanimation of rhetoric, religion, and social practices, the traditions and customs we learned so well from Kenneavy's work, Kenneth Burke's *Rhetoric of Religion*, and George Kennedy's *Classical Rhetoric and Its Christian and Secular Tradition from Antiquity through Modern Times* and *New Testament Interpretation through Rhetorical Criticism*. (Many of us Westerners—or, rather, I for one—would benefit from learning more about Eastern and African religions and rhetorics.) Working at the sites of antiquity and early Western religions taught us about both prerhetorical and codified rhetorical practices. Although the rhetoric of politics (with persuasion, or *pistis*, as the cause) dominated our study, the rhetoric of religion (with persuasion, or *pistis*, as the effect) continued to tantalize our scholarly interests, particularly because Christianity served to validate and invigorate pagan rhetorical practices. After all, political rhetoric had weakened with the fall of the Roman Empire, and educational rhetoric was enervated by the translation from Rome to Britain. When St. Augustine of Hippo demonstrated how to "take the gold out of Egypt," he fortified what would become the Christian rhetorical practices of teaching, preaching, and moving (2.4.60).

The eloquent and energetic coalescence of rhetoric, religion, and social practice in the early modern age provided rhetorical scholars another investigative site. Not only were religion and culture now inextricably laced, but educational practices were wholly informed by religion. Medieval educational opportunities were available to some men and to fewer women, producing such well-known figures as Augustine, St. Jerome, St. Bernard of Clairvaux, Heloise, Julian of Norwich, Hildegard of Bingen, Hrotsvita, Christine de Pisan, Sor Juana Inés de la Cruz, and Margery Kempe, all of whom left writings that offer opportunities to learn about religion, which was the strongest, most persistent cultural force at the time. That early modern period offered a codified rhetoric of religion that Jerry Murphy explicated in *Medieval Rhetoric*, *Rhetoric in the Middle Ages*, *Medieval Eloquence*, and *Three Medieval Rhetorical Arts*. In that last book, he gave us Robert of Basevorn and his AD 1322 art of preaching (*Forma praedicandi*), a topic that Roxanne Mountford interrogated in her 1991 dissertation, "The Feminization of *Ars Praedicandi*." In studying medieval rhetoric, we continue our study of religion and social practice and, for the first time, seriously look at the ways certain women were writing about and using rhetoric.

The expansiveness of including religion in our rhetorical study, sometimes at the expense of politics, taught us to expand even further: maybe rhetoric was more than male, public, political. Maybe it could be both male and female, maybe public and private, maybe even political and religious. And maybe rhetoric is more than argument. As we turned to and examined more and more sites of religious belief and rhetorical expertise, we automatically widened the sphere/scope of rhetoric—even when we were not sure we should be doing so or knew for sure how to do so. Together, rhetoric, religion, and social practices have promoted voting rights, citizenship, safety, freedom, and opportunity throughout the modern and postmodern eras. When the Grimké sisters, Angelina and Sarah, wrote against slavery, they knew well that only their religious convictions could provide them a discourse of power, credibility, and respectability, an idea that continues to play out when we look at the work of Dr. Martin Luther King, Jr., Frederick Douglass, Frances Ellen Watkins Harper, Anna Julia Haywood Cooper, Ida B. Wells, Sojourner Truth, and Maria Stewart. Fortunately, the scholarship of our colleagues in rhetoric, Keith Miller (*Voice of Deliverance: The Language of Martin Luther King, Jr. and Its Sources*), Jacqueline Jones Royster (*Southern Horrors* and *Voices in the Stream*), and Shirley Wilson Logan (*With Pen and Voice* and *We Are Coming*) are helping us untangle the rich complexities of this convergence.

The synergy of rhetoric and religion continues to provide ways for feminists (both male and female) to enter or reenter religious discussion, argument, and belief, often calling into question the fundamental maleness of Christian theology and of rhetoric itself. The work of academicians, some of them feminist theologians, Rosemary Radford Ruether (*Sexism and God-Talk: Toward a Feminist Theology*), Mary Daly (*Beyond God the Father*), Rebecca Chopp (*The Power to Speak: Feminism, Language, God*), and Letty Russell (*Human Liberation in a Feminist Perspective: A Theology*) have invigorated religious rhetorical study, helping us find a place for ourselves within a rhetorical tradition that has been more exclusive than inclusive, to say the least. In addition, our own colleagues (both feminists and representatives of various religious groups) are carrying out work at this intersection: Chris Anderson (*Edge Effects*); Kris Ratcliffe (*Anglo-American Feminist Challenges to the Rhetorical Tradition*); Michael Hassett ("Possibilities of a Mormon Rhetoric"); Lynell Edwards ("Struggles Inside the Contact Zone: How Students and Professional Writers Negotiate Religious with Disciplinary Ethos"); Katy Powell-Carter ("Negotiating Spiritual Sites of Composing"); and Ann Berthoff, JoAnne Campbell, Beth Daniell, James Moffett, and Jan Swearingen ("Spiritual Sites of Composing"). But so-called popular writers may well be more influential in the long run, reaching a much broader audience, as the bestselling writings of Kathleen Norris (*Dakota, Amazing Grace, Cloister Walk*) and Terry Tempest Williams (*Refuge, An Unspoken Hunger, New Genesis: Mormons Writing on the Environment*) attest.

We do not have to enter a bookstore or library to see the ways rhetoric, religion, and social practices continue to converge. Most of our towns and cities offer daily enactments in churches, with their programs ranging from Sunday services and meals-on-wheels to twelve-step and child-care programs; in shelters for the homeless, diseased, and abused; and in soup kitchens and hospices. Rosemary Winslow's work on homelessness and hospitality brings these efforts into focus, as does the work of Avis Rupert ("Religious Education via Distance Learning"), Joshua Gunn ("Towards Grounding Rhetoric in Virtues for the Twenty-First Century"), and D. B. Magee ("Emerging Responses in a Period of Uncertainty: The Religious Community's Augustinian Reaction to the HIV/AIDS Crisis").

What our colleagues have already and are continuing to open up for us are rhetorics, not "new" rhetorics, as some would say, but always/already rhetorics that fuse religious conviction with self-consciously persuasive language and social action. Ahead of us are more (not new) rhetorics, each of which illuminates a rhetorical practitioner's ethical-moral-political-spiritual-religious purpose.

Works Cited

Anderson, Chris. *Edge Effects.* Iowa City: U of Iowa P, 1997.
Augustine, Saint. *On Christian Doctrine.* Trans. D. W. Robertson, Jr. Indianapolis: Bobbs, 1958.
Berthoff, Ann, JoAnne Campbell, Beth Daniell, James Moffett, and C. Jan Swearingen. "Spiritual Sites of Composing." *College Composition and Communication* 45 (May 1994): 237-63.
Burke, Kenneth. *Rhetoric of Religion.* 1961. Berkeley: U of California P, 1970.
Chopp, Rebecca. *The Power to Speak: Feminism, Language, God.* New York: Crossroad, 1991.
Daly, Mary. *Beyond God the Father.* Boston: Beacon, 1985.
Edwards, Lynell. "Struggles Inside the Contact Zone: How Students and Professional Writers Negotiate Religious with Disciplinary Ethos." Rhetoric Society of America. Pittsburgh. June 1998.
Gunn, Joshua. "Towards Grounding Rhetoric in Virtues for the Twenty-First Century." Rhetoric Society of America. Pittsburgh. June 1998.
Hassett, Michael. "Possibilities of a Mormon Rhetoric." Rhetoric Society of America. Pittsburgh. June 1998.
Kennedy, George. *Classical Rhetoric and Its Christian and Secular Tradition from Antiquity through Modern Times.* Chapel Hill: U of North Carolina P, 1980.
—. *New Testament Interpretation through Rhetorical Criticism.* Chapel Hill: U of North Carolina P, 1985.
Kinneavy, James. *Greek Rhetorical Origins of Christian Faith.* New York: Oxford UP, 1987.
Logan, Shirley Wilson. *We Are Coming: Nineteenth-Century African-American Women's Platform Rhetoric.* Carbondale: Southern Illinois UP, 1999.
—, ed. *With Pen and Voice: A Critical Anthology of Nineteenth-Century African-American Women.* Carbondale: Southern Illinois UP, 1995.
Magee, D. B. "Emerging Responses in a Period of Uncertainty: The Religious Community's Augustinian Reaction to the HIV/AIDS Crisis." Rhetoric Society of America. Pittsburgh. June 1998.
Miller, Keith. *Voice of Deliverance: The Language of Martin Luther King, Jr. and Its Sources.* New York: Basic, 1991.
Mountford, Roxanne. "The Feminization of Ars Praedicandi." Diss. Ohio State U, 1991.
Murphy, James J., ed. *Medieval Eloquence: Studies in the Theory and Practice of Medieval Rhetoric.* Berkeley: U of California P, 1978.
—. *Medieval Rhetoric: A Select Bibliography.* Toronto: U of Toronto P, 1971.
—. *Rhetoric in the Middle Ages.* Berkeley: U of California P, 1974.
—, ed. *Three Medieval Rhetorical Arts.* Berkeley: U of California P, 1971.
Norris, Kathleen. *Amazing Grace.* New York: Putnam, 1998.
—. *Cloister Walk.* New York: Riverhead, 1997.
—. *Dakota.* New York: Houghton Mifflin, 1994.
Powell-Carter, Katy. "Negotiating Spiritual Sites of Composing." Rhetoric Society of America. Pittsburgh. June 1998.
Ratcliffe, Krista. *Anglo-American Feminist Challenges to the Rhetorical Tradition.* Carbondale: Southern Illinois UP, 1996.
Ruether, Rosemary Radford. *Sexism and God-Talk: Toward a Feminist Theology.* Boston: Beacon, 1983.
Royster, Jacqueline Jones, ed. *Southern Horrors and Other Writings: The Anti-Lynching Campaign of Ida B. Wells, 1892-1900.* Boston: Bedford, 1997.
—. *Voices in the Stream.* Pittsburgh: U of Pittsburgh P, forthcoming.
Rupert, Avis. "Religious Education via Distance Learning." Rhetoric Society of America. Pittsburgh. June 1998.

Russell, Letty. *Human Liberation in a Feminist Perspective: A Theology*. Philadelphia: Westminster, 1995.
Williams, Terry Tempest. *New Genesis: Mormons Writing on the Environment*. New York: Gibbs Smith, 1999.
—. *Refuge*. New York: Vintage, 1992.
—. *An Unspoken Hunger*. New York: Vintage, 1995.
Winslow, Rosemary. "Homelessness and Hospitality." Rhetoric Society of America. Pittsburgh. June 1998.

Keynote Address

JACQUELINE JONES ROYSTER
Ohio State University

Sarah's Story: Making a Place for Historical Ethnography in Rhetorical Studies

The thirtieth anniversary conference of the Rhetoric Society of America is a landmark occasion, suggesting to me that our field is well positioned to enter the twenty-first century with strength and considerable vitality. The theme of the conference, "Rhetoric, the Polis, and the Global Village," is a focus that certainly occupies much of my attention these days, so it was with a special enthusiasm that I accepted this role, and I am especially pleased to be able to share with you, as colleagues who are most knowledgeable about such issues, some of the work I have been doing.

I would like to fulfill three objectives. First, I want to spend some time talking about how difficult it is for some rather sensitive issues to gain presence and visibility in public arenas—still. Second, I intend to use the first part of my presentation as a springboard for unfolding the story of Sarah Kinson, hence the title of the talk, as exemplary of what it means to occupy in Gloria Wade-Gayles's words, "the narrow space of race, the dark enclosure of sex" (Wade-Gayles 3), that is, the historical place of African American women in our society. And third, I would like to use both of these two parts as illustrative of the kind of work that I do in rhetorical analysis, using a methodology that I have labeled historical ethnography.

I realize that having a threefold purpose, with the parts appearing on the surface to be rather unrelated, is an invitation to be unbearably long, but what I have tried to do is to resist sharing every single thing that I know about these three points of interest and instead to try telling, quite simply, a good and unapologetically didactic story. So bear with me, please.

La Amistad

To fulfill my first objective, I need to start with the release in 1997 of the popular film *Amistad*. I want to conduct a short survey, two questions: (1) How many of you saw the movie? (2) How many of you had more than a casual conversation about it? As you may know from the popular press, television talk show programs, and Internet Web pages, this film is based on historical fact. It chronicles the incident of *La Amistad*, a Spanish schooner that in 1839 was actively participating in the illegal kidnapping and transportation of Africans into the U.S. slave system. This ship, however, was the site of a revolt led by Sengbe Pieh, who is better known by his more anglicized name Joseph Cinque. The revolt was successful, in large part, due to the courage and determination of the African warriors on board, as well as to the smallness of the vessel and the crew: 7 white and mulatto men, who managed 49 African men, 3 African girls from age 7 to 9 (Mar-gru, Te-me, and Ke-ne), and 1 African boy (Ka-le), age 11, for a total of 53 captives.

With victory under their belts, with the captain and the cook dead, with the other sailors allowed to go free in a lifeboat, Cinque made an agreement, so he thought, with the two men remaining to sail the Africans back to Mendeland in Sierra Leone, the land from which they had been illegally captured. Cinque, being a very observant man, demanded that the two men, Jose Ruiz and Pedro Montez, sail toward the rising sun. They did this during the day, but each night they did not honor their agreement and managed to sail westward toward the shores of the United States, hoping, of course, to be picked up by southern vessels. The *Amistad* was eventually stopped by the U.S. Coast Guard off the coast of New York. The revolutionaries were arrested, jailed, and placed on trial on board the *Washington*, the ship that captured them. They were tried again in Hartford, Connecticut; again in New Haven, Connecticut; and ultimately before the U.S. Supreme Court.

The legal defense team included Seth P. Staples, a future founder of the Yale School of Law; Theodore Sedgwick, from New York and the son of a leading New York attorney; and Roger S. Baldwin, an honors graduate from Yale University, son of the governor of Connecticut, and grandson of Roger Sherman, a signer of the Declaration of Independence and a delegate to the Constitutional Convention. This team was expanded at the Supreme Court phase to include former president of the United States, John Quincy Adams, who had been keeping close watch on the proceedings and in frequent communication with various players in the scenario, including two of the children. The court process took three years, but the Africans were eventually found to have been born free in Africa and not as slaves, illegally captured and transported against their will as free people, and therefore acting, as all free men had the right to act, in self-defense. The captives were released and provided, by a substantial fund-raising effort on the part of abolitionists, with "safe" passage back to Sierra Leone, which continued to be embroiled in the illegal business of slave trading.

This is the story rendered in the film *Amistad* by Debbie Allen, who as the originator of the project took ten years to assemble the resources and connections to make the film. Allen and Colin Wilson served as co-producers, Steven Spielberg was the producer/director, David Franzoni was the screenwriter, Walter Parker and Laurie MacDonald of Dream Works Pictures were the executive producers, Janusz Kaminski was the director of photography, John Williams was the composer, Ruth Carter was the costume designer, and Michael Kahn was the editor. The filmmakers, in other words, were as stellar as the cast, which included Sir Anthony Hopkins, Matthew McConaughey, Morgan

Freeman, and Djimon Hounsou, among others. To date, the film has not received wide distribution, has been denied viewing in much of the South, and was allowed only limited distribution elsewhere. It is, nevertheless, an interestingly told tale that yielded one Oscar nomination: for Anthony Hopkins's portrayal of John Quincy Adams.

In the main, the movie has been criticized, as have other Spielberg films, for being long, for being uneven in its dramatization, for being questionable in Spielberg's choice of Matthew McConaughey as Robert (cf. Roger) Baldwin,[1] for "over-making" (i.e., making too important and unreal, several moments in the film), and for "preaching" (i.e., for becoming too ideological). One might say, in fact, that with the last two criticisms Spielberg was charged with not "entertaining" the audience.

My general sense of this film for the context at hand, that is, for its efforts to generate public conversation about slavery and racial oppression, is that it is the type of film that I have come to call a "white man's awakening story," and I rush here to emphasize that I do not quarrel much anymore with the apparently inescapable need for a film about contentious historical moments to have such a purpose, given the power structures of the United States. In their fashioning of white men's awakening stories, my sense is that filmmakers situate the participants in the discourse as performers and viewers in a way that permits concerns to become visible and thereby capable of being discussed. What we see in *Amistad*, and what in my opinion works very well, is indeed just this type of awakening, two aspects of which I want to acknowledge here. The first is the portrayal of John Quincy Adams who, as an opaque historical figure for most viewers, reaches interesting clarity as a man of principle. Though reluctant to do so, Adams ultimately stepped forward in defense of the captives and acted on his principles in the arena of our most laudable public space, the Supreme Court. The second awakening is Robert Baldwin, who experienced a major shift in the perception of his task and his commitment.

In the beginning of the movie, Baldwin is positioned as a lawyer who saw not so much the humanity and inhumanity of his case, as much as the solution of it being imbedded in a compelling legal twist. He saw the case as a legal, not a moral, problem. He recognized that the central argument was not morality or the question of piracy, revolt, and murder, but "property." If the revolutionaries were human beings and not "property," then the terms of engagement for a consideration of their revolt shifted the paradigm in a way that made the case against them null and void. What made these Africans "not property" turned on the small but concrete point of whether they were born in Africa and not in the slaveholding Caribbean or the United States. Being born in Africa made them human (i.e., not slaves). As humans, as citizens of another country who were kidnapped, they had the human right by U.S. law to defend themselves.

One of the moments in the film that best symbolizes the shift in Baldwin's thinking from a simple notion of property to a more complex notion of humanity is the moment when John Quincy Adams asks him essentially, "Who are these men? Who is Cinque? What do you know, really know, about them?" Baldwin could not provide a satisfactory answer. Despite the many months that he had spent among the men, Baldwin knew nothing about them. He knew their case, not them, and at that moment of critical questioning, we have a white man's awakening to moral complexity, social responsibility, and human ties, rather than a simple lawyer-client relationship and legal ties.

This story, as dramatic as it is in the lives of people of African descent, assumed a narrative viewpoint in the film that actually made central the white men in the story. Cinque, as the central African character, most certainly looms large as the embodiment in the movie of moral consciousness and ethical obligations. However, both he and the incident of the *Amistad* revolt become an occasion for demonstrating how a devastatingly dramatic event makes possible white men's awakening and the opportunity to make visible the previously invisible—in white men's eyes, of course, the eyes of power and the holders of the rights and authority for public policy making. The revolt becomes the instrument by which white men's duty, honor, and obligation to others are revealed amid the unarticulated systems, legal and illegal, moral and immoral, of chattel slavery and racial oppression in the United States of America. Duty, honor, obligation, freedom, justice, equality as bedrock "American" values take on new dramatic potential for both Adams and Baldwin. The movie ultimately lives up to the challenge of providing a springboard for public conversation, as did, I might add, the original historical event when it assumed in 1839 dramatic rhetorical potential as a crystallizing event for the abolitionist movement and for the formation of one of the most long-lasting organizations of political and economic support for nineteenth-century African Americans. This organization, the Amistad Committee, was formed almost immediately after the capture of the ship with the objective of mounting the defense for the Mendi and making supreme use of the occasion to further the abolitionist cause. This committee ultimately became the American Missionary Association.

The thing that I find most interesting about this film, and about the event on which it is based, is just this last point, the potential for opening a much-needed "public" discussion of issues around which we have deep desires in this country to remain silent. What I find equally interesting is the extent to which the film was actually unable to generate such a discussion. *Amistad* was neither widely seen nor widely discussed, and of course *Amistad* was not the only film that received such treatment. *Rosewood* was another limited release film about racial oppression, and this latter one, also based on historical fact, was actually sent out to the public by the studio with an "apology" (Milloy), that is, with a money-back guarantee (in the tradition, perhaps, of certification processes for slave narratives). On the surface, this guarantee was in the interest of "validating," or "authenticating," the film, and thereby declaring that it really is a good enough movie for someone to watch, that, of course, in the face of the interesting array of popular films that have not been called on to provide such guarantees. What came to mind for me with both *Amistad* and *Rosewood* was the old adage, "The more things change, the more they remain the same."

Given my viewpoint, what added yet another burning bit to this curious flame was the contrast of the internationally celebrated film *Titanic*. We now know more about the jewelry and the dinner plates on this boat than we do about the nature of chattel slavery, as a two-century-long operation in the United States, about the nature of its abolition, or about the role of *La Amistad* in the formation and work of the American Missionary Society in the interest of people of African descent.

Sarah's Story

At this point, I would like to shift attention to the dark enclosure within the small space in order to tell you the story of Sarah Kinson, that is, Sarah Mar-gru Kinson, the seven-year-old female child who was one of the captives on board *La Amistad*. If *Amistad* were our only source of information about Mar-gru, then she would remain a round-faced, dark-skinned female child, nameless among the extras, the expendables in this film, and because I assume that most, if not all of you, have not heard her name before, she would remain nameless and expendable among the pages of U.S. history and rhetorical history as well. So my effort here is to counter this erasure and say *Amistad* may be John Quincy Adams's story; it may be Roger Baldwin's story; most certainly it is Cinque's story, but *Amistad* is also Sarah's story.

Mar-gru was born in Bendembu, Mandingo country, southeast of Freetown, in Sierra Leone in 1832. She was one of seven children. According to Ellen NicKenzie Lawson, there are at least two accounts of how she came to be a captive. In one version, when she was seven years old, her parents pawned her to pay a debt and were then unable to raise the funds to reclaim her. In the second version, she was kidnapped while walking between villages. By either process, Mar-gru ended up in the slave pens at Dunbomo on the Island of Lomboko, then on the *Tecora* to Havana, Cuba, where she was sold to Pedro Montez, and ultimately taken on board *La Amistad*.

As prisoners, Mar-gru and the other *Amistad* girls, Te-me and Ke-ne, were allowed to reside in New Haven, Connecticut, in the home of their jailers, Colonel and Mrs. Stanton Pendleton. Ka-le, the male child, remained with the men. After two years, amid rumors of forced labor for the girls, both the Pendletons and the Amistad Committee (again, the abolitionists who were working on behalf of the prisoners) sued for custody. The Amistad Committee won. Mar-gru, now nine years old, was placed in the home of Reverend Noah Porter, a man of wealth. At that point, Mar-gru, Te-me, and Ke-ne were re-named Sarah, Maria, and Charlotte. During their incarceration, all of the Mende were taught to speak, read, and write English and to do math by abolitionist students from Yale Divinity School. Mar-gru proved to be academically gifted. She and the other children were frequently asked by their Christian guardians to demonstrate their adaptability to Christianity by singing hymns and reading from the Bible. Several of the Africans toured in Boston and New York, Mar-gru included, in order to raise the funds necessary for the trip back to Africa. Their program included Bible readings, African songs, Christian hymns, and a dramatic presentation of the *Amistad* story. Mar-gru was often asked to read the 124th Psalm:

> If it had not been the Lord
> who was on our side,
> let Israel now say
> if it had not been the Lord who was
>   on our side,
> when men rose up against us,
> then they would have swallowed us
>   alive,
> when their anger was kindled
>   against us;
> then the flood would have swept us
>   away,
> the torrent would have gone over
>   us,
> then over us would have gone
>   the raging waters.
>
> Blessed be the Lord,
>   who has not given us
>   as prey to their teeth!
> We have escaped as a bird
>   from the snare of the fowlers;
> the snare is broken,
>   and we have escaped!
>
> Our help is in the name of the Lord,
>   who made heaven and earth.

By this process, Mar-gru became a public speaker, one recognized in fact for her talents and abilities. You can well imagine how this psalm functioned in their program, coming from the body of a nine-year-old girl.

When the Amistad Committee had secured enough funds for the trip to Africa, they held a farewell ceremony for the Mende in November 1841 at the Broadway Tabernacle in New York City. At that ceremony, Mar-gru read the 130th Psalm:

> Out of the depths I cry to
>   thee, O lord!
> Lord, hear my voice!
> Let thy ears be attentive
>   to the voice of my supplications!
>
> If thou, O Lord, shouldst mark
>   iniquities,
> Lord, who could stand?
> But there is forgiveness with
>   thee,
>   that thou mayest be feared.
>
> I wait for the Lord, my soul
>   waits,
>   and in his word I hope;
> my soul waits for the Lord
>   more than watchmen for the
>   morning,
>   more than watchmen for the
>   morning.
>
> O Israel, hope in the Lord!
> For with the Lord there is
>   steadfast love,
>   and with him is plenteous
>   redemption.
> And he will redeem Israel
>   from all his iniquities.

Back in Sierra Leone, Mar-gru remained with Reverend William Raymond, the leader of the missionaries who traveled with the *Amistad* group on their return to Africa, and she continued her education at the mission school that he and his wife established there. In 1846, Mar-gru came back to the United States as Sarah Kinson under the sponsorship of abolitionist Lewis Tappan, a

New York merchant and organizer of the Amistad Committee, to attend Oberlin College. At Oberlin, she became the first African woman to enroll in an American college, first entering the college preparatory program and then the Ladies' Literary Course. Her roommate was Lucy Stanton, an African American woman from Cleveland, who was the first African American woman to be granted a four-year college degree in 1850, and who then went on to become a renowned teacher, public speaker, and community activist. Kinson, like Stanton, was an excellent student, who took advantage of the myriad of activities available to her at Oberlin to develop her rhetorical abilities in both speaking and writing. She spoke up in class and at local churches, and, in keeping with the habits of the day, she kept a lively correspondence between Lewis Tappan and her friends in Connecticut and Africa. To Tappan, she wrote, "I am studying very diligently so as to be qualified to do good in the world as this was my object in coming to Oberlin" (Lawson 14). Kinson did indeed study diligently, returning to Africa in 1849 as a young woman, educated well beyond the standards of her day, and well prepared for service as a missionary and teacher with the American Missionary Association (AMA). She was assigned with Hanah More, a white missionary who preferred not to work with Kinson, to Kaw Mendi Mission in Sierra Leone.

With this assignment,[2] Kinson became one of the first African-born women and one of only a few unmarried women to receive a mission assignment. A few years later, Kinson married fellow missionary Edward Henry Green, and they both continued in their commitment to missionary work. In terms of her own work, Kinson and her fellow missionary Hanah More set up an African Women's Sewing Society, called the Modest Dress Society. The thirty-six women who formed the group were required to wear Western clothes in order to attend. Kinson served as president. She told the group stories and delivered informal sermons. As Lawson reports, Kinson soon wrote to Lewis Tappan, "I am not ashamed to tell you that I am preaching to my country people . . ." (Lawson 222).

In 1855, in support of her new role as preacher, the Greens set up their own mission, believing (unlike the AMA itself) that Africans should be converted by Africans. At this point, their support from the AMA was soon withdrawn amid controversy surrounding Kinson's husband, and the historical records on Kinson blur. One version (Cable) indicates that Kinson lived out her life at Kaw Mendi Mission. The other indicates that with the controversy surrounding her husband, she fades from view and there is uncertainty about what happened to her exactly. In either case, the results are essentially the same. As an educated nineteenth-century African woman, Kinson participated in the forming of rhetorical traditions among women of African descent. I met her in the archival records of Oberlin College as I was trying to reconstruct the rise of rhetorical prowess among African American women and especially among the first generations of college-educated African American women. As one of the first female students of African descent at Oberlin, Kinson was a trailblazer whose personal history happened to include one of the most dramatic events in African American history. My job today, then, is to keep Sarah Mar-gru Kinson from being, once again, resubsumed in the dark enclosure within the narrow space of a racialized, gendered, and ideologically contentious world.

Historical Ethnography

This section makes a place for historical ethnography. As you can probably tell, I spend a lot of time in archives. So, as a rhetorician who focuses on African American women, why do I do that? One reason, of course, is that I get to discover little-known people and retell, as I have today, their stories. That, however, is really the *lagniappe*, or that little something extra, of what I do. Despite the seductive nature of storytelling as an aesthetically pleasing enterprise, unveiling little-known stories is not my primary interest. I am interested, instead, in gaining a more fully textured historical view of the rhetorical practices of African American women. I am interested in gaining a view that has the interpretive power to account for their participation as "unofficial," "unauthenticated" speakers and writers in public arenas that are typically deemed "counter." The basic question for me is this: As rhetoricians, how indeed do we account for the long-standing histories, achievements, impacts, and consequences of the "unofficial" rhetors and the "counter" discourses that have operated so consistently and with such vitality despite the hegemonic processes that support "official" rhetors and their more "mainstream" discourses.

What I have learned in looking at the rhetorical practices of African American women over time is that my viewpoint, because of its concern with "unofficial" spaces, dictates that I pay attention to the worlds that surround African American women and that I do so in two specific ways: in terms of the social, political, and ideological contexts in which these spaces are constituted; and also in terms of the material conditions under which these women are compelled to form ethos, to construct rhetorical mandates, and to operate with effect and even eloquence in language use. My viewpoint, therefore, has to be transdisciplinary and multidimensional, an agenda that fits well with ethnographic methodologies. My habit is to triangulate analyses, analyses of ethos formation, of the context for rhetorical action, and of the rhetorical event itself. I look synchronically and diachronically at the relationships of these women to the material world, looking particularly at the concrete circumstances by which they are able to live, to work, and to prosper. I look across genres or rhetorical performances to notice the resonances of a writer's habits and concerns. I chart language behavior descriptively and ideologically. I look for evidence of the relationships between ideological view and rhetorical decision making, and I draw inferences and create possible scenarios.

Mainly, I engage in processes that produce thick descriptions.[3] I gather whatever data are available about the material culture and about meaning-making processes as these processes demonstrate a convergence of personal, social, and institutional mandates. What is probably most distinctive about this approach beyond an interest in thickening descriptions is that the thickening process permits personal experience to count (both mine and theirs). Experience, not just documentary evidence, takes its place as one data set that needs to be systematically interrogated in the same way that history, traditionally defined through documentary evidence, is questioned or that rhetorical performance is questioned. The challenge, of course, is to engage in such interrogations with subjects who are often long dead. Obviously, I cannot interview my subjects or check my interpretations of their actions and achievements with them directly. What I have come to accept, however, is that historical subjects, even African American women as nontraditional historical subjects, do indeed comment with their own interpretive authority. They just do so uniquely as their rhetorical performances speak both directly and indirectly to the worlds in which they operate. I acknowledge, then, the importance of listening well, of paying careful and close attention to what they say on, between, and around the lines; of listening to what they say the day before, for example, and the day after; and of paying attention to who is in the conversation with them, where it is taking place, and how it interacts with other conversations that may be occurring simultaneously. I call this process *historical ethnography*, and I see these types of inquiries and data gathering processes to be critical to both knowledge and understanding, not simply of African American women's rhetorical practices, but of the landscape of rhetoric itself.

Coda

In fulfilling the promise of didacticism, what instruction do I want to offer? There are at least three points to which I would like to pay special note.

The first one has to do with the construction of the public sphere. Nancy Fraser and Mary Ryan are noted for the insightful ways in which they discuss the existence of alternative, parallel public spheres. I would like to underscore, through the dissatisfaction that I have inscribed here with public discourses around issues of U.S. slavery and racial oppression as two examples, that mainstream official public discourses are inadequate. They continue to boldly disregard the interests of many groups who have sustained among themselves public spheres that are lively and long-standing. My sense is that these inadequacies are becoming increasingly problematic in the global context in which we live, a context in which power relationships are shifting and the need for negotiations of various sorts are ever-present. My sense is that we need to be much more inventive in constructing a new and different concept of the public sphere, one that permits a broader array of viewpoints, experiences, and concerns to become part of the conversation, rather than peripheral to it or simultaneous with it. My view is that we need to conceptualize an arena that permits interaction and negotiation with the expectation of redress, rather than one in which there is little opportunity for cross-fertilization or even for meaningful regard.

The second point is that rhetorical traditions of women of African descent, as illustrated by the participation of Sarah Mar-gru Kinson in the formation of those traditions, are interestingly intertwined between the lines and around the edges of other traditions. My sense is that we need to bring those practices forward, to flesh them out to the extent possible, to document them, and to build interpretive frameworks that permit achievements to be acknowledged and valued. Despite the fact that these traditions have existed primarily in counterdiscourses, their long existence suggests that they have the capacity to add in a more dynamic way than we have been giving credit to the history of language well used.

Third, what these two points suggest to me about rhetorical knowledge and training is that our rhetorical past remains too narrowly rendered. We need to open up the vistas by which we set the terms of valuation so that we do not just glorify one view of the past but position and reposition ourselves to see other values easily missed if we focus too exclusively in one arena. We need research methodologies that permit us to see what is there and not there and to be imaginative and articulate about what could be there instead. My sense is that we live in a world that insists now that definitions of what constitutes the "polis" be extended. Certainly, we live in a world that is beginning to be insistent also about the need to re-vision the world as a multisplendored conglomeration of competing interests and alliances. What I see also is that contemporary research methodologies in rhetorical studies are called on to match contemporary challenges in dynamic ways. Salient among those challenges is the need to develop paradigms and practices that facilitate cross-boundary communication and cultural exchange. My sense is that language is increasingly our most invaluable cultural commodity. It is the capital by which we have the capacity to negotiate differences as we learn, sometimes under fire, to live, breathe, and prosper in the presence of others, in fact, in the presence of a whole slew of others who these days rather insistently constitute this little village called Earth and our little street called the United States of America.

With all of this said, however, I suppose in all fairness that my most didactic message is this: Given the ways of our contemporary world, rhetorical studies may just be (like "Babylon Five," for those of you who are fellow science fiction buffs) our last and best hope for the future. More than that, given the ways of our historical world, African American women and other groups who have honed their crafts in the margins may be the rhetors from whom we can learn and be inspired. So, in tribute to Sarah Mar-gru Kinson and other women of African descent who have played roles in the formation of rhetorical history as "counter" space, I want to end by quoting from a poem by Mari Evans, entitled "I Am a Black Woman" (105-06):

> I am a Black woman
> The music of my song
> Some sweet arpeggio of tears
> Is written in a minor key...
>
> I
> am a Black woman
> Tall as a cypress
> strong
> Beyond all definition—still
> Defying place and time
> and circumstance
> assailed
> impervious
> indestructible.
>
> Look
> on me and be
> renewed.

Look on Sarah Mar-gru Kinson and the landscape of unknown others like her whom we do not know but could, and yes indeed, look on them and be renewed.

Notes

1. Please note that, whereas this film conforms to the broad sweep of historical fact with the *Amistad* case, it nevertheless takes many liberties with some of the specific details (e.g., who the defenders actually were, the role of black abolitionists in this story, the close attention and consistent involvement of John Quincy Adams as advisor in the case).

2. Please note that I also discuss Sarah Mar-gru Kinson in *Traces of a Stream: Literacy and Social Change Among African American Women* (University of Pittsburgh Press). In this project, my intent is to secure for Kinson an appropriate place in the history of higher education for women of African descent, highlighting her participation as one of the first students to attend Oberlin College and to situate her work in Africa as part of a tradition of social activism.

3. The term "thick description" was popularized by anthropologist Clifford Geertz (*The Interpretation of Cultures*) as a methodological process for reaching deeper levels of understanding in interpreting data relative to specific cultural events and practices. He says that "ethnography is thick description. What the ethnographer is in fact faced with ... is a multiplicity of complex conceptual structures, many of them superimposed upon or knotted into one another, which are at once strange, irregular, and inexplicit, and which he must continue somehow first to grasp and then to render" (9-10). Geertz advocated looking, looking again, and looking again and again to push oneself as an observer to go below the surface and beyond the obvious for interpretations that are more meaningful.

Works Cited

http://hollywood.com/sites/amistad/notes/makers.html
Cable, Mary. *Black Odyssey: The Case of the Slave Ship* Amistad. New York: Penguin, 1971.
Evans, Mari. "I Am a Black Woman." *Confirmations: An Anthology of African American Women*. Ed. Amiri Baraka and Amina Baraka. New York: Quill, 1983. 105-06.
Fraser, Nancy. *Justice Interruptus: Critical Reflections on the Postsocialist Condition*. New York: Routledge, 1997.
Geertz, Clifford. *The Interpretation of Cultures*. New York: Basic, 1973.
Lawson, Ellen NicKenzie. *The Three Sarahs: Documents of Antebellum Black College Women*. Studies in Women and Religion 13. New York: Edwin Mellen, 1984.
Milloy, Courtland. "Washington Post Reporter Discovers Rosewood Refund Offer Discounting a Disturbing Truth." *The Washington Post* 12 Nov. 1997: B1.
Psalm 124. The Holy Bible. Revised Standard Version.
Psalm 130. The Holy Bible. Revised Standard Version.
Ryan, Mary P. *Women in Public: Between Banners and Ballots, 1825-1880*. Baltimore: Johns Hopkins UP, 1990.
Royster, Jacqueline Jones. *Traces of a Stream: Literacy and Social Change Among African American Women*. Pittsburgh: U of Pittsburgh P, forthcoming.
Wade-Gayles, Gloria. *No Crystal Stair: Visions of Race and Sex in Black Women's Fiction*. New York: Pilgrim, 1984.

Selections from the Charles Kneupper Memorial Lecture

GEORGE A. KENNEDY
University of North Carolina, Chapel Hill

Rhetoric and Culture/Rhetoric and Technology

Most of us probably come to an understanding of the nature of rhetoric from Aristotle, and many Aristotelian concepts can be used to describe rhetoric throughout the global village. My recent comparative studies, however, have led me to the conclusion that some Aristotelian concepts—his view of epideictic, for example—need revision if they are to be valid cross-culturally.[1] In addition to what I have said earlier, one might, on cultural grounds, question some of the logical methods Aristotle applied to describing rhetoric. Aristotle was a formalist and a structuralist, and he often relied on binary logic that would not have appealed to some non-Western thinkers, not to his near contemporary the Chinese philosopher Mencius, for example, who developed a theory of multiple definitions. Every audience, Aristotle says (*Rhetoric* 1.3.2), is either a judge or not a judge. Subsequently (2.18.1), he admits that an audience is in some sense a judge even when it is not asked to make a formal decision, and in practice the three species of Aristotelian rhetoric—judicial, deliberative, and epideictic—are rarely pure. A second binary distinction made by Aristotle (1.2.1) is that between atechnic (or nonartistic) and technic (or artistic) means of persuasion, the latter divided into what may conveniently be labeled *ethos, logos,* and *pathos*. Most of us would probably agree that these are useful general categories of rhetoric, even though there may be others, and even though there are overlapping features among these three. Ethical, logical, and emotional means of persuasion are found in all cultures, but the effectiveness of a composition often derives almost exclusively from ethos. We need to recognize, however, something Aristotle did not make clear, that all three of his means of persuasion have nonartistic and artistic elements. The nonartistic element of ethos is the authority that the speaker—or writer—brings to the occasion or context. Its artistic element, which is the only feature discussed by Aristotle, is how a speaker creates trust by what is actually said and how it is said. The nonartistic element in logos is the material that the rhetor chooses and uses in the discourse, applying artistic technique to it. Is there any real difference between, on the one hand, a rhetor's citation of witnesses, which Aristotle regarded as nonartistic but which includes quotation of proverbs (1.15.14), and on the other hand the use of historical examples, which he regards as artistic (1.2.8-10)? The nonartistic element of pathos is the emotion already existing in an audience, which the speaker then artistically enhances or mollifies. Aristotle's discussion of the emotions (2.2-11) seems to imply as much.

One might propose that many of the categories of Western rhetorical theory, and thus what we think of as rhetorical techniques, are general features in many—perhaps all—cultures, though some categories, including epideictic and nonartistic means of persuasion, need revision to describe what actually occurs. What differs is not the psychology and dialectic inherent in our traditional system of rhetoric, but primarily the materials the rhetor uses: the examples, specific topics, images, symbols, and gestures. Cultural differences can be discovered in what is available and acceptable as an example—the extent to which examples from myth or from documented history can be found and used. Dialectical topics (e.g., cause and effect) are in themselves culturally neutral, though there may be cultural differences in what members of a society regard as a cause (e.g., whether the culture admits magic and sorcery as causal). Rhetoric is a potentiality, inherent in nature, that is actualized in particular contexts, where it undergoes cultural evolution. Another way of looking at it might be to say that rhetoric utilizes both hardware and software. The hardware is the way our minds are wired to create and receive discourse; the software is the programming supplied by culture. Discourse is programmed by features of each culture, the natural environment, religious and social values, and historical experience, but in turn it helps to create, mold, preserve, and change cultural programs. A theory or way of teaching rhetoric emerged in classical Greece to meet the needs of democracy, but it is equally clear that the existence of vigorous rhetorical practice in archaic Greece was one of the factors making possible the development of democracy.

Technological developments are also actualizations of potentials and systems of organizing energy. The invention of writing in Mesopotamia was a rhetorical act in that the earliest uses of writing were to identify and thus preserve ownership by impressing seals on objects, or listing objects belonging to temples or individuals. Although writing may have helped to actualize some potential features of rhetoric and given a particular emphasis to others, and although it probably both aided and weakened memory, its contribution to rhetoric was largely in terms of the materials available for the rhetor to use: documents that could be introduced in proof, historical examples known from records, written speeches that could be studied and imitated, rhetorical handbooks that suggested effective techniques, and the like. It should be kept in mind, however, that except in certain places and certain periods (e.g., in classical Athens and imperial Rome), the literacy rate was low, and fluent literacy was often limited to a small elite in the court or the church. Any psychological effects attributed to writing by scholars were hardly felt by the general populace until modern times. Written texts were more often heard when read aloud than by private silent reading, the goal of ancient schools of rhetoric was to teach public speaking, for which writing was regarded as an aid, and the dominant images applied to communication were and have remained verbal. We still regularly use phrases like an author or text "says," poets still "sing," and controversialists "speak out" in their writings.

It is not clear to me that modern technology has altered the basic structures or techniques of rhetoric, whether theoretical or applied. It has not, you might say, rewired our rhetorical hardware. Technology clearly has facilitated the storage and access to information on a vast scale, the process begun by the invention of writing and amplified by the introduction of printing. But a recent article in *Business Week*[2] reveals the present limitations: computerized data can decay before you know it and only archival quality microfilm has anything comparable to the durability of a book.

Writing and printing reduced the role of delivery in rhetoric. Both of course had a delivery system of their own, and manuscripts—Islamic, Indic, and Chinese, as well as Western—show how artistic these can be, but the techniques are necessarily limited and rather static. Modern technology, especially cinema and television but to an increasing extent also the Internet, has brought back delivery as a major—perhaps the major—part of rhetoric.

Understanding of the creation of visual effects in artistic representations goes back at least thirty thousand years to the cave paintings in France, and was exploited by architects and artists in Egypt, the Near East, India, Rome, and elsewhere as political propaganda in support of the regime in power or of religious belief. Artists understood how to vary the arrangement, size, stance, and expression of figures, the iconography of represented symbols, and the angle at which representations would be viewed to convey a message to the populace. There are some accounts of the reactions of those who saw these works, and a general recognition of analogies between rhetoric or poetics and painting or sculpture, but no surviving theoretical discussions to reveal the extent to which visual rhetoric was conceptualized earlier than the Renaissance. In the sixteenth and seventeenth centuries, theorists of painting (e.g., Francisco Junius) began to use rhetorical terminology to describe techniques of visual representations.

That modern technology has vastly increased the role of visual rhetoric in our lives is widely recognized, especially in the case of cinema, television, and advertising, and there is an extensive body of research that explores in detail the effects of color, form, motion, staging, camera angle and lens, cutting and pasting, and all the possible manipulation of images, together with sound, to create psychological effects. A recent book that supplies a good introduction to this rhetoric is *Visual Intelligence: Perception, Image, and Manipulation in Visual Communication*, by Ann Marie Seward Barry.[3] Unlike many who discuss these subjects, Barry actually uses the word "rhetoric"! Cinema clearly employs invention, arrangement, style, memory, and delivery, and cinema studies use some terms borrowed from rhetoric (e.g., troping, metonymy, and synecdoche) while borrowing others from semiotics or narratology or giving special meaning to other terms (e.g., frame, mise-en-scène, or montage as describing the rhetorical arrangement of a film). What has not been done, so far as I know, is an integration of this practical knowledge with rhetorical theory of speech and writing, whether Aristotelian, Burkean, or other, into a comprehensive general theory of rhetoric. It is a formidable task. My expectation is that many traditional rhetorical concepts would survive this test, especially concepts of invention and style, and that many new techniques would be identified, especially in the parts of rhetoric we call arrangement and delivery.

Less clear, at least to me, are the rhetorical consequences of the hypertext, including the Internet, the World Wide Web, and e-mail. The electronic word carries on the work of writing and printing in greatly facilitating communication over distance; in some other ways, it would seem to reduce or undermine effects introduced by writing or printing. Both writing and printing encouraged the standardization of language, the use of formal language determined by conventions of genre, and probably also the use of complex, hypotactic, or periodic sentence construction that would be easily understood only when read slowly. Electronic communication is characteristically colloquial, informal, antihierarchical, and paratactic. It facilitates quick reaction to a situation or communication, in contrast to writing a letter or publishing a statement. E-mail encourages an abrupt style that can be perceived as insensitive and discourteous. There is often only a weak perception of audience; electronic communication lessens the responsibility for what is said, provides an opening not only for quick reaction but for gossip and slander. Conversely, in the case of serious and responsible discourse, it creates problems for the protection of intellectual property and copyright to ideas. These issues have recently been discussed by Laura Gurak in *Persuasion and Privacy in Cyberspace*.[4] Plagiarism, deliberate or inadvertent, is not solely a modern phenomenon, but the demand of the modern university for original scholarship as the basis of tenure and salary decisions puts a particularly sharp edge on authorship and creativity. Ideas on the Internet seem to be in the public domain in a way that written or printed ideas are not. Instant response by e-mail or in chat groups may seem to return us to something like the conditions of an oral situation and lively debate, but there are important differences: it is not face-to-face communication; it lacks the nuances of tone and body language,[5] the constraints imposed by someone presiding in the chair, or the physical presence of an audience; and it does not have the modulating conventions of public address. In a word, there is less inclination to allow an opponent to save face.

Among recent discussions of the effects of the new technology, one of the liveliest is Richard A. Lanham's book, *The Electronic Word*,[6] which James Arnt Aune has called "the most important book on the Third Wave" (of communication technology).[7] It is a fascinating, impressive book in many ways, but some of Lanham's observations about the history and function of rhetoric need revision. One of his themes is the negative effect of specialization of the academic disciplines and the value of rhetoric as an arch-discipline in the human sciences and education. In general, I agree with this, but not in placing the blame for the situation so heavily on Peter Ramus in the sixteenth century. Ramus's influence on the teaching of rhetoric, restricting it in practice to the study of tropes and figures, was very regrettable and had negative repercussions, but it was an extreme example of a trend in his time, its direct influence lasted for only about 150 years, it was strongly resisted by some other major thinkers, and its indirect influence continued primarily in France and some other parts of the European continent, not in Britain and America after about 1750. More importantly, Ramus did not invent the organization of specialized academic disciplines, as Lanham seems to think; their history goes back to Plato and Aristotle and suffered through the academic imperialism of both grammar and logic in the Middle Ages. Modern academic disciplines in the humanities and social sciences are creations of the nineteenth century, when their increasing specialization largely resulted from their imitation of the methods of the natural sciences. This is a cultural phenomenon. Outside the West, rhetoric has usually been integrated into the study of politics and ethics, as it was by the Greek sophists.

Elsewhere in his book, Professor Lanham raises what he calls the "Q Question." The Q Question as he formulates it is, at the most general level, the question of whether education in the humanities, including the study of literature and rhetoric, can create moral virtue, and if so, how? That is indeed a challenging question, and as Professor Lanham says, it is rarely directly faced. My problem is his placing special blame for a failure to face the question on Quintilian, and thus labeling the whole question after the initial of Quintilian's name. Quintilian is indeed the classic source for the thesis that only a good man can be a good orator, but there is very little textual support in Quintilian's *Institutio* for the view that he believed education in rhetoric could create a moral person. From my reading of what he says, I would summarize his view as follows: moral virtue results in part from nature, or what we would call genetic inheritance; partly from the example of parents and role models; from the imposition of rewards and punishments on the young (and Quintilian would emphasize the carrot more than the stick); and finally from the thoughtful study of moral philosophy and the examples of history, the kind of study undertaken by Quintilian's contemporary Plutarch. The student's moral values are largely formed before undertaking study of rhetoric, but can be reinforced or undermined by the example of the teacher and the conditions the teacher creates in class. Oratory requires an ability to discuss moral issues, and the orator who believes in them will be more successful than one who does not, but moral character is essentially something distinct from rhetorical skill; indeed, it is the recognition of this distinction that leads Quintilian to demand moral character as a prerequisite to great oratory. What Lanham calls the Q Question would be better called the "Iota

Question," because among ancient rhetoricians it was Isocrates who comes closest to the view that a student can develop moral values by rhetorical compositions in favor of ethical and civic virtue.

Lanham (154-94) distinguishes a weak and a strong defense of rhetoric. The weak defense is the traditional one, originating with Aristotle. It argues that rhetoric is in itself neither good nor bad; it is a neutral tool that can be used by good or bad purposes. The strong defense assumes that truth is determined by social dramas, such as a courtroom trial. As Michael Leff restates it, "The strong defense reorders the relationship between theory and practice, giving priority to practice. From this perspective, ethical and political knowledge is not based in a priori, abstract truth but is formed through rhetorical engagement in concrete situations." "This shift in attitude," Leff continues, "characterizes a variety of new approaches to rhetoric, known variously as 'rhetoric as epistemic,' 'constitutive rhetoric,' 'generative rhetoric,' and 'the rhetoric of the human sciences.'"[8] One might argue that the weak defense is an example of structuralism, the strong defense of poststructuralism.

I have considerable respect for the strong defense of rhetoric at the level of practice, some reservations at the level of theory, where it seems to me the strong defense has to be justified by the weak defense. The strong defense works best in a democratic society where the majority grant some measure of toleration to minorities. On the global level it seems to justify any values and beliefs in society that are rhetorically constituted and accepted by an audience, which includes fascism, anti-Semitism, misleading advertising, chauvinism, religious fundamentalism, and most of the ills of history. At this level of description, we then have to fall back to defend rhetoric as a neutral tool that can be used equally for beneficial or exploitative purposes.

The study and practice of rhetoric, oral and written, certainly facilitates the student's development of skills of argumentation and expression, and equally important an ability to evaluate the discourse of others. Today it seems important for this to include an ability to understand and criticize the rhetoric of modern technological communication, sometimes with appreciation of its artistic qualities while discounting its propaganda, sometimes consciously accepting, sometimes consciously rejecting or modifying the message. The citizens of today and tomorrow need a knowledge of many things, of science and technology and economics and languages and of issues of class and gender, and of cultural differences. But there is probably nothing in which they are in greater need than of an ability to evaluate the rhetoric of others, oral, written, printed, or electronic, domestic or foreign, political, religious, or commercial, and to become themselves effective artists in composition and communication.

Notes

1. See *Comparative Rhetoric: An Historical and Cross-Cultural Introduction* (New York: Oxford UP, 1997) 222.
2. "From Digits to Dust," *Business Week* 20 Apr. 1998: 128-30.
3. (State U of New York P, 1997).
4. *Persuasion and Privacy in Cyberspace: The Online Protests Over Lotus Marketplace and the Clipper Chip* (New Haven: Yale UP, 1997).
5. The lack can be supplied in part from the use of "smilies," the code of glyphs developed by Scott Fahlman at Carnegie Mellon University that picture the state of mind of the writer or the tone in which something is said.
6. *The Electronic Word: Democracy, Technology, and the Arts* (Chicago: U of Chicago P, 1993).
7. *Quarterly Journal of Speech* 83 (1997): 234.
8. "Cicero's *Pro Murena* and the Strong Case for Rhetoric," *Rhetoric and Public Affairs* 1 (1998): 63.

Part I
Classical Roots

SHAWN SMITH
Yale University

Pity and the *Polis*

Quintilian writes: "Athens, the wisest of all states, regarded pity not merely as an emotion, but even as a god" (5.11.38). Although the social dimension of this apotheosis of pity is not entirely clear, a few recent studies of ancient Greek literature and culture have shown an interest in the role of pity (or more properly, *eleos* and *oiktos*) in the cultivation of ethical, social, and political values in the Greek *polis* (Crotty; Salkever; Zak). Such studies usually associate the experience of tragic *katharsis* in Aristotelian poetics (where pity plays a major role)[1] with a kind of learning that corresponds to the political education of the *demos*.[2] Some of these scholars have been influenced by Leon Golden's interpretation of *katharsis*, which defines it as a form of intellectual clarification (Golden, *Aristotle*; Golden, "Clarification Theory"), rather than medical or moral purgation. Martha Nussbaum has modified Golden's argument somewhat by saying that *katharsis* is not a purely cognitive process, but one that also involves a kind of emotional clarification (Nussbaum, *Fragility of Goodness*, 383-91).[3] Nussbaum has taken the idea a step further, suggesting that Greek conceptions of pity in drama are useful not only personally and psychologically, but that they can also inform discussions of pity and compassion in modern political and legal discourse (Nussbaum, *Poetic Justice*, 65-66).[4] At least one modern political theorist has made an even stronger appeal for incorporating ancient ideas about pity into modern discussions of public policy. C. Fred Alford, drawing extensively on the work of Nussbaum, has argued that "pity is the paradigmatic civilizing passion" (265) and his essay on the subject seeks to inaugurate a modern "dialogue of the passions" in which "a policy for pity, or a regime based upon compassion" can be formulated (277).

Because ideas of compassion and cruelty dominate a wide range of modern political and social issues such as welfare and capital punishment, the proposition seems to be an appropriate one. A number of modern moral philosophers (Blum; Callan; Greenspan; Hamburger; Solomon) and legal scholars (Murphy and Hampton) have begun to consider the role of compassion, mercy, pity, and sympathy in modern culture, but such studies rarely allude to classical authors, or to any sources before the eighteenth-century studies of sympathy by David Hume and Adam Smith.

The purpose of this chapter is not to show how ancient Greek ideas about pity are relevant for modern society, but rather to fill in some blanks before we begin the modern "dialogue of the passions" called for by Alford. In doing so, I want to emphasize the role of rhetoric in this dialogue by briefly outlining the history of the idea of pity in rhetorical theory between Greek antiquity and the Renaissance. I will use this history as a context for discussing some of the problems that arise when theoretical formulations of pity intersect with actual and literary rhetorical situations. I also want to focus my comments on a particular kind of rhetorical situation. Although the rhetorical significance of pity in a community is often casual—the cultivation of civic harmony through philanthropy, charity, and tolerance[5]—other kinds of rhetorical experiences situate pity in more formal contexts of political and judicial power. I specifically want to discuss pity as an emotional means of persuasion in the forensic relationship between judge and advocate, a relationship that manifests itself in numerous other forms in political and social discourse when a petitioner's appeal for compassion attempts to persuade a higher power to act in a particular way. The judge or magistrate to whom the appeal is directed has an obligation to make rulings according to the established laws, but he also has the power—and some would say the responsibility—to mitigate punishments, pardon crimes, or otherwise show mercy toward an offender in an equitable way and according to the relative merits of a case. The judge's prerogative to show mercy depends, to some degree, on an understanding of and sympathy with an individual's suffering, especially when the judge determines that suffering to be unmerited. But the nature of the judge's emotional and cognitive involvement with the details and contingencies of a particular situation are extremely difficult to define in theoretical terms, although many philosophers have tried to establish rules for judges to follow.

The respective rhetorical responsibilities of judge and advocate can be seen in the disagreement between Plato and Aristotle about the social and political merits of pity. Plato, who seeks to define the kind of wisdom required for proper judgment and justice, believes that pity diminishes the judge's ability to reason and should therefore play no role in the administration of justice (*Republic* 604d-605c). His position is indeed an extreme one; even when Socrates finds himself before a judicial authority, he explicitly refuses to make the customary appeal for pity (*Apology* 34c-35b). Plato recognizes that even the best of men can be moved to tears by epic and tragic poetry, but he emphasizes that this is not a proper way to respond to afflictions in real life (*Republic* 605c-e).

For Aristotle, pity arises naturally in people and can play a useful role in society by cultivating feelings of philanthropy and fellow-feeling.[6] Like the other emotions, pity should be moderated, and moderation requires an education in pity as an ethical value (Alford 262-63; Nussbaum, *Fragility of Goodness* 308-09). This education in pity, especially as understood in relation to the "clarification" theory of *katharsis* advanced by Golden and Nussbaum, disputes the Platonic separation of dramatic experience from actual experience. Tragic pity becomes socially relevant as Aristotelian poetics constructs a kind of "theater of pity" in which the rhetorical relationship between judge and advocate is opened up both for public reflection and public participation in a double rhetorical situation.[7] In the first rhetorical context, the audience reflects on the rhetorical situation of pity by watching rhetorical encounters on the stage or by reading about them (or hearing them) in epic narrative. Priam's appeal to Achilles for the return of Hector's body in *Iliad* 24 is an appeal to pity, as is Hecuba's appeal to Odysseus for the life of Polyxena in Euripides's *Hecuba*. As in modern courtroom dramas, scenes such as these allow the audience to see and reflect on both the rhetorical techniques commonly used to arouse pity and the ways in which judges respond to such appeals. But, at the same time, the audience is part of a second, indirect rhetorical context in which they are in a position of judging the words and actions of characters dramatizing the rhetoric of pity on the stage. The actors and playwright are, in effect, making an appeal to the audience to feel pity[8]— not in order to effect a political or legal judgment, but to convey ideas about the phenomenon of pity and to validate the literary work by showing that it can move and persuade. In the prologue to *Henry VIII*, Shakespeare writes: "Those that can pity, here / May (if they think it well) let fall a tear; / The subject will deserve it" (pr. 5-7). This authorial statement is not substantially different from the character Antony's remark to the crowd in *Julius Caesar*: "If you have tears, prepare to shed them now" (3.2.169). When we watch a play, the two rhetorical contexts intermingle, allowing the audience to both think about and experience the emotion.

Whereas the less formal, indirect rhetoric of pity is informed by Aristotle's *Poetics*, the more formal, oratorical context of pity is informed by Aristotle's *Rhetoric*. In book 2 of the *Rhetoric*, Aristotle devotes an entire chapter to pity (*eleos*) as an emotional means of persuasion, and another chapter considers its opposite, indignance (*to nemesan*). Aristotle defines pity as "a certain pain at seeing [*phainomenoi*] a destructive or painful evil happening to one who does not deserve it and which a person might expect himself or one of his own to suffer, and this when it is seen [*phainetai*] close at hand" (1385b).[9] Later in the same chapter Aristotle outlines useful rhetorical techniques for arousing pity:

> [S]ufferings are pitiable when they are seen near at hand . . . necessarily those are more pitiable who contribute to the effect by gestures and cries and display of feelings and generally in their acting [*hypokrisis*]; for they make the evil seem near by making it appear before [our] eyes either as something about to happen or as something that has happened. . . . For this reason signs and actions [contribute to pity]; for example, the clothes of those who have suffered and any other such things. (1386a-b)

This emphasis on the need to employ acting and visual signs in the appeal to pity is clearly relevant to the "theater of pity" I have outlined earlier as a component of Aristotelian poetics.[10] It is also an important part of the "clarification" theory of *katharsis*, in which an audience's emotional and intellectual response depends entirely on tragic *mimesis*.

Aristotle's emphasis on the importance of visual signs in appeals to pity was considerably amplified by Roman rhetoricians. Quintilian gives us an insight into the techniques of the Roman lawyer when he writes:

> Actions as well as words may be employed to move the court to tears. Hence the custom of bringing accused persons into court wearing squalid and unkempt attire, and of introducing their children and parents, and it is with this in view that we see blood-stained swords, fragments of bone taken from the wound, and garments spotted with blood, displayed by the accusers, wounds stripped of their dressings, and scourged bodies bared to view. The impression produced by such exhibitions is generally enormous, since they seem to bring the spectators face to face with the cruel facts. For example, the sight of the bloodstains on the purple-bordered toga of Gaius Caesar, which was carried at the head of his funeral procession, aroused the Roman people to fury. (6.1.30-31)

The audience for such advice is the advocate, but earlier in the same century Seneca had warned judges and princes about the dangers of such appeals:

> Good men will all display clemency [*clementia*] and gentleness, but pity [*misericordia*] they will avoid; for it is the failing of a weak nature that succumbs to the sight [*ad speciem*] of others' ills. And so it is most often seen in the poorest types of persons; there are old women and wretched females who are moved by the tears of the worst criminals, who, if they could, would break open their prison. Pity regards [*spectat*] the plight, not the cause of it; clemency is combined with reason. (*De Clementia* 2.5.1)

The passage is more than simply a reflection of Seneca's Stoicism; it allows the prince to employ a form of compassion that is guided by reason and equity, and it is useful in that it formulates a vigorous and confident form of political compassion that can stand against barbarism and cruelty. But it also exposes the vulnerability and instability that arises when the judge is confronted by the sight of suffering and suggests that the appeal for pity can be problematic in situations of judgment even when, and perhaps especially when, ocular proofs are presented. Although an understanding of this vulnerability may be instructive on a personal level, it is problematic for the development of public policy, especially if we begin to question the ease with which Seneca distinguishes *clementia* from *misericordia*.

Even for the advocate, the appeal to pity does not always guarantee success. Quintilian is aware of the great power of pity when he says that "the appeal which will carry most weight is the appeal to pity, which not merely forces the judge to change his views, but even to betray his emotion by tears" (6.1.23). But because pity's role in society and politics is rhetorical and situational, the experience of pity and the range of possible responses to its presence in our lives is difficult to establish in theoretical terms, and this applies to both advocates and judges. In the face of unlimited and arbitrary powers of judgment and punishment, the petitioner for pity, no matter how carefully he constructs his argument, can never be absolutely sure of obtaining the desired result.[11]

Seneca's comments raise another important question about pity in political rhetoric: What happens if the person appealing for pity is lying? The problem is aggravated by the advocate's dependence on histrionics in appeals for pity, but Quintilian says that both actor and lawyer should actually experience the emotion as they represent it:

> I have often seen actors, both in tragedy and comedy, leave the theater still drowned in tears after concluding performance of some moving role.... I have frequently been so much moved while speaking, that I have not merely been wrought upon to tears, but have turned pale and shown all the symptoms of genuine grief. (6.2.34-36)

Quintilian's ideal orator is a *vir bonus dicendi peritus* (a good man skilled in speaking), and like most classical rhetoricians he assumes a high degree of ethical responsibility in rhetorical and civic activities. This is not to say that ancient Greek and Roman lawyers were always honest, only that there was no philosophical or moral tradition in which deceptive rhetoric could be considered a legitimate attribute of political and judicial power.

If classical political and rhetorical theory tends to avoid thinking about deceptive rhetoric in political discourse, then classical literature more fully addresses the kinds of problems Seneca identified in the rhetoric of pity. Aeneas's description of Sinon's appeal to the Trojans for pity in *Aeneid* 2, for example, shows how a culture dedicated to ideas of equity and compassion could be destroyed by the same emotion. Troy is defeated, Aeneas tells Dido, not by Achilles or the thousand Greek ships, but by "a tall tale and fake tears" (*Aeneid* 2.196). Left behind with the wooden horse, Sinon is captured and dragged in before Priam and a growing crowd of Trojans. He tells them he has deserted the Greek army having long suffered the cruel treatment of Ulysses. He weeps at the thought of never seeing his home or family again, and begs the Trojans to pity him. Sinon's appeal is successful, and his explanation of the horse is almost an afterthought. By this time, the Trojans have been won over and the horse is brought inside the city walls.

Whereas the wooden horse is a tool of deception used by the Greeks to bring down their enemy, Sinon's false appeal for pity is the rhetorical means of persuasion that facilitates the trick. The great power of the appeal for pity is demonstrated by the fact that in this case words and acting destroy an entire civilization that has withstood ten years of battle. Because pity here is deceptive, and because it results in violent discord rather than social harmony, the enormous problems of pity in social and political discourse are amplified. The story of Sinon is a reminder that the compassion that is so valuable in cultivating fellow-feeling and philanthropy in the *polis* can also be its greatest enemy.[12]

This ambivalence about pity in political and rhetorical situations is an important part of how Renaissance thinkers approached classical ideas about the rhetoric of pity. Victoria Kahn has written that as Machiavelli relativizes the competing interests of political and moral discourse he creates

> a rhetoric of de facto political power—a rhetoric of theatrical violence, sembling and dissembling, whether in the service of the commonwealth . . . or in the interests of the self-aggrandizing tyrant. (237)

When Machiavelli rejects traditional humanist rhetoric—that of Aristotle, Cicero, and Quintilian—he makes it possible to recognize more fully pity's power as a tool for deception in rhetoric. Henry Peacham is a Renaissance rhetorician who was particularly aware of the ambivalence of rhetorical pity. The second edition of his *Garden of Eloquence* (1593), a treatise on elocution, contains a number of what he calls "figures of affection," many of which are related to the problematic role of compassion in rhetoric. Peacham's formula in the book is to give a general description of each figure followed by a separate section on "use" and another section called "the caution." *Tollerantia*, he says, "helpeth mightily to move compassion," but it is "most abused when the sufferance and despair is counterfeited" (84). *Syngnome* "doth aptly serve to commend the clemency, charity and mercy of the speaker," but he adds the caution that "foolish pity, undoeth many a city" (98). Peacham's definition of *threnos* declares that it "is most forcible and mighty to move pity and compassion in the hearer," but he also emphasizes the problems of counterfeit pity:

> As this form of speech is most passionate so ought it to be most serious and void of fiction and feigning; for counterfeit lamentation doth seldom move pity, for it is commonly bewrayed or known either by the cause or by the person; by the cause, as feigned lamentations in tragedies; by the person . . . as the lamentations of common beggars, which are commonly counterfeited. . . . (67)

However much Peacham wants counterfeit lamentation to expose itself as a fraud, he is probably wrong, especially in light of everything he has already said about the ambiguous power of the appeal for compassion. In Sinon's case, counterfeit pity destroyed an old and wise civilization, and for many Renaissance thinkers Sinon's deception corresponded to the strategies of Machiavellian rhetoric. In Shakespeare's *Henry VI, Part 3,* Richard, Duke of Gloucester (later King Richard III), describes his political ambitions:

> I'll play the orator as well as Nestor,
> Deceive more slily than Ulysses could,
> And like a Sinon, take another Troy.
> I can add colors to the chameleon,
> Change shapes with Proteus for advantages,
> And set the murtherous Machevil to school.
> Can I do this, and cannot get a crown? (3.2.188-95)

In *Titus Andronicus*—a play that begins with Titus refusing to pity a vanquished queen, and that becomes perhaps the most piteous spectacle of cruelty and bloodshed in the history of drama—a Roman Lord enters at one point and asks:

> Tell us what Sinon hath bewitched our ears,
> Or who hath brought the fatal engine in
> That gives our Troy, our Rome, the civil wound. (5.3.84-86)

In *The Rape of Lucrece*, Lucrece contemplates a tapestry depicting the story of Troy. When her eyes fall upon Sinon, she exclaims:

> Look, look how list'ning Priam wets his eyes,
> To see those borrowed tears that Sinon sheds!
> Priam, why art thou old, and yet not wise?
> For every tear he falls a Trojan bleeds;
> His eye drops fire, no water thence proceeds;
>   Those round clear pearls of his, that move thy pity,
>   Are balls of quenchless fire to burn thy city. (1548-54)

Shakespeare is equally aware of the importance of compassion both for establishing bonds of charity and fellow-feeling in the community and for guiding the administration of justice, as in Portia's oration on the "quality of mercy" in *The Merchant of Venice* (4.1.180). But like Vergil, he always has an eye on the dangers of pity in society, and he recognizes the dramatic and tragic potential of situations in which pity fails, or in which a rhetoric of compassion turns into an action of cruelty.

If we follow Golden, Nussbaum, and Alford in their belief that dramatic representations and narratives help us understand the role of emotions in our lives, part of our learning must recognize that pity's great potential for social harmony is balanced by a competing potential for deception and discord. The vulnerabilities that the rhetoric of pity exposes in our lives do not always lead to disaster; in fact, by sharing and talking about such vulnerabilities as they arise both in life and in literature, we learn much about ourselves and the people around us. But the story of Sinon reminds us that rhetoric is a neutral discipline that cannot always assume an ethical ideal, especially in a world where Machiavellian rhetoric thrives. The value of the rhetoric of pity for modern culture and politics, then, is not at all clear. We clearly should establish a dialogue of compassion as a way of cultivating tolerance, peace, and civility in the world, but we should also beware of Greeks bearing gifts.

Notes

1. Aristotle defines *katharsis* as a process that involves two emotions, pity and fear, but pity (which depends on the fear of a danger that is near, *Rhetoric* 1385b) is often given priority over fear in discussions of both Aristotelian and non-Aristotelian theories of tragedy. W. B. Stanford calls *eleos* the "supreme tragic emotion" (23).

2. The correspondence of the two ideas is suggested by Aristotle's use of the word *katharsis* at *Politics* 1341b37. The most influential recent article on the role of *katharsis* for the *demos* is Stephen Salkever's, though the degree to which Aristotelian poetics makes assumptions about the *polis* has recently been questioned by Edith Hall.

3. Christian Wagner has suggested a third version of Golden's interpretation, *katharsis* as "ethical clarification" ("ethische Aufklärung").

4. Nussbaum's comments on the relevance of pity for modern thought depend not only on ancient Greek thinkers, but Hellenistic philosophy as well. See Nussbaum, *Therapy of Desire*.

5. In his *Familiares*, Petrarch defines rhetoric as "the cultivation of charity towards others" ("ceterorum hominum caritas," 1.9). See also Vickers, "Bacon's So-Called Utilitarianism," and Vickers, *In Defence of Rhetoric*, 276). For an example of how classical definitions of pity were incorporated into Christian definitions of mercy and compassion as late as the eighteenth century, see Zedler, who refers the reader looking for a definition of *caritas* to *Barmherzigkeit*, which is defined as "diejenige Gemüths-Neigung, welche aus der Menschen Liebe entstehet, da wir durch das Elend eines andern gerühret werden, und ihn, weil wir sein Uebel als unser eigenes ansehen, auf alle Art und Weise davon zu befreyen suchen." The first classical reference is to Aristotle's definition of *eleos* in the *Rhetoric*.

6. On the relation between *philanthropia* and *eleos* in Aristotle, see Grimaldi, 137-38.

7. For a theory of narrative as both direct and indirect rhetoric, see Kirby.

8. Aristotle discusses "acting" (*hypokrisis*) as an attribute of both actors and rhetoricians in *Rhetoric* 3.1 (1403b).

9. Quotations from Aristotle's *Rhetoric* are from the Kennedy translation, though I have occasionally made slight modifications.

10. See also *Metaphysics* 980a, where Aristotle identifies the visual experience as the most important form of learning.

11. Montaigne considers this idea in his first essay, "Par divers moens on arrive a pareille fin" ("By Diverse Means We Arrive at the Same End"). A recent book by David Quint argues that the

theme of mercy in this essay is important for understanding ethical themes in the *Essais*, especially as they relate to ideas of cruelty, compassion, and trust between individuals (Quint, *Montaigne and the Quality of Mercy*).

12. The emphasis on clemency in the first half of the *Aeneid*, especially in Anchises's instructions to Aeneas "to spare the conquered" (6.853), illustrates the value of pardon to Trojan culture. But, as David Quint has shown, the second half of the poem is dedicated to the theme of vengeful *pietas*, and corresponds to the contradictory ideology of Augustan Rome, which promises "to pardon and avenge at the same time" (Quint, *Epic and Empire* 78). Michael Putnam has argued that *pietas* carries an important secondary meaning of compassion and clemency, and he suggests that Aeneas's actions in the second half of the poem taint his position as an icon of *pietas*. By the Middle Ages and the Renaissance, after *pietas* had evolved into both "piety" and "pity" in the European vernacular languages, *pietas* and *pius* were usually defined as both compassion and "devotion to family"; see both Ball and Burrow.

Works Cited

Alford, C. Fred. "Greek Tragedy and Civilization: The Cultivation of Pity." *Political Research Quarterly* 46 (1993): 259-81.
Aristotle. *On Rhetoric: A Theory of Civic Discourse*. Trans. George A. Kennedy. Oxford: Oxford UP, 1991.
—. *The Complete Works of Aristotle*. Trans. Jonathan Barnes. 2 vols. Princeton: Princeton UP, 1984.
Ball, Robert. "Theological Semantics: Virgil's *Pietas* and Dante's *Pietà*." *Stanford Italian Review* 2 (1981): 59-79.
Blum, Lawrence. "Compassion." *Explaining Emotions*. Ed. Amelie Rorty. Berkeley: U of California P, 1980.
Burrow, Colin. *Epic Romance: Homer to Milton*. Oxford: Oxford UP, 1993.
Callan, Eamonn. "The Moral Status of Pity." *Canadian Journal of Philosophy* 18 (1988): 1-12.
Crotty, Kevin. *The Poetics of Supplication*. Ithaca: Cornell UP, 1994.
Golden, Leon. *Aristotle on Tragic and Comic Mimesis*. Atlanta: Scholars, 1992.
—. "The Clarification Theory of *Katharsis*." *Hermes* 104 (1976): 437-52.
Greenspan, Patricia. *Emotions and Reasons: An Inquiry into Emotional Justification*. London: Routledge, 1988.
Grimaldi, William. *Aristotle, Rhetoric II: A Commentary*. New York: Fordham UP, 1988.
Hall, Edith. "Is there a *Polis* in Aristotle's *Poetics*?" *Tragedy and the Tragic*. Ed. M. S. Silk. Oxford: Clarendon, 1996. 295-309.
Hamburger, Käte. *Das Mitleid*. Stuttgart: Klett-Cotta, 1985.
Hume, David. *A Treatise of Human Nature*. London, 1739.
Kahn, Victoria. *Machiavellian Rhetoric: From the Counter-Reformation to Milton*. Princeton: Princeton UP, 1994.
Kirby, John T. "Toward a Rhetoric of Poetics: Rhetor as Author and Narrator." *Journal of Narrative Technique* 22 (1992): 1-22.
Montaigne, Michel de. *The Complete Essays of Montaigne*. Trans. Donald M. Frame. Stanford: Stanford UP, 1958.
Murphy, Jeffrie G., and Jean Hampton. *Forgiveness and Mercy*. Cambridge: Cambridge UP, 1988.
Nussbaum, Martha. *The Fragility of Goodness: Luck and Ethics in Greek Tragedy and Philosophy*. Cambridge: Cambridge UP, 1986.
—. *The Therapy of Desire: Theory and Practice in Hellenistic Ethics*. Princeton: Princeton UP, 1994.
—. *Poetic Justice: The Literary Imagination and Public Life*. Boston: Beacon, 1995.
Peacham, Henry. *The Garden of Eloquence*. London, 1593.

Petrarch, Francesco. *Rerum Familiarum Libri*. Trans. Aldo S. Bernardo. 3 vols. Albany: State U of New York P, 1975-85.
Plato. *The Collected Dialogues of Plato*. Ed. Edith Hamilton and Huntington Carins. Princeton: Princeton UP, 1961.
Putnam, Michael C. J. *Virgil's Aeneid: Interpretation and Influence*. Chapel Hill: U of North Carolina P, 1995.
Quint, David. *Epic and Empire: Politics and Generic Form from Virgil to Milton*. Princeton: Princeton UP, 1993.
—. *Montaigne and the Quality of Mercy: Ethical and Political Themes in the Essais*. Princeton: Princeton UP, 1998.
Quintilian. *Institutio Oratoria*. Trans. H. E. Butler. Loeb Classical Library. 4 vols. Cambridge: Harvard UP, 1920.
Salkever, Stephen G. "Tragedy and the Education of the *Demos*: Aristotle's Response to Plato." *Greek Tragedy and Political Theory*. Ed. J. Peter Euben. Berkeley: U of California P, 1986. 274-303.
Seneca, Lucius Annaeus. *Moral Essays*. Trans. John Basore. Loeb Classical Library. Cambridge: Harvard UP, 1928.
Shakespeare, William. *The Riverside Shakespeare*. Ed. G. Blakemore Evans. Boston: Houghton, 1974.
Smith, Adam. *Theory of Moral Sentiments*. London, 1759.
Solomon, Robert C. *The Passions*. Garden City, NY: Anchor, 1976.
Stanford, W. B. *Greek Tragedy and the Emotions*. London: Routledge, 1983.
Virgil. *The Aeneid*. Trans. Robert Fitzgerald. New York: Random, 1981.
Vickers, Brian. "Bacon's So-Called 'Utilitarianism': Sources and Influence." *Francis Bacon: Terminologia e fortuna nel XVII secolo*. Ed. M. Fattori. Rome: Edizioni dell'Ateneo, 1984. 281-313.
—. *In Defence of Rhetoric*. Oxford: Clarendon, 1988.
Wagner, Christian. "'Katharsis' in der aristotelischen Tragödiendefinition." *Grazer Beiträge* 11 (1984): 67-87.
Zak, William F. *The Polis and the Divine Order*. Lewisburg: Bucknell UP, 1995.
Zedler, Johann Heinrich. *Grosses vollständiges Universal-Lexikon Aller Wissenschafften und Künste*. Leipzig, 1732-50.

BRUCE MCCOMISKEY
University of Alabama, Birmingham

The Global Village, Multiculturalism, and the Functions of Sophistic Rhetoric

In his final and most generative work, *Rhetorics, Poetics, and Cultures* (1996), James Berlin argues that theories and practices of rhetoric are both the products and producers of particular economic, political, and social conditions. I accept Berlin's premise as axiomatic; and thus I begin my journey into rhetoric with the following question: if we agree (though certainly not all of us will) that our present and future economic, political, and social conditions may generally be described as a "global village," then how *do*, *will*, and *should* the conditions of globalization affect our present and future theories and practices of rhetoric?

Communication in the Global Village

In *The Global Village* (1989), Marshal McLuhan and Bruce Powers argue that our twentieth-century high-tech telecommunications and high-speed modes of travel have linked once disparate and isolated cultures into a single unit, and that so-called global village requires new approaches to social understanding and communication. Computer technologies in particular, according to McLuhan and Powers, have caused a biological paradigm shift from left brain to right brain dominance in human thought processes (103). They propose that the "ultimate interactive nature of some video-related technologies will produce the dominant right-hemisphere social patterns of the next century" (83). Indeed, McLuhan and Powers predict that the "United States by [the year] 2020 will achieve a distinct psychological shift from a dependence on visual, uniform, homogenous thinking, of a left-hemisphere variety, to a multifaceted configurational mentality, . . . [or] right-hemisphere thinking" (86).

One problem with McLuhan and Powers' global village, according to Ien Ang, is that "the creation of the 'global village' implies the progressive homogenization—through successful communication—of the world as a whole" (194). But the reality is that the global village is marked by "uncertainty" (193), not homogenization; it is "a thoroughly paradoxical place, unified yet multiple, totalized yet deeply unstable, closed and open-ended at the same time" (194). Ang contends that the very scope and function of the global village rely inherently on the successful *transmission* of homogenizing discourse, unmediated by culture and perspective (194-95). According to Ang, "communication-as-transmission has generally implied a concern with social order and social management," an "(unstated) desire for a disciplined population and therefore a belief in the possibility of an ordered and stable 'society'" where "social integration (e.g., through the dissemination of a 'central value system' throughout the entire social fabric) is the main concern" (195). At least as theoretical constructs, transmission models of communication "inherently privilege the position of the Sender as legitimate source and originator of meaning and action, the centre from which both spatial and social/cultural integration is effectuated," and "[c]ommunication is deemed successful if and when the intentions of the Sender, packaged in the Message, arrive unscathed at the Receiver" (195).

I prefer to view the global village not as a structure, not as a standard or measure against which to compare lived culture, but as a *heuristic* with which to explore the process of culture as it is lived. The global village, or more accurately the "process of globalization," is not a structure or a place but a discursive practice, a collection of universalizing rhetorical "strategies" to which individuals and communities may respond with "tactics" designed to negotiate globalizing rhetoric from local perspectives. I borrow these two terms, "strategies" and "tactics," from Michel de Certeau's *The Practice of Everyday Life* (1984), and it is in their contradistinction that I believe we can find a useful model for communication within the complex discursive process of globalization.

Rhetorical Strategies and Tactics

In *The Practice of Everyday Life*, de Certeau describes a "strategy," on the one hand, as

> the calculation (or manipulation) of power relationships that becomes possible as soon as a subject with will and power (a business, an army, a city, a scientific institution) can be isolated. It postulates a place that can be delimited as its *own* and serve as the base from which relations with an exteriority composed of targets or threats (customers or competitors, enemies, the country surrounding the city, objectives and objects of research, etc.) can be managed. As in management, every "strategic" rationalization seeks first of all to distinguish its "own" place, that is, the place of its own power and will, from an "environment".... [I]t is an effort to delimit one's own place in a world bewitched by the invisible powers of the Other. (36)

The manifestations of these "calculations of power relationships," these "places of power" (as opposed to real "environments"), take their ultimate shape in the discursive process of globalization.

On the other hand, de Certeau describes a "tactic" as "a calculated action determined by the absence of a proper locus. No delimitation of an exteriority, then, provides it with the condition necessary for autonomy. The space of a tactic is the space of the other" (i.e., the space constructed by the strategy). "Thus it must play on and with a terrain imposed on it and organized by the law of a foreign power." A tactic "does not have the means to *keep to itself*, at a distance, in a position of withdrawal, foresight, and self-collection; it is a maneuver . . . within enemy territory. It does not, therefore, have the options of planning general strategy and viewing the adversary as a whole within a distinct, visible, and objectifiable space." A tactic "operates in isolated actions, blow by blow. It takes advantage of 'opportunities' and depends on them, being without any base where it could stockpile its winnings, build up its own position, and plan raids." This nowhereness "gives a tactic mobility, to be sure, but a mobility that must accept the chance offerings of the moment, and seize on the wing the possibilities that offer themselves at any given moment. It must vigilantly make use of the cracks that particular conjunctions open in the surveillance of the proprietary powers. It poaches in them. It creates surprises in them. It can be where it is least expected" (37). Tactics are rhetorical practices that can work to subvert a dominant order while operating within the very order they mean to subvert.

Universalizing, essentialist, and utopian global village discourses (i.e., the discursive processes of globalization) are inevitable—they are inescapable; they are an inherent aspect of many of our most powerful economic, political, and cultural institutions. These are the strategies. And because strategies are universalizing, essentialist, and utopian, they are not consciously applied in situations but are assumed applicable to any circumstance. Yet I argue that what characterize intercultural communications within this context are the different ways in which communicators subvert and negotiate the discourses of globalization according to the exigencies of particular situations. These are the tactics, and tactics comprise the practice(s) of everyday life. Further, tactics are "sophistic" in nature, a point that de Certeau himself makes clear: "In the enormous rhetorical corpus devoted to the art of speaking," de Certeau writes, "the Sophists have a privileged place, from the point of view of tactics. The principle was, according to the Greek rhetorician Corax, to make the weaker position seem the stronger, and they claimed to have the power of turning the tables on the powerful by the way in which they made use of the opportunities offered by the particular situation" (xx). One of the earliest technologized aspects of the sophistic theories of rhetoric in the fifth century BCE was, according to Edward Schiappa, the conception of *kairos* (73), a qualitative view of time (*chronos*) and usually translated as the "right," or "opportune," moment.

Kairos—seizing the opportune moment, choosing arguments depending on the demands of the situation—was one of the fundamental tactics of sophistic rhetoric and was intended to confound powerful, perhaps even institutionalized, rhetorical strategies. (For further useful treatments of *kairos*, see

Kinneavy, White, and Untersteiner). The following is a selection of sophistic and presocratic treatments of *kairos*, all of which can be found in Hermann Diels and Walther Kranz's *Die Fragmente der Vorsokratiker* (1956):

Democritus

- "One must be on one's guard against the bad man, lest he seize his opportunity [*mê kairou labêtai*]" (Freeman, sec. B 87).

- "Freedom of speech is the sign of freedom; but the danger lies in discerning the right occasion [*hê tou kairou diagnôsis*]" (Freeman, sec. B 226).

Anaxarchus

- "Much learning can help much, but also can greatly harm him who has it. It helps the clever man, but harms him who readily utters every word in any company. One must know the measure of the right time [*kairou metra*], for this is the boundary of wisdom. Those who recite a saying outside the right time [*eksô kairou*], even if their saying is wise, are reproached with folly, because they do not mix intelligence with wisdom" (Freeman, sec. B 1).

Anonymous *Dissoi Logoi*

- Quotes an anonymous poet: "There is nothing that is in every respect seemly or shameful, but the right moment [*ho kairos*] takes the same things and makes them shameful and then changes them round and makes them seemly" (Robinson, sec. 2.19).

- Comments on the previous quotation: "All things are seemly when done at the right moment [*kairôi*], but shameful when done at the wrong moment [*akairiai*]" (Robinson, sec. 2.20).

These ancient uses and descriptions of *kairos* resemble in many ways de Certeau's tactics: they do not speak of argument from institutional authority, or of an immutable base from which relations to others might be consistently managed; they speak not a discourse of globalization, as Plato and others did, but a discourse of "uncertainty," that is, a discourse of tactics among powerful strategic discourses. When exploiting *kairos*, there is no steady locus of power, no universal strategy to follow; its operations are blow-by-blow, as fleeting as the right moment itself, taking advantage of opportunities as they arise.

Twenty-four hundred years after the sophists, we see another arena in which *kairos* is thrust into the foreground (i.e., in what we now call "multiculturalism"). One of the key concepts at the foundation of multiculturalism as a theory and practice is the idea of "hegemony." In the

Prison Notebooks, Antonio Gramsci describes hegemony in structuralist terms: it is a cultural condition in which, first, a dominator has power over a dominated, and second, the dominated views the power exerted by the dominator as natural, a universal and inalterable reality. However, in *Marxism and Literature*, Raymond Williams introduces a third definition of hegemony, one that turns "hegemony" from a structure into a process. According to Williams, not only is there domination that is viewed as natural, but there must also be a perpetual process of consensus building: hegemony "does not just passively exist as a form of dominance. It has continually to be renewed, recreated, defended, and modified. It is also continually resisted, limited, altered, challenged by pressures not at all its own" (Williams 112).

If we combine the sophists, Gramsci, Williams, and de Certeau into a big pot of theory stew, we arrive at the following view of power: dominators establish universalizing "strategies" as a means to gain consensus among the dominated, and the dominated negotiate these "strategies" with timely localized "tactics" as a means to gain control over their own lived experience. Multicultural theory in particular critiques the deployment of universalizing strategies and promotes the development of timely localizing tactics, and we can see this view of hegemonic power clearly at work in the evolution of multiculturalism over the past two centuries.

In his introduction to *Multiculturalism: A Critical Reader*, David Theo Goldberg provides a three-phase genealogical analysis of multiculturalism in an institutional (particularly academic) context. In the first phase of multiculturalism, during the nineteenth and early twentieth centuries, a phase that Goldberg calls *assimilation*, the university "gave way immediately to (if it did not already conceptually presuppose) the discourse of universality, the insistence that the university stood for and on the unwavering and singular standard of universal truth. Local knowledge was effaced in the name of universalizing local standards as rationally required" (3). According to Goldberg, "By mid-[twentieth]century, this monocultural, ethnoracial Eurovision had become cemented in the United States as hegemonic intellectual ideology and institutional practice. It was virtually impossible without extreme marginalization to think and do other than in and through its terms" (4). Further, "the United States was taken in its dominant self-representation to have a core set of cultural and political values, and assimilation meant giving up all those 'un-American' values to be able to assume those that would fashion one American subject to the warrant of monocultural interpretation" (4-5). Here we find universities wielding discursive strategies of globalization at the tragic expense of local knowledge and identities, effacing not only the appearance of cultural differences but, more significantly, also denying their epistemic salience.

The discursive practices associated with monocultural assimilation occupy the lion's share of American history. But as Goldberg points out,

> [T]he civil rights and countercultural movements of the 1960s signaled a shift from the prevailing standard [of assimilation] to the new one of *integration*. Confronted by demographic shifts as well as by committed, vocal, and active social movements, the fragile grounds sustaining monoculturalism began to buckle. The new model of integration that emerged left cultural groups (including races) with effective control of their private autonomous cultural determinations and expressions at the sociocultural margins, while maintaining a supposedly separate and, thus, neutral set of common values (especially, but not only economic and legal ones) to mediate their relations at the center. . . . The common (re)public(an) culture was to furnish the grounds for cohesion, the conditions of Americanness. (6)

Goldberg continues, "The dualism of this model is reflected in its pluralist allowances at the margins with its univocal core insistences at the center. The central values continued to be defined monoculturally. Where insurgent cultural expressions emerged, . . . they either were quickly suppressed or diluted through the tokenism of economic and cultural appropriation" (6). These, according to Goldberg, are the integrative multiculturalisms of a "centrist academy and multinational corporations that take themselves to be committed to the broad tenets of philosophical liberalism which are unconcerned . . . with the redistribution of power or resources" (7); they become "mantric administrative instruments that serve to contain and restrain resistance and transformation as they displace any appeal to economic difference by paying lip service to the celebration of cultural distinction" (7-8).

Goldberg ends his genealogy of multiculturalism with a forward-looking third phase, "*incorporation*," which "involves the dual transformations that take place in the dominant values and in those of the insurgent group as the latter insists on more complete incorporations into the body politic and the former grudgingly gives way. . . . The body politic becomes a medium for transformative incorporation, a political arena of contestation, rather than a base from which exclusions can be more or less silently extended, managed, and manipulated" (9). Finally, "The body of political relations" in the incorporation phase of multiculturalism "is irreversibly altered as new parts attach themselves to and then work their own ways into its mechanisms of power and cultural expression" (9). Goldberg argues that "incorporative undertakings are transgressive, engaged by definition in infringing and exceeding the norms of the monocultural status quo and transforming the values and representations that have held racist culture together" (10).

What Goldberg's genealogy of multiculturalism tells us (and what de Certeau does not) is that strategies over time can be changed. Repeated efforts at the level of tactics can have permanently altering effects on institutionalized strategies. What de Certeau tells us (and what Goldberg does not) is how tactics might be used in timely ways to begin moving social institutions in the direction of incorporation.

Turning finally to pedagogical concerns, what elsewhere I have called " social-process rhetorical inquiry" focuses students' composing energies on inventing tactics in response to institutionalized strategies (McComiskey). Social-process rhetorical inquiry usually takes the form of heuristic questions based on the cycle of cultural production, contextual distribution, and critical consumption. Applying these heuristics in institutional contexts, students discover some ways in which texts and their contexts promote certain cultural and social values over others, and students are encouraged to take a critical stance toward the encoded values they find in institutional discourses. This heuristic cycle helps students understand how different institutions' rhetorical strategies operate; they are ongoing, everchanging, and critical analysis serves to describe the strategies that are in place at the point of observation. But this heuristic cycle is not complete until students produce their own discourses intended to participate in the institutionalized discursive processes that they are studying. Understanding institutionalized strategies at any given point in time provides students with the discursive knowledge they need to compose their own timely rhetorical tactics, tactics that, a little at a time, work toward challenging marginalizing strategies and supporting the strategies already in place that might be used in the process of "incorporation." The study of individual texts, removed from institutional contexts, can help students develop critical sensibilities, but it does little to help them understand the shifting temporal discursive flow of institutional strategies; and that, I argue, is where the real power of language is played out.

Works Cited

Ang, Ien. "In the Realm of Uncertainty: The Global Village and Capitalist Postmodernity." *Communication Theory Today*. Ed. David Crowley and David Mitchell. Stanford: Stanford UP, 1994. 193-213.

Berlin, James A. *Rhetorics, Poetics, and Cultures: Refiguring College English Studies*. Urbana: NCTE, 1996.

de Certeau, Michel. *The Practice of Everyday Life*. Trans. S. Rendall. Berkeley: U of California P, 1984.

Diels, Hermann, and Walther Kranz. *Die Fragmente der Vorsokratiker*. 3 vols. Berlin: Weidmann, 1956.

Freeman, K. *Ancilla to the Pre-Socratic Philosophers*. Cambridge: Harvard UP, 1948.

Goldberg, David Theo. "Introduction: Multicultural Conditions." *Multiculturalism: A Critical Reader*. Cambridge, MA: Blackwell, 1994. 1-41.

Gramsci, Antonio. *Selections from the Prison Notebooks*. Ed. and Trans. Q. Hoare and G. Nowell-Smith. London: Lawrence and Wishart, 1974.

Kinneavy, J. L. "*Kairos*: A Neglected Concept in Classical Rhetoric." *Rhetoric and Praxis: The Contribution of Classical Rhetoric to Practical Reasoning*. Ed. J. D. Moss. Washington, DC: Catholic U of America P, 1986. 79-105.

McComiskey, Bruce. "Social-Process Rhetorical Inquiry: Cultural Studies Methodologies for Critical Writing About Advertisements." *JAC: A Journal of Composition Theory* 17.3 (1997): 381-400.

McLuhan, Marshal, and Bruce Powers. *The Global Village: Transformations in World Life and Media in the 21st Century.* New York: Oxford UP, 1989.

Robinson, T. M. *Contrasting Arguments: An Edition of the* Dissoi Logoi. Salem, NH: Ayer, 1984.

Schiappa, E. *Protagoras and* Logos: *A Study in Greek Philosophy and Rhetoric.* Columbia: U of South Carolina P, 1991.

Untersteiner, M. *The Sophists.* Trans. K. Freeman. Oxford: Blackwell, 1948.

White, E. C. *Kaironomia: On the Will-to-Invent.* Ithaca: Cornell UP, 1987.

Williams, Raymond. *Marxism and Literature.* Oxford: Oxford UP, 1977.

EKATERINA HASKINS
University of Iowa

Orality, Literacy, and Isocrates' Political Aesthetics

During the past thirty years, the concepts of orality and literacy have become powerful critical lenses for historians of rhetoric. Following the work of pioneers like Havelock and Ong, scholars have begun to question the "literary" assumptions of traditional rhetorical principles and have thus yielded a better understanding of rhetoric's oral, performative aspects. No longer can we view rhetoric as a timeless compendium of statements on the art of speaking well; instead, we are urged to appreciate the web of technological and cultural forces that give rise to rhetorical practices and theories.

Orality and literacy are not abstract terms conjured in a political vacuum. In the twentieth century, "the rediscovery of rhetoric" as a social force occurred in conjunction with major technological and political changes—the introduction of radio and the political upheavals of the 1920s and 1930s. For Havelock, the thirties were marked by the influence of the two "masters of myth-making"—Franklin D. Roosevelt and Adolph Hitler—whose "power and persuasion over men's minds was electronically transmitted" (*Muse Learns to Write* 31). Instantaneous impact of the human voice augmented by electronic technology was, perhaps, one of the reasons scholars started paying greater attention to rhetoric as a practice. However, the introduction of the electronic media did not supplant the written and printed message; instead, as Havelock points out, "what had happened was a forced marriage, or remarriage, between the resources of the written word and of the spoken" (33).

It is this gray area between orality and literacy that provides historical and theoretical contexts for the exploration of rhetoric's ambivalent political potential. This chapter applies Havelock's observations about the "marriage" between the spoken and written word to the rhetorical practices of Isocrates. Isocrates appears to represent the "literate" culture of the fourth century BCE. After all, his orations are elaborate literary compositions addressed to mostly literate audiences. Yet, his writings display a remarkable interpenetration between the traditions of poetry and oratory and the newer literary medium. Isocrates presented himself as an inheritor of the oral mythopoetic tradition; his aesthetic task was to preserve the forcefulness of oral poetic performance in written prose.

The political thrust of Isocrates' rhetorical practice—the shaping of the cultural knowledge that had secured the unity of the Greeks in the past—deserves no less critical attention. In the twentieth century, "political aesthetics" has become suspect due to its association with fascism and totalitarianism. Here, Havelock's stress on the myth-making quality of discourse of both Roosevelt and Hitler is instructive as a parallel, because it indicates very divergent political possibilities of rhetoric conceived as performance under conditions of secondary orality. I therefore draw a distinction between the legacy of the Isocratean Pan-Hellenic *paideia* and his own vision of rhetoric as civic performance. The former, represented by the interpretation of Isocrates by the German philological tradition, appears to some as a justification of cultural imperialism and even Nazism. By contrast, civic performance, with its capacity for aesthetic and cultural resonance, is not locked into a predetermined political path but constitutes the condition of possibility for a pluralistic democracy. Accordingly, I will first discuss Isocrates' complex relation with the oral culture and his literary appropriation of the mythopoeic tradition. I will then address the problems that arise when we try to tease out political implications of his aesthetics.

Orality and Literacy in Isocrates' *Logos Politikos*

Isocrates' use of writing may seem paradoxical. On the one hand, he explicitly shuns and even attacks the oral culture of his contemporaries. On the other, he promotes the type of rhetoric that relies on oral elements of composition and address for its political impact. In this section, I examine Isocrates' seemingly antidemocratic "quietist" literary strategy and the oral resources of his *logos politikos*, which he proposes as an alternative to rhetorical practices of fourth-century Athens.

Contrary to ancient biographers and some contemporary critics, Isocrates' preference for writing was not due to his physical lack as an orator. As Too demonstrates, Isocrates' *ipsissima verba*, on which the traditional accounts are based, constitute a deliberate strategy of self-depiction. Isocrates engaged in writing not simply to compensate for his bodily weakness or lack of courage; he pursued writing with a dual goal of shifting the focus of contemporary rhetorical-political practices from their traditional sites and crafting his own distinct civic identity. At the same time, his shunning of the courts and the assembly—the places where citizens could influence the affairs of the polis through the power of their oral performance—marks Isocrates as one of the "quietists," or *apragmones*. According to Deborah Steiner, these individuals' choice of reading and writing, as well as their absence from public spaces of the polis, signal "disenchantment with democracy and the desire for different social and political discourse" (187). Gunter Heilbrunn confirms this interpretation when he reads Isocrates' quasi-biographical statement about the lack of "voice and daring" in *To Philip* as an "accusation of the Athenian democracy" (175). Yet unlike other literary *apragmones* of his generation, especially Plato and other Socratics, Isocrates adopts the quietist stance in order to reinvent democratic rhetoric, not to disavow its legitimacy altogether. Let us first inspect what Isocrates finds objectionable in rhetorical practices of his age.

Isocrates' criticisms of his contemporary rhetoricians are well-known: he seldom misses the opportunity to berate demagogues in the assembly, sycophants in law courts, logographers, and teachers of eristic disputation. Demagogic orators, who have undermined the civic potential of Periclean democracy, exemplify the excesses of orality. In *On the Peace*, Isocrates puts his outrage at the abuse of public performance in the mouth of a pacifist speaker, who faces a hostile audience:

> I observe that you do not hear with equal favor the speakers who address you, but that, while you give your attention to some, in the case of others you do not even suffer their voice to be heard. And it is not surprising that you do this; for in the past you have formed the habit of driving all the orators from the platform except those who support your desires. . . . Indeed, you have caused the orators to practice and study, not what will be advantageous to the state, but how they may discourse in a manner pleasing to you. (Isocrates 2: 3-5)

One may conclude from this passage that Isocrates objects to aesthetically pleasing oral performance, just as Plato does in his *Gorgias*, when he chastises loudmouthed politicians who pander to their audiences in order to achieve selfish ends, or when he banishes poets from the city in the *Republic*. Plato's animosity, however, targets rhetorical instruction and poetic performance because they fail to measure up to the philosophical ideals of justice and truth. Unlike Plato, Isocrates does not condemn the aesthetic dimension of rhetoric. It is not the power of the spoken word that he questions, but the unrestrained pursuit of individual gain at the expense of the polis that has become the dominant type of rhetoric in the courts and the assembly.

By abandoning the traditional venues of public performance for writing, Isocrates attempts to foster a different type of democratic rhetoric that he terms *logos politikos*. Such a rhetoric, according to Takis Poulakos (68), "was an indistinguishably ethical and political art," for it combined both *eu legein* (the art of speaking well) and *phronein* (prudential thinking) for the benefit of the polis. The difficulty in articulating the difference and value of this educational project had to do not only with the lack of the immediacy and power of oral address, but also with the suspect status of writing in the fourth century BCE. Despite the use of writing by historians Herodotus and Thucydides, as well as by dramatists of the late fifth century, Athens was still mainly an oral culture, where writing functioned either as a supplement to oral communication, or, among the elites, as a diversion (*paignon*) (Harris 65-92).

To distinguish his art from both functions of writing, Isocrates attacks logography (ghost writing) and the intellectual exercises of the literate elites. To Isocrates, the former is contemptible because it is an instrument of the new politician and the litigious sycophant. The latter, although it does not promote unscrupulous quest for political power or material gain at the expense of others, is self-indulgent and often inconsequential. But it is precisely the novelty and elite nature of such writing that may cast doubt on Isocrates' own compositions. That is why, in a famous passage in *Antidosis*, Isocrates explicitly contrasts his version of rhetoric (*logous Hellenikous kai politikous*) with other types of prose writing: "genealogies of the demigods," "studies in the poets," "histories of war," "dialogues," and "private disputes" (Isocrates 2: 45-46).

What, then, should be the model of *logos politikos*, that is, the discourse that is at once aesthetically pleasurable and politically beneficial to the state? Isocrates looks to the mythopoetic tradition as his resource. In *To Nicocles*, he instructs a rhetorician seeking consensus of the audience to follow the example of Homer. "Those who aim to write anything in verse or prose which will make a popular appeal should seek out," he writes, "not the most profitable discourses, but those which most abound in fictions; for the ear delights in these just as the eye delights in games and contests. Wherefore we may well admire the poet Homer and the first inventors of tragedy, seeing that they, with true insight into human nature, have embodied both kinds of pleasure in their poetry" (Isocrates 1: 48). The appeal of mythopoetic discourse is not purely thematic (in the sense of the audience's recognition of familiar characters and stories)—it relies on the reactivation of shared cultural knowledge (the Greek expedition against the Trojans) through a rhapsodic performance. Impact of such a performance depended not only on the skill of a rhapsode, but on the audience's direct involvement in "the performance event" (Bakker 2).

But Isocrates is not a rhapsode who captivates the hearers by his mimesis of Homeric verses. He is a prose writer who adapts mythopoetic discourse for his educational and political project. Isocrates appreciates the potential of oral performance even as he disdains the uses to which it is put by demagogic orators. Too points out that Isocrates repeatedly draws attention to the lack of his bodily presence in his writings; on several occasions, he describes his prose as "bereft" (*eremos*). However, Too also suggests that repeated references to the apparent weakness of discourse stripped of the speaker's voice and the immediacy of the occasion "anticipate and defuse the criticisms that may be brought against the written text, above all the *logos politikos* which he produces" (120). Furthermore, although Isocrates loses the advantages of the oral performative situation, he gains something that only literacy can grant: time. According to T. Poulakos, "with time on its side, eloquence would have a chance to develop its intrinsic qualities even as it continued to cater to an external situation, and to become a self-sufficient art even as it continued to be shaped by a purpose outside its form" (70). A question arises from this characterization: how would the writer's discourse, which now is "more closely tied now to the cultural and the thematic" (Poulakos 70), exercise its influence on the audience? What elements of the written text, in the absence of the author's body and voice, would secure the delight and wisdom embedded in common cultural references?

As I have proposed, Isocrates presents himself as an inheritor of the mythopoetic tradition. He takes upon himself the rhapsodic labor of re-activating the familiar cultural themes, yet his mimesis is at once akin to and radically different from that of an oral rhapsode. The similarity between Isocrates and his poetic predecessors (variously referred to as *aoidoi* or *rhapsoidoi*) rests on the mode of composition and address. As *rhapsoidoi*, whose name derives from *rhapto* ("sew together") and *aoide* ("song"), Isocrates weaves his texts with a poet's attention to the rhythm of his utterance (Lentz 131). This link to the poetic tradition is not confined to the phonetic and syntactical levels of discourse. Like *rhapsoidoi*, who often stitched together "many and various fabrics of a song, each one already made" (Nagy 66), Isocrates inserts into his compositions fragments of already completed writings. Thus, intertextuality becomes a form of rhapsodizing. In *Antidosis*, a piece dramatized as a courtroom defense speech, "Isocrates" asks the clerk to read from previously published speeches—*Panegyricus, On the Peace, To Nicocles*—to display "what sort of eloquence it is which occupied me and given me so great a reputation" (Isocrates 2: 43).

It is certainly possible to conceive of the *Antidosis* as a panoply of examples of eloquence intended primarily as instructional showpieces. However, a reading attuned to the performative aspect of this lengthy "court speech" shows Isocrates' writing as a response to challenges against his character and his educational agenda. It would not be too much of a leap, I think, to compare Isocratean defense in *Antidosis* and other writings to the *mythoi* of epic heroes. As Martin's (1989) study of language taxonomy in the *Iliad* explains, *mythos* in Homer is "a speech-act indicating authority, performed at length, usually in public, with a focus on full attention to every detail" (12). As such, *mythos* tends to be "the speech of one in power, or of someone, for example of boasting warrior who is laying claim to power over his opponents" (22). In *Antidosis*, too, the reputation (*doxa*) of the speaker is contested and speech performs an authoritative function. Isocrates himself draws a parallel between his discourse and "works composed in rhythm and set in music" (47). In addition, he urges the audience "to fix their attention even more on what is about to be said than on what has been said before" and "not to seek to run through the whole of it at the first sitting" (12). Significantly, written discourse is presented as an answer to previously uttered speech, and as a composition to be heard (or read aloud) by "those present" rather than a solitary reader. Whether such word choice is a matter of convention, as Norlin suggests, is a different matter (Isocrates 2: 192). Despite the written mode of composition, Isocrates emphasizes the act performed by the speech rather than presenting it as a mere expression of his thoughts. His logos, in other words, is not an autonomous medium that guarantees transmission of the message; the author portrays himself in a constant agonistic dialogue with the audience.

The main distinction between rhapsodic and Isocratean performance resides in the identity of the performer. Whereas the fabric of Homeric epics is held together by recurring performances of the *Iliad* and *Odyssey* at the Feast of the Panathenaia in Athens (Nagy 69), textual integrity in Isocratean writing is secured by the author's constructed identity. Rhapsodic mimesis brought to life the characters of an Achilles or an Agamemnon or even Homer himself, whereas the rhapsode's persona remained in the shadow despite considerable inventiveness and variation that he could bring to the performance. Nagy argues that when "the rhapsode is re-enacting Homer by performing Homer, ... he *is* Homer so long as the mimesis stays in effect, so long as the performance lasts" (61). In Isocrates, on the other hand, the author's "I" refers to himself, and mythopoetic material is often employed to highlight his own constructed identity as a citizen-rhetor and educator (Too 113-50).

Panathenaicus, a speech composed to celebrate Athenian leadership among the Hellenes, illustrates the construction of the author's identity by its association with mythical personae. Here Isocrates invokes the memory of Agamemnon not simply to underscore the common heritage of the Greeks, but to draw an analogy between the Homeric hero's *doxa* and his own lifelong literary labors of promoting *homonoia*, or unity, among the Greek states:

> Although he took command of the Hellenes when they were in a state of mutual warfare and confusion and many troubles, [Agamemnon] delivered them from these. Having established concord (*homonoian*) among them and despising deeds which were superfluous, prodigious and without benefit to others, he assembled the army and led it against the barbarians. None of those with a good reputation at that time or coming later will be found to have engaged in an expedition finer or more useful to the Greeks than this individual. (Isocrates, *Panathenaicus* 2: 77-78)

Isocrates, although not a military leader, sees his *doxa* resting on his being a leader of words—*ton logon hegemon* (*Panathenaicus* 2:13), who through his logos had worked to foster concord and goodwill between the Athenians and other Greeks. And, thanks to the literary medium, he can appeal to the textual record of his statements as a proof of his identity as a citizen-rhetor.

The Legacy of Isocratean Paideia and Civic Performance

Isocratean use of mythopoetic tradition to promote cultural unification against the backdrop of the agonistic Athenian democracy appears problematic to contemporary rhetorical historians. This section, then, deals with charges of "elitism" and "cultural imperialism" leveled at Isocrates. These charges come most forcefully from Victor Vitanza's *Negation, Subjectivity, and the History of Rhetoric* (1997). Vitanza argues that Isocrates' paideia and his vision of logos lead to the class bias of the modern European educational system and, in retrospect, justify the ideology of the Third Reich. These claims cannot be dismissed simply by calling attention to the critic's anachronistic (or "metaleptic" as he prefers to call it) "reading protocol" (140). After all, by invoking the past—archaic, classical, or medieval—we illuminate our present condition in order to better articulate terms that constitute our pedagogical and political "equipment for living" (Burke 293). We need carefully to distinguish between reactionary appropriations of Isocrates' corpus, and the potential of his vision of civic performance in a contemporary democracy.

First, let us examine the claim of "elitism" associated with Isocrates' appeal to the past. This claim is based on M. I. Finley's 1972 lecture, later reprinted under the title "The Heritage of Isocrates," in which Finley critiques modern historians' nostalgia for "traditional" education, of the sort often connected to institutions like Oxford and Cambridge (Vitanza 153; Finley). Finley links Isocratean literary paideia to socioeconomic bias of educational institutions "designed for members of the ruling elite, a socially and culturally homogeneous group, whose common values were formed and repeatedly reinforced by their continuous association and shared experience" (208). For Finley, such paideia, if it serves merely as a "common code," a mark of social status, inevitably degenerates into a "cult of the past" (210). As an example of such cultlike elitism, Finley quotes Dean Gaisford of Christ Church, who is "supposed to have said early in the nineteenth century that a classical education 'enables us to look down with contempt on those who have not shared its advantages'"(203). What Finley wants to teach to modern students—and I wholeheartedly support him—is "a relevant past" (213). I disagree, however, that Isocrates' critique of Athenian rhetorical practices and his use of the mythopoetic tradition have nothing to teach modern Americans. Ironically, the original title of Finley's lecture is "Knowledge for What?"—a resoundingly Isocratean concern. Isocrates, as I have shown earlier, also questioned the purpose of contemporary rhetorical education and literary exercises, faulting the former for its service to political and material self-advancement and the latter for furthering esoteric knowledge. Indeed, the problem with today's university training, even within the humanities, is its increasing stress on technical skills, "a general cultural drift which may reduce Anglo-American democracy to an oligarchy of expertise" (McGee 9).

Furthermore, Finley's remark about the "literary" emphasis, and hence, elitism, of Isocratean paideia is only partially true: despite their literary medium, his compositions and training were oriented toward what can be called "mass culture" of the Hellenic world. Epic poetry and drama in antiquity were popular genres. It is modern philological tradition that has severed them from their performative context, rendered their civic character into timeless expression of the Greek genius, and transformed them into a corpus of texts to be perused by the elites. Isocrates' legacy did not escape this process of formalization—or, if you will, mummification, with the resulting attitudes of protective nostalgia on the part of the "traditionalists," and resentment toward "the dead white males" on the part of the younger generation of academics.

Having adopted Finley's "elitism" claim as a point of departure, Vitanza goes on to find a more politically malevolent ramification of Isocratean Panhellenism—its cultural imperialism. In Vitanza's words, "It becomes a forerunner of 'manifest destiny' and the Third Reich" (140). The basis for Vitanza's causal argument is the identification of reactionary German philosophical historiography and philology with the Greco-Roman ideal. I will bracket the validity of Vitanza's "reading protocol," which, he claims, is a "language game" like any other "canonized protocol of reading" (140). Nevertheless, I would like to object to the lack of differentiation between the discourses that have appropriated Isocrates to their reactionary political agenda and the ambivalent political potential of his rhetorical practice.

The association of Isocrates with proto-Nazism emerges from Vitanza's reading of Jaeger's *Paideia*, which epitomizes a rhetorical historiography predicated on "an *abstract timeless* conception of the mind as a realm of eternal truth and beauty high above the troubled destinies of any one nation" (Jaeger, qtd. in Vitanza 146). Vitanza shows how Jaeger constructs two links: "the Greece-Rome-Germany continuum," and a parallel between Isocrates and himself (147). Vitanza explains the Isocrates-Jaeger construction as follows: "The hero of *Paideia* story is not Plato, though he is commonly considered to be of a greater intellectual weight; instead, the hero is Isocrates—either the pragmatic or xenophobic political strategist—in his constant attempt to argue for Panhellenism and war against the barbarians" (147).

It is easy to see how Jaeger's idealistic abstraction, or extraction of Isocrates from his historicopolitical context could implicitly justify the logic of cultural chauvinism culminating with Nazi ideology that equated culture with race. If read as programmatic philosophical or moral positions, Isocrates' references to the war of the Hellenes against the barbarians might sound unequivocally xenophobic. But so would Aeschylus, Herodotus, and Aristotle. Within the context of Athenian democracy of the fifth and fourth century BCE, the term *barbarian* fulfills the role of a rhetorical placeholder, ready to be filled with insignia of Greekness. The barbarian, in fact, is "invented" in order to delineate the Greek identity (Hall). In Aeschylus's *Persians*, the "barbarian" servitude to King Xerxes is depicted to highlight the freedom (*eleutheria*) of the Athenian democratic polity. Herodotus goes even further by framing the Trojan War as the conflict between the Greeks and the Barbarians (3-5). In Aristotle, the opposition between the Greek and the Barbarian achieves theoretical status in the *Politics*, where "barbarians" are presented as "natural slaves" (26-27).

If Isocrates resembles Jaeger, it is only because his appeal to the cultural capital of the Greeks is treated as a transcendental principle and not as a series of statements crafted in response to a concrete historical situation. As McGee points out, in Isocrates the past does not work as a model to be reproduced in the present as it does in the rhetoric of Fascist nationalism. Rather, "the past is related to the present through analogy, as memory to action. The analogy does not prove—it illustrates and clarifies" (11). Distancing himself from rhetorical practices that have led to oligarchy in Athens and war among the Greek city states, Isocrates adopts the old theme of Panhellenism in order to criticize the contemporary historical situation by comparing it with mythologized historical past and to remind the audience of its collective identity. However, as distinct from the Homeric rhapsodes of the oral tradition, Isocrates promotes the rhetoric of civic responsibility by assuming in his writing the identity of the "leader of words."

In an era that has accepted, at least in theory, the concept of universal suffrage, the democratic potential of Isocratean political aesthetics may seem problematic, for it is complicated—if not tarnished—by the nationalism of Athenian democracy and misappropriations of Isocrates' heritage by modern nationalistic historians. Yet, by acknowledging both of these tendencies—one past, the other still present—we can move beyond labeling Isocrates' rhetoric as progressive or reactionary. Taking into consideration the gray area between the oral and the written word, we can ponder what can be accomplished through the rhetoric that is culturally sensitive, pragmatically oriented, and aesthetically influential.

Works Cited

Aeschylus. *Aeschylus*. Vol. 1. Trans. H. W. Smyth. Cambridge: Harvard UP, 1927.
Aristotle. *The Politics*. Trans. T. A. Sinclair. New York: Penguin, 1962.
Bakker, E. J. "Discourse and Performance: Involvement, Visualization and 'Presence' in Homeric Poetry." *Classical Antiquity* 12 (1993): 1-29.
Burke, K. *Philosophy of Literary Form*. Berkeley: U of California P, 1973.
Finley, M. I. *The Use and Abuse of History*. New York: Penguin, 1975.
Hall, E. *Inventing the Barbarian*. Oxford: Clarendon, 1989.
Harris, W. V. *Ancient Literacy*. Cambridge: Harvard UP, 1989.
Havelock, E. *The Muse Learns to Write: Reflections on Orality and Literacy from Antiquity to Present*. New Haven: Yale UP, 1986.
—. *Preface to Plato*. Cambridge: Harvard UP, 1963.
Heilbrunn, G. "Isocrates on Rhetoric and Power." *Hermes* 103 (1975): 154-78.
Herodotus. *The Persian Wars*. Trans. G. Rawlinson. New York: Modern Library, 1942.
Isocrates. *Isocrates*. Trans. G. Norlin. 2 vols. Cambridge: Harvard UP, 1928-29.
Lentz, T. M. *Orality and Literacy in Hellenic Greece*. Carbondale: Southern Illinois UP, 1989.
Martin, R. *The Language of Heroes: Speech and Performance in the* Iliad. Ithaca: Cornell UP, 1989.
McGee, M. C. "The Moral Problem of *Argumentum per Argumentum*." *Argument and Social*

Practice: Proceedings of the Fourth SCA/AFA Conference on Argumentation. Annandale, VA: Speech Communication Association, 1985. 1-15.

Nagy, G. *Poetry as Performance: Homer and Beyond.* Cambridge: Cambridge UP, 1996.

Ong, Walter. *Orality and Literacy: The Technologizing of the Word.* London: Methuen, 1982.

Poulakos, T. *Speaking for the Polis: Isocrates'* Rhetorical Education. Columbia, SC: U of South Carolina P, 1997.

Steiner, Deborah T. *The Tyrant's Writ: Myths and Images of Writing in Ancient Greece.* Princeton: Princeton UP, 1994.

Too, Y. L. *The Rhetoric of Identity in Isocrates: Text, Power, Pedagogy.* Cambridge: Cambridge UP, 1995.

Vitanza, V. *Negation, Subjectivity, and the History of Rhetoric.* Albany: State U of New York P, 1997.

MARGARET IMBER
Bates College

Pudentilla's Anger:
The Indirect Discourse of a Roman Matron

What do women want? This eternal question grows even more difficult when we ask it about women of the ancient Roman world, whose voices have not merely been lost by the accidents of a history two millennia in the making, but ignored by the ideological presuppositions of those who sought to maintain that history and write its narratives. We have little evidence that records directly the "voice(s)" of Roman women. The evidence we do have records these voices indirectly, and thus poses profound methodological problems.[1] In this chapter I want to consider one tantalizing source of indirect evidence of a woman's "voice," Apuleius' *Apology*.[2] I find this text tantalizing for two reasons. First, it tells a story of domestic drama and intrigue—a woman's story, in the male, public genre of courtroom oratory. Second, the *Apology* contains the story of what one woman wanted. Indeed, it is the simple fact of this woman's desire that initiated the events that Apuleius recounts.

Pudentilla, daughter of a very wealthy North African family, in her teens, had married Sicinius Amicus, the son of a local prominent family. She had two sons by her husband, who died when the older boy was about nine (*Apol.* 68). Her husband's family was very keen on keeping Pudentilla's personal fortune in the family, and her father-in-law went so far as to threaten that he would disinherit his grandsons if Pudentilla married *extrario* (*Apol.* 68). Pudentilla responded to this threat by agreeing to become engaged to, but never to marry, one of her dead husband's brothers (*Apol.* 68). This action, Pudentilla reminded her son when she later decided to remarry, had secured the boys' inheritance of their paternal estate (*Apol.* 70). During her long widowhood, Pudentilla managed the considerable estate she had inherited and supervised the investment of funds that her sons would receive from their grandfather (*Apol.* 70, 93).

Eventually, Pudentilla's father-in-law died. Her oldest son was now a young man, studying rhetoric at Rome (*Apol.* 70). Her younger son was ready to receive the *toga virilis*, the mark of adulthood for Roman males. Pudentilla announced that she wanted to remarry and told her oldest son she would marry whomever he chose for her (*Apol.* 70-71). Her son chose Apuleius, a brilliant *rhetor* whom he knew from school days in Athens (*Apol.* 72-73), and who came from a reasonably wealthy family.[3] At first things went well, but eventually Pudentilla's in-laws fought back, waging a campaign of gossip and slander against Pudentilla and Apuleius and persuading her son to withdraw support from the very marriage candidate he had named (*Apol.* 1, 74, 77-78, 82, 87, 103). Nevertheless, Apuleius and Pudentilla married (*Apol.* 88). Apuleius claimed that he subsequently effected a reconciliation between Pudentilla and her sons (*Apol.* 87, 93-94). However, Pontianus, the older son, died shortly thereafter in Carthage, where he had returned to pursue his education and career (*Apol.* 97). Pudens, Pudentilla's younger son, fell under the influence of his father's family and their friends (*Apol.* 98) and the quarrel resumed. The conflict eventually resulted in a lawsuit against Apuleius. Although his enemies had gossiped that Apuleius had played a role in Pontianus' death (*Apol.* 1), the trial itself turned on their allegation that Apuleius was a magician who had used his arts to seduce Pudentilla (*Apol.* 2).

Pudentilla's story is a great one. It is not, however, the story that survives. The *Apology*, Apuleius's defense speech, is his own tale. If Apuleius told this story, moreover, he told it for very high stakes in defense of a capital charge. If Apuleius's story is occasioned by Pudentilla's domestic drama, then it is also true that to tell his own tale, he usurps and encapsulates Pudentilla's story within a larger narrative framework, one preoccupied with his own masculine exploits in philosophy, rhetoric, magic, and science. To add to the tantalizing nature of the text, however, I must emphasize the "ifs." Scholars have long questioned the veracity of the text, some claiming it is all a fiction, a rhetorical *jeu d'esprit*. Others speculate that the speech we have recorded bears little relation to the speech Apuleius gave in court.[4] Even if we posit the veracity of the text, we must concede that the only evidence of these events is Apuleius's speech. Thus, the *Apology* is the most untenable of texts, oscillating somewhere between two quite distant poles of representation. At one extreme, we may read it as Apuleius's whimsical imagination of how he might explain a woman's desire. At the other extreme, we might say that his very life depended on his ability to explain what his woman wanted to an audience suspicious of women who dared to want at all.

If we cannot be sure that Apuleius ever gave the Apology in court, then we cannot, it seems, say what it was that Pudentilla wanted. But we can read the *Apology* to see how one man imagined her desire. And that effort is instructive. Apuleius deliberately creates and exploits a gap between his representation of Pudentilla's articulation of her desire, and his own understanding of it. Our author mediates this tension through references to both positive and negative idealizations of Roman women. He constantly compares his Pudentilla to the perfect Roman matron and her awful opposite, the wicked stepmother.

We can explore one particular source for these idealized portraits of Roman women in some detail. That source is the corpus of Roman declamations.[5] Declamation was the crowning glory of Roman pedagogy. School boys wrote, practiced, and gave mock trial court speeches about wicked stepmothers and evil tyrants for the last several years of their formal education.

As adults they attended public declamations by professional teachers and held private declamation contests for entertainment, much the way moderns play cards or go to movies with friends after dinner. Apuleius, the *rhetor*, knew them well, and even refers to studying with Pudentilla's sons (*Apol.* 73). The complete familiarity Apuleius' audience would have had with the plots and characters of declamation cannot be overestimated.

The declamations that are concerned with the character and conduct of women offer us two polarized ideals of Roman women: the good and bad matron. The ideal declamatory mother completely subsumes herself to the identity of the husband and the house into which she marries. This good Roman wife and mother has no male kin of her own that might intrude on her husband's family and challenge her husband's decisions. The ideal declamatory mother, moreover, manages to be both the perfect wife and the perfect mother, satisfying the fantasies of both father and son that her first loyalty is to each of them. The ideal mother has no money of her own, which might lead to her having some power and authority that declamatory men might have to recognize. Finally, this paragon, when she has lost sons and husband, wants to commit suicide.

The bad women of declamation are adulteresses and stepmothers who actively hate and frequently poison their children. Bad mothers possess some form of identity distinct from that of wife and mother to their husband's children, represented either by adultery, or by a continued relationship with their own fathers. The bad mother's actions against son and husband (often blinding or murder) are often ascribed by declaimers to her desire to rule in the house without effective male supervision. Even where a mother does not connive at power, her failure to repress her identity is inevitably an assertion of power, if not authority, over her sons.

In every reference Apuleius makes to Pudentilla's desire he alludes to these iconic figures, the good matron and the evil stepmother. These declamatory figures shape the variety of ways Apuleius describes Pudentilla's desire to remarry. He argues that Pudentilla wanted to remarry after her first husband's death, but was prevented from doing so by her father-in-law. She did not, he assures us "in the very flower of her youth, willingly remain so long a widow" (*Apol.* 68). Apuleius could scarcely deny that Pudentilla desired remarriage. Her desire and her wealth were the principal reasons he was a defendant in court. Accordingly, he argues that it was a fact that everyone knew. Aemilianus, her brother-in-law, for example, wrote to Pontianus after the elder Sicinius had died, acknowledging that she would and should now want to remarry (*Apol.* 69).

Apuleius's concession of the fact of Pudentilla's desire would seem to argue against a presentation of Pudentilla as an idealized Roman matron who lives only for her husband, and after his death, for her sons. Acknowledging her desire, however, allows Apuleius to characterize Pudentilla's in-laws as the overreaching, tyrannical fathers and husbands of Roman declamation who misunderstand and abuse their daughters and wives. Although Apuleius could not dispute the fact that Pudentilla wanted to remarry, he could, however, treat the years she spent as an unwilling widow as an unfair punishment that she, an idealized, good mother, suffered willingly for her sons' sake.

It is interesting, then, to compare the explanation Apuleius gave for Pudentilla's decision, and the explanation Pudentilla offered for herself, according to Apuleius:

> But she, herself, wrote to her son Pontianus about this matter while he was in Rome, and furthermore, explained completely the reason for her decision. She told him all the medical reasons: there was, moreover, no longer any reason for her to further persist—the very paternal inheritance which she had sought, despite the consequences to her own health, she had increased by her own efforts.... Finally, [she asked] that her sons at last allow her to attend to her own loneliness and illness; and that about her devotion and her final choice [of husband], they should fear nothing—what she was to them as a widow, so she would be as a wife. I direct that the copy of this letter sent to her son be read aloud. (*Apol.* 70)

Apuleius did not question Pudentilla's decision to remarry, and suggested that Aemilianus did not as well. Conversely, Pudentilla suggests that she has no personal desire to remarry. Her interests have always been in her sons and the preservation of their inheritance. It is only the external compulsion of medical reasons that require her to take this step. Pudentilla closes her letter to Pontianus, moreover, with an assurance to her son that she will achieve the maternal ideal of maintaining perfect devotion to both her sons and her new husband.

Apuleius himself argued, however, that the abnegation of her own personality implicit in such a promise is not something that Pudentilla should have been required to attempt. Indeed, he criticizes Pudens for not respecting Pudentilla's right to maintain an identity distinct from that of her sons: "Do you then snoop out what she does in her bedroom, lest your mother be thought—I don't say a paramour—but simply a woman? Do you consider her love to be worthless unless you have it all?" (*Apol.* 85). By articulating this range of perspectives on Pudentilla's decision to remarry, Apuleius can have the best of two arguments and minimize his own role in the conflict over Pudentilla's decision. Pudens's position is that of an immature schoolboy who wants his mother all to himself and wants her to act like the perfect mothers he reads about in school. Grown men understand this fantasy, but in the real world of marriages and wills they do not expect to see it realized. Grown women like Pudentilla, conversely, Apuleius can suggest, do not contest this idealizing vision of their devotion to family. Voicing Pudentilla's position that she is motivated by dire medical necessity alone, moreover, permits Apuleius to characterize her as a passive victim of life's fortunes, not an autonomous woman seeking personal fulfillment. Apuleius's Pudentilla is, in Bourdieu's formulation, a "well-meaning rule-breaker," one who presents herself as a victim of circumstances that prevent her compliance with a rule that she herself believes valid. Thus, her conduct, which appears to contradict the social norm, actually reinforces it.[6]

Apuleius tells us, furthermore, that Pudentilla's description of her decision to marry, in which she masks her own agency, is typical of women. Thus, even if she had called Apuleius a magician in a second letter that she wrote to Pontianus after he withdrew his support for Apuleius's marriage candidacy, her use of this epithet would merely have been "the device employed by all women—that when they begin to want something of this sort, they prefer to appear compelled" (*Apol.* 79). Our author, again, is having it both ways. First, the letter demonstrates that Pudentilla had not called him a magician, as his enemies had alleged. Second, even if she had, it would not have been a meaningful utterance—women, by definition, should not speak their own desire directly or literally. Pudentilla, in contrast to the villainesses of rhetorical exercises, explains the aspects of her behavior that violate the ideology of Roman matrons in terms that uphold the validity of its idealizing norms.[7]

Finally, Apuleius insists that Pudentilla left the decision of what man she would marry entirely in the hands of Pontianus. He assures us that "she obeyed her son more than her heart in doing this (choosing Apuleius), which even Aemilianus can't deny" (*Apol.* 71; see also 73 and 83). Of all the men in Oea to whom Pudentilla might nominally defer, Pontianus was the one she could most easily influence. Apuleius several times describes Pontianus as torn between his affection for his mother and his concern for his inheritance. Apuleius's ability to further Pontianus in his chosen career as a rhetor through his connections in Carthage also added to Pudentilla's ability to influence Pontianus (*Apol.* 94).

Pudentilla, however, could not control Pontianus completely. When Herrenius Rufinus, his father-in-law and friend of the Sicinii, persuaded Pontianus to abandon his support for Apuleius's suit for Pudentilla, the son discovered that his mother now refused his guidance:

> Pontianus went to his mother, a messenger of Rufinus' tidings. But when he made no headway at all against her purposefulness, and instead was rebuked for his own fickleness and inconstancy, he brought back scarcely pleasant news to his father-in-law: that his mother, a woman of the most easy going temperament, was unyielding, and what's more, that he had inflamed her anger by his importuning (and that would increase her resistance in no small measure); and that she had finally answered him that it was obvi-

ous that he was browbeating her at Rufinus' request—all the more reason why she needed a husband as a defense against his desperate greed. (77)

Apuleius's portrayal of Pontianus as a hapless messenger boy caught between powerful masters undercuts in two respects any claim Pontianus might have had to impose his change of heart on Pudentilla. First, Pontianus appears to lack the strength of character to assert his own will—he was still a boy, not a *pater familias*. Second, his change of heart regarding Apuleius's spousal candidacy appears inauthentic. Pontianus seems to be only the mouthpiece of Rufinus. Because Rufinus's choice in the matter is inherently invalid—he has no right to involve himself in Pudentilla's marriage decision, and because his interest in doing so presumably derives solely from his greed for her estate, Pontianus's position is especially suspect.

The most interesting feature of Apuleius's description of Pudentilla's behavior is that she nowhere challenges the notion that she should be subject to some man's authority. She is not, like the evil mothers of declamation, struggling to rule the house, unrestrained by paternal authority. Rather, she is struggling to obtain a paternal authority figure to whom she may properly defer. Pontianus, in allowing himself to be used by Rufinus, has lost his right to that status. Apuleius, as her husband, however, can play this role. Thus, Pudentilla, as Apuleius describes her, is careful to articulate her own desires—which in declamatory terms she ought not to have at all—in terms that efface that desire. As Apuleius's Pudentilla would describe it, she is obeying the wishes of Pontianus's true and better self, not pursuing her own. It is he who is fickle and inconstant.

Apuleius's description of this scene, with its passing mention of Pudentilla's anger, is linked to his subsequent descriptions of the negotiation of a financial settlement between Pudentilla and her sons, and Pudentilla's testamentary dispositions after the unexpected death of Pontianus. In Apuleius's account of the financial settlement Pudentilla made with her sons, through which Apuleius effected the reconciliation between Pudentilla, Pontianus, and Pudens, he was "the instigator, the supporter, the conciliator of tranquillity, peace and family feeling" (*Apol.* 93). Pudentilla, on the other hand, was angry and unwilling to come to terms with her sons (*Apol.* 93). Apuleius had to win the terms of the settlement from her with "ingentibus precibus [immense entreaties]" (*Apol.* 93).

This description is meant to suggest the possibility of a Pudentilla unrestrained by Apuleius's paternal authority, who in womanly fashion might give vent to a deserved but ultimately destructive anger that would destroy her family. In a nice touch, Apuleius also tells us that Pudentilla herself has given him leave to so describe these events (*Apol.* 93). His delicacy here is meant to highlight Pontianus's unfilial behavior in permitting Rufinus to publish misleading excerpts of Pudentilla's second letter (*Apol.* 78, 82), an act that also inspired Pudentilla's anger (*Apol.* 87). Thus, with his wife's permission, he offers a portrait of Pudentilla to serve as an alternative to the one his enemies circulated in Oea. According to the plaintiffs, Pudentilla was an aging, bewitched, lovesick matron. Apuleius tells us that she objected to this depiction because it was false and because it arose from an unfilial breach of respect for her privacy. Pudentilla approved, however, of Apuleius's image of Pudentilla as a barely restrained Medea. Pudentilla authorized this self-portrait because it highlighted her legitimate need for Apuleius, a husband who could protect her from Rufinus and Aemilianus, and from her own worst instincts.

Apuleius emphasizes this characterization of Pudentilla again, when he describes the will she wrote on Pontianus's death. By now, outraged by Pudens's behavior, Pudentilla had amended her will to disinherit her remaining son (*Apol.* 99). Pudentilla was so adamant that Apuleius had to threaten to leave her in order to persuade her to rewrite her will and name Pudens as her heir (99). It is at this point in his narration that Apuleius explicitly invokes the plots and characters of the declamatory corpus:

> A stepfather, I battled with an angry mother on behalf of my wicked stepson, just as a father takes the part of a loyal son against a stepmother. Nor was I satisfied until I had, far more than fairness required, checked my good wife's indulgent generosity towards me. (*Apol.* 99)

Apuleius's irony works here because of his own ambiguous position in Pudentilla's family. Stepfathers are not a stock character of declamation. Indeed, Noy argues that the wicked stepfather did not become a character of folklore in Roman culture until the fourth century of the common era, when Christian writers, adapting language typically used of stepmothers, castigated the figure.[8]

There is some evidence in the *Apologia*, however, that Apuleius's opponents may have anticipated the Christian fathers and attempted to assimilate Apuleius to the declamatory figure of the wicked stepmother. They charged that he was a magician (*Apol.* 1). Apuleius's enemies also claimed in gossip, if not in the indictment, that he had a hand in the death of his stepson, Pontianus (*Apol.* 1). They alleged that he bewitched Pudentilla, carried her off to the isolation of the country to marry her, and forced her (against the interest of her own children) to make over the bulk of her estate to him in a marriage settlement (*Apol.* 96). His behavior, according to the plaintiffs, was very like the declamatory stepmother who sought to rule her husband's house, and the evil wife or stepmother, who sought her husband's patrimony against the interests of her children or stepchildren.

Apuleius counters this characterization by claiming the role of the beneficent father in declamation and casting Pudens in the role of the evil stepson.

Stepsons in declamation, however, are evil sons only when they engage in illicit sexual relations with their stepmothers and thus demonstrate their disloyalty to their father. Although Apuleius is happy to paint Pudens with as black a brush as he can, he cannot suggest anything sexually illicit in Pudentilla's behavior toward Pudens. More typically, declamatory stepsons suffer at the hands of evil stepmothers. Apuleius's identification of Pudens with the evil stepson of declamation, accordingly, is inherently unstable, because Apuleius himself plays an anomalous role in the story that declamation does not provide for, the stepfather.

The angry Pudentilla of Apuleius's defense, who writes her son out of her will, is a similarly unstable character in the rhetor's analogy. The good mother of declamation subsumes her identity to the interests of her son. The evil stepmother is hostile to those interests. Apuleius went to great lengths in the *Apologia* to recast many aspects of Pudentilla's conduct so that he might characterize her as a good declamatory mother. Why then, at the close of the speech, would he, by emphasizing her anger, undermine his characterization of Pudentilla as a good matron?

The answer lies, I think, in his assimilation of his own conduct to that of the good father of declamation. He begins by claiming to be a good stepfather. Like the only example declamation offers of the good stepmother, he attends to the interest of his stepson at the expense of his own (*"nimio plus aequo,"* i.e., far more than fairness required), abandoning reasonable financial expectations of his marriage to Pudentilla to ensure that Pudens and Pontianus in the financial settlement with their mother, and Pudens in her will, are treated well.

Apuleius's analogy to the declamatory family, however, concludes by comparing his position to that of a father protecting his own son against the hostility of a stepmother. It is in offering himself as the good father that Apuleius resolves the instability of his analogy. As the good father, he has protected Pudens from Pudentilla's anger. He has, moreover, enabled Pudentilla to achieve the declamatory matron's ideal, if elusive, goal of completely serving the interests of both father and son.

Similarly, Apuleius suggests that as Pudentilla's husband he has been able to resolve the potential conflicts her role as wife and mother have raised. Pudentilla alone cannot. Her anger, unchecked by Apuleius, will transform Pudentilla into the hostile stepmother Pudens deserves. Thus, only if Pudens accepts Apuleius's authority as father and his place as Pudentilla's husband will Pudens be able to play the role of loyal son and Pudentilla that of good mother. Apuleius explicitly threatens in the conclusion of his speech, moreover, to abandon his role as good declamatory father, and leave mother and son in a permanent state of stepmother-son hostility, if Pudens will not accept his authority:

Now he, if you please, can entreat his mother hereafter, since he has made it impossible for me to plead on his behalf. Now he's his own master. Let him rewrite his mother's angriest codicils, let him appease her wrath. The man who can make orations against his mother surely will be able to talk her around. (*Apol.* 101)

Thus, by manipulating the characters of the declamatory family, Apuleius is able to recast Pudentilla's behavior, transforming her from a wealthy, willful widow into a dutiful matron. He similarly transforms himself from a fortune-hunting interloper into an ideal declamatory father whose good offices alone will enable Pudentilla to conform to the declamatory ideals that govern maternal behavior.

In Apuleius's *Apologia*, we find the story of one wealthy Roman matron whose behavior did not accord with that of the idealized matrons of the declamatory corpus—she wanted, she acted, she spoke, she wrote. If we accept Apuleius's description of Pudentilla's letters and conversations as accurate, then we have seen—at least through Apuleius's eyes—Pudentilla's own efforts to shape the perception of and account for her conduct in terms of declamatory ideology about good and bad mothers. We cannot reconstruct the subjectivity of Roman women from a text as difficult as the *Apology*. But Apuleius's treatment, whether fictional or realistic, indicates both that female subjectivity did exist and, more importantly, that women like Pudentilla did negotiate their desire, did speak, if with varying degrees of effectiveness, against a dominant ideology that sought to silence their voices. Our difficulty in hearing Pudentilla's voice lies less with Pudentilla and Apuleius and the two thousand years of historical narrative that did not attend to the woman's voice, than it does with us. If we want to say what it is that women like Pudentilla wanted, then we must seek better tools to listen to their silence, to apprehend their indirect discourse.

Notes

1. See S. Joshel, *Work, Identity, and Legal Status at Rome: A Study of the Occupational Inscriptions* (Norman and London: U of Oklahoma P, 1992, 3-15) for a summary of the methodological and ideological issues at stake in "listening to silence" for those whose voices have been suppressed.

2. Translations from Helm's Teuber edition of the *Apologia* are mine.

3. Apuleius claimed that his father, a *duumvir* of Maudura, a veterans' *colonia* in Numidia (*Apol.* 24), left an estate of two million sesterces to Apuleius and his brother (*Apol.* 23). He conceded, however, that his life of travel, study, and his frequent generosity to friends and students made serious inroads on his inheritance (*id.*). Stok's analysis of Apuleius's "dissimulation of poverty" as a style of elite Roman self-fashioning should caution against relying too literally on Apuleius's economic descriptions. F. Stok, "Il pauperismo di Apuleio," *Index* 13 (1985): 353-86, 364-67.

4. See G. B. Conte, *Latin Literature: A History* (Baltimore and London: Johns Hopkins UP,

1994) 557. Conte, himself, concludes the work was produced by a real historical circumstance, but that the text we have reflects a substantial reworking, with deliberate literary goals and purposes, of the speech given at trial (*id.*). See also A. Abt, *Die Apologie des Apuleius von Madaura und die antike Zauberei: Beiträge zur Erläuterung der Schrift de magia* (Gießen: Alfred Töpelmann, 1908) 6-9; F. Gaide, "Apulée de Madaure a-t-il prononcé le *De Magia* devant le proconsul d'Afrique?" *Les Études Classiques* 61.3 (1993): 227-31; K. Sallmann, "Erzählendes in der *Apologia* des Apuleius, oder Argumentation als Unterhaltung," *Groningen Colloquia on the Novel* 6 (1995): 137-57; F. Amarelli, "Il Processo Di Sabrata," *Studia et Documenta Historiae Iuris* 54 (1988): 110-46; and Stok 354-55 (our text is an adequate re-elaboration of the trial speech). Winter and Callebat argue that the *Apologia* is substantially the speech Apuleius gave before Claudius Maximus. T. N. Winter, "The Publication of Apuleius' *Apology*," *TAPA* 100 (1969): 607-12; L. Callebat, "La prose d'Apulée dans le De Magia," *Wiener Studien* 97 (1984): 143-67.

5. The surviving corpus consists of the 145 Minor Declamations and the 19 Major Declamations ascribed to Quintilian, the excerpts of *controversiae* and *suasoriae* recorded in the Elder Seneca, and the excerpts of 53 *controversiae* ascribed to Calpurnius Flaccus. See M. Winterbottom, *The Elder Seneca: Declamations*, Loeb Classical Library (Cambridge, MA and London: Harvard UP, 1974); L. Håkanson, *Calpurnii Flacci Declamationum excerpta* (Stuttgart: Teubner, 1978); L. Håkanson, *Declamationes XIX maiores Quintiliano falso ascriptae* (Stuttgart: Teubner, 1982); L. A. Sussman, *The Major Declamations Ascribed to Quintilian: A Translation* (Frankfurt am Main: Verlag Peter Lang, 1987); M. Winterbottom, *The Minor Declamations Ascribed to Quintilian (Texte und Kommentare)* (Berlin: Gruyter, 1984). See S. F. Bonner, *Roman Declamation* (Berkeley: U of California P, 1949) for a discussion of the social and educational practice of declamation.

6. P. Bourdieu, *Outline of a Theory of Practice* (Cambridge and New York: Cambridge UP, 1977) 17-21, 41. See also Cohen's review of anthropological literature describing modern Mediterranean cultures in which social norms calling for the limitation of female activity to the home coexist with social practices that tolerate public economic and social activity by women. D. J. Cohen, *Law, Sexuality, and Society: The Enforcement of Morals in Classical Athens* (Cambridge, England and New York: Cambridge UP, 1991) 139-63.

7. The obvious contradiction here is that she must speak to explain that she is not speaking. Her letters announce her desire, the first to marry, the second to marry Apuleius despite the fact that Pontianus has withdrawn his support for the marriage. The contradictory nature of Pudentilla's letters, then, capture the essence of the tension between ideological expectation and the realities of social existence.

8. D. Noy, "Wicked Stepmothers in Roman Society and Imagination," *Journal of Family History* 16.4 (1991): 345-62.

STEPHEN MCKENNA
Catholic University of America

Advertising as Epideictic Rhetoric

The largest, most pervasive, and most successful rhetorical enterprise on the planet is advertising. If it is possible to think of advertising as becoming even larger, even more pervasive, and even more successful in the future, then in this dawn of the global economy it is reasonable to think that it will become so. Granting even modest truth to these observations, it is perplexing to note that scholars of rhetoric give advertising scant attention. Of the 360 items in the *MLA* bibliography for the period from 1980 to the present that deal with advertising, the majority are in journals of linguistics, followed by journals of cultural studies, literature, and folklore. Exactly one cites an article in a scholarly journal devoted to rhetoric (see Kehl and Heidt). The best place to read scholarly studies of advertising rhetoric—including some that draw quite ably on the rhetorical tradition—are in journals of consumer research that probably cross the desks of few rhetoricians (e.g., Leigh, McQuarrie and Mick, Scott, and Stern). No book length study of advertising draws in any sustained way on the resources of the rhetorical tradition; few papers delivered at rhetoric conferences concern advertising. Why should this be?

Perhaps ads, which are generally very short in duration, fail to invite the kind of analysis typically done by rhetoricians, who tend to focus on lengthier forms of discourse. We would rather leave ads to the linguists, who are more at home with the speech act and the fragmentary semantic or syntactic unit. Or perhaps, because ads are typically so image-driven, so multiply mediated, so seemingly heterogeneous in character, we textualists feel ourselves ill-equipped to deal with them. Hence we prefer to leave the work to the semiologists, the structural anthropologists, or those in media studies. Or maybe we find that the rhetorical criticism of advertising is simply uninspiring or dull: upon scrutiny, it often seems that every ad shrivels, with numbing repetition, into more or less the same spiritually desiccated piece of propaganda. Perhaps, again, it is only that we are a bit elitist: advertising is literally vulgar and at most points glaringly unsubtle in its rhetoric, and so it is not the proper object of "serious" study. Or, contrarily, perhaps we recognize that this is one of advertising's most ingenious rhetorical strategies: in late twentieth-century consumer capitalism, the critical prerogative is perpetually co-opted by advertising, which usually already deconstructs itself and hence is self-inoculated against serious consideration. The advertising critic is then apt to be seen as an obligatory but tiresome court jester, who in the end only imitates the object of study, at best identifying rhetorical devices that will soon be ironically appropriated into the commercial enterprise and played back endlessly. (Another place where the criticism of advertising rhetoric is taken seriously is in the industry's own trade magazine, *Advertising Age*.) Whatever the cause, the inattention of rhetoric scholars to advertising is probably best seen as a mark of its success.

Yet another possible reason for our near silence about advertising is the fact that the bulk of rhetorical theory—or at least the seminal set of ideas that nearly all later theory in some way refracts—was conceived over two millennia ago amidst social and political conditions vastly different from those of the world in which advertising is a force. What could any theory devised to aid the practice of public speaking in the polis have to say about direct mail, Times Square neon, or "Tippy" the Taco Bell Chihuahua? Of course, it is simple enough to plug the square pegs of advertising devices into the round holes of classical rhetorical concepts—tracing, say, the topology of commercial invention, unraveling ad enthymemes, sketching visual analogues of the figures of speech, and so on—but in the end, would this not be a mostly trivial and ahistorical exercise in mere taxonomy? Would it not serve mainly to obfuscate the critical political and social dislocations of 2,500 years of human history?

Classical rhetoric was public in a way that modern rhetoric cannot be. The public of classical rhetoric was a privileged sphere of life wholly opposed to the private—a realm wherein, as Hannah Arendt describes it, men of property escaped the anonymous futility of private life in the *oikos* and the biological needs it existed to service. In the public sphere, men sought the freedom and immortality in public memory afforded by speech and action (26-31). Advertising rhetoric, on the other hand, is consumed with (and in) private life, which is now our privileged realm of existence. It is no coincidence that the triumph of consumer capitalism occurs in an age and culture whose politics can be described as having undergone a wholesale "privatization of good" (McIntyre 353). To the classical rhetoricians, "private good" would have been an oxymoron.

The prospect of bringing the rhetorical tradition to an analysis of modern advertising is further impeded by equipment that emphasizes choice and agency. Rhetoricians from the sophists to the belletrists devised a variety of theories, but all of these shared the assumption of situational determinacy in the constitutive elements of rhetorical practice: speaker, speech, subject, audience, and occasion. Calling the eloquent response to these conditions *to prepon* (Aristotle), *decorum* (Cicero), "seemelynesse" (Thomas Wilson), propriety (Adam Smith), and still other names, theorists of rhetoric have long recognized that the right words spoken in the right way at the right moment make speech a kind of morally and politically significant action, quite apart from its communicative or informational function. In contrast, the defining situation of rhetoric in the age of mass media is an antisituation, "the context of no context" (Trow). Advertising's "speaker" is corporate; its "speech" is multiply mediated; its audience is massive and heterogeneous, but physically isolated or compartmentalized; its occasions are repeated through time and across space. The conditions of its reception are neither entirely public nor wholly private, but rather a variety of situational and social amalgamations of the two. In short, the kairotic core of classical rhetoric has mostly disappeared from the construction and reception of advertising media. "Global village" joins "private good" as another term that would have struck the ancient rhetoricians as self-contradictory.

Perhaps the attempt to apply classical concepts to modern rhetoric is no more anachronistic than in applying classical genre criticism to modern discourse. This is so especially in the case of epideictic, which at first seems to have a vastly diminished role in modern public discourse, at least in comparison to its prominent place in the polis. And certainly advertising would seem to be the wrong substrate, because epideictic in its broadest sense is display rhetoric with "no ulterior motive," whereas with advertising, an ulterior motive is understood to be present from the moment the audience recognizes that it is being exposed to an ad (Burke, *Motives* 71).

Despite all of this, there may be some cause for looking at advertising through the lens of epideictic. In the polis, epideictic was probably the type of speech most likely to be witnessed by *hoi polloi*: it is not entirely unreasonable, considering these parallels in audience, to seek affinities between ancient display rhetoric and modern advertising as the rhetoric of what Arendt calls the "social sphere," or that realm of life that surfaced fully with the rise of nation states and capitalism, in which issues of mutual dependence and private survival were pushed under the ambit of public concern (68). In addition, although in Aristotle's *Rhetoric* epideictic's time frame is said to be the present moment (1358b18), the intent of epideictic was a celebration of the timeless, a characteristic that increased its tendency to transcend the usual kairotic determinacy of situated practice. Perhaps this element of timelessness gives epideictic, among the three species of rhetoric, something in common with the practice of advertising (though surely not its subject matter). In further support, there is Kenneth Burke's observation that epideictic tends naturally to thrive in periods when other forms of public rhetoric are in decay (*Motives* 71). It goes without saying that such a condition is continually said to be that of our historical moment.

And there are, prima facie, other reasons for interpreting advertising rhetoric as epideictic discourse. The most obvious among these is that at this stage in the history of capitalism, the need for a deliberative rhetoric to persuade people not only to buy specific products but to see consumption as a valid way of life is long past. Whereas in the embryonic era of industrial capitalism businesses used advertising in explicitly exhortatory ways to create new concepts of good (including the virtue of advertising itself) before a working-class audience that was largely resistant to such persuasion, this is no longer the case (Ewen 33). Even where today's ads use exhortation, more often than not all trace of the economic nature of the buying objective is coyly suppressed: consumers are urged to "Get to know" Geo; they are advised, "Don't miss" the Hyundai Sonata; or they are told, in the voice of a gruff but lovable athletic coach, to "Just do it." As if to dramatize the irrelevance of a deliberative mode in contemporary advertising, the makers of Macallan whiskey ran a campaign in the late eighties telling consumers in banner headlines *not* to buy Macallan. So complete is the advertising audience's conversion, so taken for granted are the practical aims and endoxic underpinnings of the ads themselves, that the epideictic element is allowed greater play.

This is not a particularly new point, just one whose ramifications have not been sufficiently explored by rhetoric scholars. Although Leo Spitzer never used the term *epideictic*, the epideictic function of advertising was a strong current in his brilliant 1946 essay, "American Advertising as Popular Art." Following an intricate explication of a simple lunch counter placard advertising Sunkist orange juice, Spitzer drew a prescient conclusion.

> American advertising [is] one of the greatest forces working to perpetuate a national ideal: in their own way the pictures of happy family life or of private enjoyment have a conservative function comparable to that of the statues in the old Greek Polis; though the American images are not embodiments of gods or heroes, they preach an exemplary well-being as an idea accessible to every man [sic] in the American community. (356)

More than half a century before Volvo claimed to sell an automobile that can "save your soul," Spitzer saw that this epideictic motive in advertising was fundamentally religious in nature—that the celebration of capitalism's invisible, Providential hand was informed by a "eudaemonistic deism."

Indeed, almost as if it were trying to head off some incipient weariness in the consumer audience for all those pseudo-claims and puffed promises of worldly "happiness," advertising today has become increasingly explicit in its use of the religious, the spiritual, and the other-worldly as special topics of argument. Perhaps rhetoric scholars should have seen this coming: thirty-five years ago, when Amos Wilder described a species of rhetoric marked by creative novelty in style, dramatic immediacy, use of common idiom and media, addiction to narrative, and subordination of the role of the sender to the spirit of the audience, he was addressing himself to early Christian rhetoric, but the characterization fits the discourse of advertising tolerably well (43). Of course, the religious argument in advertising is designed, like all publicity tactics, to cut through the cluttered mediascape by being shocking or just different, which is to say that its aims are ulterior rather than ultimate. But it would be a mistake to dismiss the possibility that, in the very unsubtlety of its irony, the openly religious turn in some recent advertising discloses some deep human yearnings that the epideictic element in all rhetoric seeks in some way to address.

Consider Volvo's recent TV commercials. There are several versions of the spot, but all of them share a serious male voiceover claiming, "It is perhaps our most impressive safety feature ever: a Volvo that can save your soul." One version crudely but unmistakably manages to allude to Islam (the opening music recalls a muezzin's call to prayer), Buddhism (an Asian woman gazes contemplatively at the audience through a slowly revolving bicycle wheel), and Christianity (closing matched shots of a man and then a Volvo being "baptized" in a purifying cascade of water). Although these ads are perhaps the most explicitly kerygmatic in their message, they are not unique. One recent Toyota print ad, for example, explicitly brings together advertising's tendency to use praise in place of argument with the religious motive lurking in epideictic discourse generally. In it, the Toyota Land Cruiser appears (as so often is the case in car and truck ads) in the vast emptiness of the desert Southwest's mesa country. The copy touts the vehicle as having "the qualities man has revered and respected for thousands of years": namely, "the power to tame the forces of nature," "the prowess to navigate any terrain," but also "authenticity" and the ability to "inspire awe." The headline copy immodestly announces, "In primitive times, it would've been a god."

A similar rhetoric operates in a recent ad for Absolut Vodka, one that breaks from the long-running pattern in which the Absolut bottle appears as a visual metaphor for anything and everything, as if anticipating the hallucinatory effect of overindulgence in the product. Instead, this ad offers a short-short story (a small display-narrative) by Latina writer Julia Alvarez. The story tells of an encounter on some magical-realist island between a writer and a mystical priest who performs his Eucharistic rite with the aid of an Absolut bottle, the very name on which, the priest says, is that of "God Almighty." For all its offensiveness (a ciborium full of bad Easter candy is mentioned), this ad is ingenious in its own meta-hermeneutic offerings. Through its sacrilegious rhetoric it both evidences a spiritual poverty in its audience and simultaneously suggests that the transmutating appearances of the Absolut bottle in those many other ads seek to address a still present human yearning for divine omnipresence. This last point may seem extreme, but at the very least, the religious turn in recent advertising should prompt scholars of rhetoric to make a serious reconsideration of the arguments about the religious motive lurking in all rhetoric made in different ways by Kenneth Burke, Richard Weaver, and more recently Wayne Booth.

Walter Beale too has remarked (albeit in passing) on the essentially epideictic character of advertising in support of his view that the multiple criteria historically used to distinguish epideictic discourse (stylistic display, temporal present-ness, and/or value reinforcement) are insufficient (243). Beale uses speech act theory to reinterpret epideictic as "rhetorical performative discourse": speech that not only refers to or proposes action(s) but participates in the sphere of action itself (225-26). It is this species of rhetoric that Aristotle terms an "activity," or "actualization" (*energeia*), as opposed to a purposive process or motion (*kinêsis*)—a distinction he develops in his discussion of pleasure (*Nicomachean Ethics* 1153a8). An *energeia* carries its end (*telos*) with it at all points; it is always complete in its being-done, as opposed to terminating in the achievement of a sought-after goal. So in what way(s) does advertising epideictic participate in the sphere of action? One likely answer is that it helps create that very sphere and consecrates it as the privileged space of appearance in which things are made present as "real" and their moral significance made apparent. Hence, the epideictic purpose of every ad is simply to say: "this product is advertised." A recent print ad for Chevrolet trucks illustrates this plainly: it pairs two photographs, one of a barren landscape (again) with the truck in it, the other the same photo but without the truck. The former is labeled "ours," the latter "theirs."

From this perspective, the epideictic element in advertising draws attention to itself as a making-present function. It is evident not so much in connection with the things that actually appear in ads or are even praised or blamed therein, but as the background against and amid which those objects appear, whether it is a desert landscape, the white space on the page, or the blue-gray ether of the TV screen. This view tolerably agrees with that of Lawrence W. Rosenfield, who argues that epideictic's essential function is to disclose the "radiance" of being (135), and it also accords with Richard Weaver's undeveloped thoughts about the confluence of rhetoric's roles as both a presenter of reality and an expression of a "very primitive" and "quasi-religious" metaphysics (173). Taken together with the insights advertising affords about the nature of rhetoric, these views suggest a need to rethink epideictic as serving a phenomenological function in all its manifestations, including its more traditional ones.

Rhetoric achieved its prominent place in the life of the ancient polis not only because of its obvious usefulness in pursuing justice and in getting things done, but because it was, through epideictic practice, the medium by which the good was brought to public light. Classical rhetoricians took for granted that an appropriate space for this appearance was available. It was made available in part by epideictic practice itself. We may well wonder what the implications are for our spaces of moral appearance when the largest, most pervasive, most successful rhetorical enterprise on the planet is so strongly epideictic in character. To pursue this question, scholars of rhetoric need to examine more deeply the intersections between the rhetorical tradition and contemporary forms of rhetoric. In the case of advertising, we stand to advance our understanding not only of advertising rhetoric's role in our culture, but also of the culture of advertising in all our rhetoric.

Works Cited

Arendt, Hannah. *The Human Condition*. Chicago: U of Chicago P, 1958.
Aristotle. *The "Art" of Rhetoric*. Trans. J. H. Freese. Cambridge: Harvard UP, 1982.
—. *Nicomachean Ethics*. Trans. David Ross. Oxford: Oxford UP, 1988.
Beale, Walter. "Rhetorical Performative Discourse: A New Theory of Epideictic." *Philosophy and Rhetoric* 11.4 (1978): 221-46.
Booth, Wayne. "Rhetoric and Religion: Are They Essentially Wedded?" *Radical Pluralism and Truth: David Tracy and the Hermeneutics of Truth*. Ed. Werner G. Jeanrond and Jennifer Rike. New York: Crossroad, 1991. 62-80.
Burke, Kenneth. *A Rhetoric of Motives*. Berkeley: U of California P, 1950.
—. *The Rhetoric of Religion: Studies in Logology*. Boston: Beacon, 1961.
Ewen, Stuart. *Captains of Consciousness: Advertising and the Social Roots of the Consumer Culture*. New York: McGraw, 1976.
Kehl, D. G., and Donald Heidt. "The Rhetoric of Cow and the Rhetoric of Bull." *Rhetoric Society Quarterly* 14.3-4 (1984): 129-38.
Leigh, James H. "The Uses of Figures of Speech in Print Ad Headlines." *Journal of Advertising* 23.2 (1994): 17-34.
McIntyre, Alasdair. "The Privatization of Good: An Inaugural Lecture." *Review of Politics* 52.3 (1990): 344-77.
McQuarrie, Edward F., and David Glen Mick. "On Resonance: A Critical Pluralistic Inquiry into Advertising Rhetoric." *Journal of Consumer Research* 19.2 (1992): 196-214.
—. "Figures of Rhetoric in Advertising Language." *Journal of Consumer Research* 22.4 (1996): 38-52.
Rosenfield, Lawrence W. "The Practical Celebration of Epideictic." *Rhetoric in Transition: Studies in the Nature and Uses of Rhetoric*. Ed. Eugene E. White. University Park: Pennsylvania State UP, 1980. 131-55.
Scott, Linda M. "Understanding Jingles and Needledrop: A Rhetorical Approach to Music in Advertising." *Journal of Consumer Research* 17.2 (1990): 223-36.
—. "Images in Advertising: The Need for a Theory of Visual Rhetoric." *Journal of Consumer Research* 21.2 (1994): 252-73.
Spitzer, Leo. *Representative Essays*. Ed. Alban K. Forcione, Herbert Lindenberger, and Madeline Sutherland. Stanford: Stanford UP, 1988.
Stern, Barbara B. "Pleasure and Persuasion in Advertising: Rhetorical Irony as a Humor Technique." *Current Issues and Research in Advertising* 12 (1990): 25-42.
Trow, George W. S. *In the Context of No Context*. Boston: Little, Brown, 1981.
Weaver, Richard M. "Language Is Sermonic." *Language Is Sermonic: Richard M. Weaver on the Nature of Rhetoric*. Ed. Richard L. Johannesen, Rennard Strickland, and Ralph T. Eubanks. Baton Rouge: Louisiana State UP, 1970. Rpt. in *The Rhetoric of Western Thought*. Ed. James L. Golden, Goodwin F. Berquist, and William E. Coleman. Dubuque: Kendall/Hunt, 1997. 169-78.
Wilder, Amos N. *The Language of the Gospel: Early Christian Rhetoric*. New York: Harper, 1964.

Part II
Rhetorics of Culture/Recovering RhetoricalCultures

LOIS AGNEW
Texas Christian University

Unstifling the Rhetorical Impulse: Style and Invention in Thomas De Quincey's Rhetoric

A striking number of scholarly articles have focused on the question of whether Thomas De Quincey's essays on rhetoric offer any coherent and substantive statement about rhetoric's basic function. De Quincey himself would probably be among the first to acknowledge that they do not, and further to assert that our tendency to search through his writings for precise and efficient guidelines that explain the way rhetoric works is in itself symptomatic of the utilitarian approach to knowledge that his essays attempt to challenge. Although De Quincey's interest in style resonates with the British rhetorical tradition that preceded him, De Quincey diverges from earlier theorists in demonstrating the intellectual play with words that he advocates rather than methodically describing the central features of rhetoric or providing practical instructions for its proper use. In assuming for his own writing the freedom to explore the subtleties of his topic in an unsystematic fashion, De Quincey directly responds to a modern culture that he diagnoses as too exclusively oriented toward the immediate and practical goals of science and public business. In De Quincey's view, the creative impulse that preserves the vitality of society can only be recaptured through a rhetorical theory that recognizes the essential unity of style and invention.

De Quincey's unconventional approach reflects a turning point in the evolution of British rhetoric. His anxiety over the limitations that industrial society has placed on the creative use of rhetoric builds on a concern demonstrated by writers from the eighteenth century forward. However, his proposed solution—to conceive of rhetorical invention as the dynamic interplay between form and substance that unleashes the individual's creative energy—anticipates a nineteenth-century trend, more fully developed in the Victorian aesthetic movement, to replace theoretical approaches to rhetorical training with practices that reveal the lasting social value of the individual's imaginative activity. This view alters rhetoric's traditional social function of making judgment possible. Rather than engaging the rhetor and audience in a common effort to achieve consensus about specific questions, rhetoric becomes the means for transforming society indirectly through serving as a site of resistance to the mechanization associated with modern life.

De Quincey serves as an early proponent of this new conception of rhetoric as he advocates a shift from a theory that emphasizes the specific results of discourse, its persuasive intent, to a process significant primarily because of its ability to engage the intellect. For De Quincey, rhetoric's potential to stimulate the intellect is vital to a society in which creativity has been increasingly sacrificed to scientific materialism. He identifies the early seventeenth century as the last era in which rhetoric flourished in England, for at that time "science was unborn as a popular interest" ("Rhetoric" 100). He argues that from that point forward, the imaginative potential of invention fully developed through style has been limited by a growing emphasis on the mere substance of discourse, dictated by "that same love for the practical and the tangible which has so memorably governed the course of our higher speculations from Bacon to Newton" ("Style" 141). De Quincey's objective in his writings about rhetoric is to challenge the prevailing view that language must promote the scientific efficiency that governs the rest of the world.

In adopting this position, De Quincey implicitly counters the scientific orientation toward language exemplified in the seventeenth century by Thomas Sprat in his well-known *History of the Royal Society*, which places rhetoric in the service of an accurate and objective accounting of the world of external appearances. Sprat insists that rhetoric that simply explores different sides of an issue—an enterprise that De Quincey later advocates as an important means of sharpening the mental powers—in fact holds little value, for true knowledge only comes about through attaining greater familiarity with "the *solid substance of Science* itself" (18). In Sprat's view, the purpose of language is not to engage in abstract speculation in order to refine intellectual ability, but instead to provide the means for accurately describing the external world. It is in this area that Sprat believes that ancient philosophy, which includes previous attempts to define the province of rhetoric, has gone wrong, because it has not promoted the "wariness, and coldness of thinking" that ultimately leads "to a solid *assent*, and to a lasting *conclusion*, on the whole frame of Nature" (102). Perceiving the "coldness" of objective observation as a desirable attribute leads Sprat to denigrate ancient philosophers on general principle; he states that Plato, Aristotle, Zeno, and Epicurus would be better respected in later ages "if they had only set things in a way of propagating Experiences down to us; and not impos'd their *imaginations* on us, as the only *Truths*" (117). Boasting of the Royal Society's emphasis on "the things themselves" (18), Sprat argues for a conception of knowledge based on direct observation of the external world. In Sprat's view, science transforms the purpose of discourse from the classical realm of discovery and negotiation to a modern concern with efficiently recording data obtained through observation and experimentation.

In resisting such scientific appropriations of rhetoric, De Quincey identifies his thought with that of Aristotle, as he maintains that rhetoric resides within the realm of opinion and the probable rather than addressing matters of fact or intuition. His attempt to counter scientific assumptions about the intrinsic value of certainty leads him to place particular emphasis on rhetoric's importance in mediating between extremes, "amongst that vast field of cases where there is a *pro* and a *con*, with the chance of right and wrong, true and false, distributed in varying proportions between them" ("Rhetoric" 91). Moreover, he adds that "[t]here is also an immense range of truths where there are no chances at all concerned, but the affirmative and negative are both true" ("Rhetoric" 91). The focus of rhetoric therefore should not be on achieving a definite conclusion, because "where it is possible for the understanding to be convinced, no field is open for rhetorical persuasion" ("Rhetoric" 91). Rhetoric's role involves "giving an impulse to one side, and by withdrawing the mind so steadily from all thoughts or images which support the other as to leave it practically under the possession of a one-sided estimate" ("Rhetoric" 91). Those who seek to free themselves from the constraints of the practical in order to realize the creative potential of rhetoric must be willing to involve themselves in an activity that balances varied perspectives, recognizing the persuasive features of other positions even as they make the advantages of one side more vivid to others.

De Quincey's view of rhetoric directly counters the view that the foundation of knowledge must be the observation of an external reality that requires little interpretation. He emphasizes the notion that rhetoric constantly negotiates between the extremes of objective observation and subjective exploration. In contrast with Sprat's emphasis on the value of language in describing "the things themselves" (18), De Quincey insists that English style has been damaged by the belief that "the right of occupying the attention of the company seems to inhere in *things* rather than in persons" ("Style" 156). On the other hand, he notes that French style is focused to excess on feelings without regard for intellectual content, which potentially leads to eloquence that does not necessarily fulfill the objectives of rhetoric: "There is no eddying about their own thoughts . . . but strains of feeling, genuine or not, supported at every step from the excitement of independent external objects" ("Rhetoric" 121). In De Quincey's view, the perfection of style can only come about through the recognition that rhetoric occupies a middle ground distinct from both scientific objectivity and spontaneous personal feelings.

In keeping with his own view, De Quincey writes essays that reflect on rhetoric rather than methodically detailing the steps one should follow in its production. He views the tendency to seek rules for rhetorical practice as limiting the free play of thought that forms the inventive process. Although Frederick Burwick is accurate in characterizing De Quincey's orientation toward rhetoric as belletristic (xi), the keen interest De Quincey consistently maintains in the written text is balanced by his desire to preserve rhetoric's capacity to respond to the immediate needs of the situation in a manner that is more easily attained through oral discourse.

De Quincey further recognizes that the transition from an oral to a literary culture has in some ways accentuated the division between true style and mere ornamentation. He maintains that there are two distinct features of style: the *mechanical*, which includes the rules of grammar and word use, and the *organic*, which involves "the function by which style maintains a commerce with thought" ("Style" 164). He notes that the development of writing has promoted attention to mechanical style at the expense of the organic; for example, punctuation serves as an artificial tool for preserving the writer's meaning that draws attention from concern that at one time was fittingly directed toward "the natural machinery, which lay in just and careful arrangement" ("Style" 165). Thus, although De Quincey sees the potential of writing for enhancing the development of thought, he recognizes at the same time that writing possesses the danger of focusing too much attention on the mechanical features of discourse, indirectly promoting the perception that style constitutes the extraneous ornamentation of language rather than the essence of invention. The mark of the "truly splendid rhetorician," however, is the individual whose imagery has "grown up in the loom, and concurrently with the texture of the thoughts" ("Rhetoric" 110). Attention to style provides a source of intellectual pleasure in itself, because style should be seen as inextricably linked to rhetorical invention.

De Quincey repeatedly states his view that the ability to appreciate the vital function of style has been gradually eclipsed by a growing concern with science and public business. Greater attention to style can restore society's intellectual vitality through breaking the boundaries of practicality that otherwise "stifle the rhetorical impulses" ("Rhetoric" 121). De Quincey notes that it is a simple matter to construct "a shorthand memorandum of a great truth"; the challenge of composing "begins when you have to put your separate threads of thought into a loom; to weave them into a continuous whole" ("Style" 181). He argues that such careful weaving of thought cannot be found in the print media, which widely distributes written material that lacks the intellectual depth and stylistic quality that encourages critical thought. Blaming newspapers for limiting the intellectual development of his society, De Quincey argues that texts written hastily with the intention of being merely efficient encourage people to develop habits of "desultory reading," as they rapidly seek out the key words that contain the essential information of a news story. Such habits can have disastrous consequences for the community as a whole, for "it is by the effects reflected upon his judging and reasoning powers, that loose habits of reading tell eventually. And these are durable effects" ("Style" 162). De Quincey anticipates later theories about orality and literacy in maintaining that the process of composing written texts provides people with an opportunity to develop new insights through reflecting on their use of language. However, he nevertheless expresses his concern that the British orientation toward literary language might eventually limit the imaginative process; although the immediate consequence of the "bookish idiom" that has suffused the nation is pedantic sentences, De Quincey fears that the appropriation of literary language in daily conversation may in time "weave fetters about the free movement of human thought" ("Style" 152). Only written style that self-consciously embarks on a leisurely course of intellectual exploration can preserve the power of rhetoric that ultimately revitalizes society.

De Quincey was not alone in believing in this relation between rhetorical practices and the strength of the community. The development of British rhetoric is consistently marked by an assumed link between style and moral philosophy, a connection that assumes new force during the eighteenth century as industrialization and the growth of literacy both enhance and challenge traditional approaches to rhetoric. Elocutionists and belletristic rhetoricians of that period share the belief that the character of society is both reflected and formed through the way in which people use language. In his 1762 treatise on elocution, Thomas Sheridan explains that his goal is to provide guidelines for delivery that can restore the moral and imaginative power of oral language, the gift of God "by which all the faculties of the mind" are formed (xiii), in place of written language that he describes as having arisen solely through human efforts. In *Elements of Criticism* (1762), Kames articulates the role of aesthetic appreciation in restoring the ethical sense of a society in which "flourishing commerce begets opulence" (v) that can be constructively curbed through public criticism. For Hugh Blair, also, the quality of language is important both to the individual and to society at large, for language receives "its predominant tincture from the national character of the people who speak it" (Lecture IX, 97). The belletristic rhetoricians who precede De Quincey generally do not treat invention as one of the canons of rhetoric, but they implicitly anticipate De Quincey's assumption that the manner of expression has a direct bearing on the thoughts being expressed.

While De Quincey's interest in style preserves an important link to belletristic rhetoric, his essays reflect a shift in the way in which nineteenth-century thinkers were beginning to conceive of the central function of rhetoric. Belletristic rhetoric generally emphasizes the connection between style and *ethos* as it relates to moral character. Adam Smith argues that "[t]he style of an author is generally of the same stamp as their character" (31), whereas Blair claims that language that is rhetorically appropriate is beautiful as "it is conceived to show of internal moral dispositions" (Lecture V, 53). Such ethical qualities are socially constructed and reflected in the rhetor's ability to assess the needs of the audience. Kames insists that a complete understanding of human nature and rhetorical responsibility only arises within a social setting, "because from the constitution both of his body and mind, he cannot live comfortably but in society. It is thus we discover for what end we were designed by nature, or the author of nature" (*Essays* 28). For both Blair and Smith, as well, style is necessarily defined according to the rhetor's sensitivity to the needs of the rhetorical moment: Smith comments that various styles "may be considered as good in their kind and suited to the circumstances of the author" (30-31), and Blair summarizes his advice on style by pointing out that "[n]othing merits the name of eloquent or beautiful, which is not suited to the occasion, and to the persons to whom it is addressed" (Lecture XIX, 215). Belletristic rhetoricians share De Quincey's belief that the responsible rhetor's interest in the aesthetic features of discourse must arise not simply due to an interest in ornamentation for its own sake; however, they insist that the value of discourse derives not from the internal exploration of an individual's thought, but from its merit in communicating meaningfully with others.

De Quincey's disenchantment with nineteenth-century society leads him to reject the optimistic classical and belletristic vision of rhetoric that unites the rhetor and audience in a common search for the most virtuous course of action. He replaces this model with a proposal for intellectual play with language that indirectly enables the individual to challenge others to new ways of thinking. De Quincey attempts to resist the power of the print culture to construct within society an artificial sense of unity, or what Christopher A. Kent calls "creating the code of realism that affected the way readers conceived and perceived the world" (4). For De Quincey, the potential of style is achieved not through attending to the demands of the external world, but through adopting a subjective perspective, for "the more closely any exercise of mind is connected with what is philosophically termed *subjective* . . . does the style or the embodying of the thoughts cease to be a mere separable ornament" ("Style" 229). Even to instruct people in the fine points of rhetorical practice holds the danger of stifling rather than promoting the creative impulse that springs from within. De Quincey insists that even ignorance is preferable to a mechanical system of instruction that teaches everyone to write according to a formula that restricts individuality ("Style" 193).

De Quincey's attempt to identify rhetoric's capacity to restore creative energy to a society overwhelmed with monotony ultimately places the responsibility for preserving the vitality of rhetoric in the hands of the individual. In comparing De Quincey's subjective orientation with Aristotle's view of rhetoric's capacity for promoting collective judgment, Wilbur Samuel Howell states that De Quincey's idea of rhetoric is

> so far divorced from actual human experience, so completely devoid of connection with the urgent issues of politics and law, that we can only wonder why De Quincey would think it worth while for Aristotle or any serious-minded person to bother with it in any theoretical or practical way. (3)

Anyone who reads De Quincey's essays on rhetoric might be tempted to share Howell's view that they have nothing to offer the real world. However, De

Quincey's notion of uniting style and invention in a transformative subjective realm in itself constitutes a social statement that responds to the unique cultural conditions that he faced. De Quincey's significance to the history of our discipline lies not in his presentation of a coherent theory of rhetoric, but in his refusal to attempt such a task. De Quincey's musings on rhetoric deliberately fail to offer the practical statement on his subject that he knows his society to be anxiously seeking. In the process, De Quincey provides an early model for a new rhetoric whose foundation derives from the inventive process of the individual rather than from the desire to resolve the immediate pragmatic concerns of the community.

Works Cited

Blair, Hugh. *Lectures on Rhetoric and Belles Lettres.* 1783. Pittsburgh: C. H. Kay, 1833.
Burwick, Frederick. "Introduction." *Essays on Rhetoric by Thomas De Quincey.* Ed. Frederick Burwick. Carbondale: Southern Illinois UP, 1967. xi-xlviii.
De Quincey, Thomas. "Rhetoric." 1828. *Essays on Rhetoric by Thomas De Quincey.* Ed. Frederick Burwick. Carbondale: Southern Illinois UP, 1967. 81-133.
—. "Style." 1840. *Essays on Rhetoric by Thomas De Quincey.* Ed. Frederick Burwick. Carbondale: Southern Illinois UP, 1967. 134-245.
Howell, Wilbur Samuel. "De Quincey on Science, Rhetoric, and Poetry." *Speech Monographs* 13 (1946): 1-13.
Kames, Henry Home, Lord. *Elements of Criticism.* 3 vols. 1762. New York: Georg Olms Verlag, 1970.
—. *Essays On the Principles of Morality and Natural Religion.* 1758. Hildesheim, New York: Georg Olms Verlag, 1976.
Kent, Christopher A. "Victorian Periodicals and the Constructing of Victorian Reality." *Victorian Periodicals: A Guide to Research.* Ed. J. Don Vann and Rosemary T. VanArsdel. New York: MLA, 1989. 1-12.
Sheridan, Thomas. *A Course of Lectures on Elocution.* 1762. New York: Benjamin Blom, 1968.
Smith, Adam. *Lectures on Rhetoric and Belles Lettres Delivered in the University of Glasgow by Adam Smith Reported by a Student in 1762-63.* Ed. John M. Lothian. Carbondale: Southern Illinois UP, 1971.
Sprat, Thomas. *History of the Royal Society.* 1667. St. Louis: Washington U Studies, 1959.

JILL SWIENCICKI
Miami University

Performing Conversion: Washingtonian (In)Temperance Rhetorics

The Washington Temperance Society was inaugurated in 1840 when six men in a Baltimore tavern thought it might be interesting to check out the temperance lecture across the street. As the story goes, two of them left the meeting having taken a pledge of abstinence. They decided to form a temperance group made up of laborers and artisans like themselves—workers who were reeling from the aftermath of the financial panic of 1837 and looking to secure social and economic stability and respectability (Blocker 37). During this period, many working-class men and women turned to temperance as a strategy for enfranchisement into public spheres of business and civil society when their attempts to establish unions and "benevolent societies" largely failed against the relentless power of burgeoning industrial corporations.[1] In hopes of accommodating to the new constraints placed upon their labor, they created a public sphere that was a "hybrid" of proletarian interests and universalized bourgeois norms (Negt and Kluge 59). By 1841, the Washingtonians had 100 thousand members enrolled; two years later they were half a million (Reynolds 26). It became the largest and most diverse reform movement of the antebellum period; it was one in which such societies, and the associations they facilitated, were crucial access routes to public life and personal ascendancy.[2]

Washingtonians spread their message through temperance novels, newspapers, plays, and especially lectures. Indeed, it was the group's intervention into the period's thriving oratorical culture that afforded them the greatest social impact, most notably through the practice of what they called "experience speeches." During meetings, which were held in town halls and music halls, intemperate men literally made spectacles of themselves as each stood before crowds of hundreds, confessed the circumstances of his past intemperance, and solidified his conversion to sobriety by signing a pledge of abstinence.[3] This confession serves as the bridge that joins what Negt and Kluge might call a proletarian "context of living"—the material conditions of experience—with codes of bourgeois subjectivity (Hansen 201). One of these confessors was John Gough, a Welsh immigrant, fledgling stage actor, and reformed drunkard who became one of the most popular orators in American history. Dubbed "the Demosthenes of total abstinence" (Furnas 150), Gough wrote an autobiography at the end of his career as a temperance speaker in which he described his affection for the public confession that was the cornerstone of most meetings: "I loved the temperance pledge," he writes. "No one could value it more than I, for, standing as I did, a redeemed man, enabled to hold up my head in society, I owed everything to it[—]painful as I said this event in my life was in the act and humiliating in the contemplation . . ." (77). Here, in a tone of resigned masochism, Gough expresses a "love" for an act that was "painful" because the "humiliating" ritual allowed him, for the first time, to be recognized as attaining a form of publicity that had cultural capital.

This essay is an attempt to understand the pleasure and the pain of casting one's experience into the public as rhetorical spectacle and social currency; and it is interested in the extent to which the working class can utilize the public sphere as "a horizon for the organization of experience" (Negt and Kluge 1, 56). Gough's temperance autobiography is characteristic of the hundreds of Washingtonian temperance narratives that were published for public consumption in the period. As a written narrative, it reveals what the experience speech alone does not, exposing what at first glance is a hybrid public sphere where differences are bridged via the rhetoricizing of experience as in fact a deeply ambivalent space. At times, such as the representation of the confession itself and what it gained for him, the autobiography idealizes the public sphere as a normative space offering universal access. Other moments express the temperate experience as deeply restrictive and alienating, adding a critical edge to the narrative. More than sensationalized, hackneyed rhetorics of assimilation, these experiential narratives display an ambivalence that furthers the revisionist work that has been undertaken on the public sphere since Habermas.

Washingtonian temperance uses the concept of experience rhetorically as a way to make its marginalized members worthy of sympathy and association with an ostensibly bourgeois audience whose subjectivity is seen as normative. This makes sense in a social and rhetorical moment where a truth based in experience was valued as a way to discern virtuous citizens who act on behalf of the public good from confidence men, who perform virtuous ideals for personal gain.[4] Such anxieties over threats to a more traditional social order were actually conveyed through analogies that linked rhetorical practice to intemperance. An example is provided by E. L. Godkin, editor of *The Nation*, who claimed that the effects of rhetorical study had become deleterious, "almost as baneful as those of excessive alcohol; as destructive of manliness, of simplicity; and of power, as productive of fatuous conceit and self-worship. It is almost certain to produce too, a love of notoriety; and when once this takes possession of a rhetorician, it consumes him utterly" (145-46). Godkin's analogy of rhetoric to intemperance evinces the gendered and classed concerns over both rhetoric's and alcohol's supposed propensity to jeopardize manly simplicity; to pull its subject away from an imagined community of peers and consume the speaker in his obsessive, narcissistic performance.

The experiential meeting's use of public confessions addressed these concerns by staging "true" accounts of human experience at a time when, as Henry Beecher argued, "the person who acknowledged suffering as the inevitable human condition had a firm hold on the truth of human emotion" (qtd. in Gabler-Hover 50). The strategy worked, according to public figures such as Frederick Douglass, who argued that, unlike rhetoric coming from the bar, pulpit, and senate, a "mightier and more thrilling eloquence is that which has come up from the dram shop and gutter. The simple, straightforward, unvarnished narration of individual suffering—the graphic pictures of family distress and ruin—the painful exhibitions of shattered and broken constitutions . . . have nearly all come from this class of persons . . ." (2: 106-07). Arguments based on experience, particularly the experience of suffering, had the effect of making the confessor-orator transparent, legible, and therefore true.

A characteristic example of this form is provided in the *Life of J. B. Gough: An Autobiography*. The following passage recounts his first speech at an experiential meeting. One day, while Gough was debilitated by liquor (which he used as a buffer to numb the death of his mother, his poverty, and the loss of yet another acting job), a stranger approached him and implored him to "take the pledge" at the next Washingtonian meeting. He consented:

> I was invited to the stand . . . and, on turning to face the audience, I recognized my acquaintance who had asked me to sign. It was Mr. Joel Stratton. He greeted me with a smile of approbation, which nerved and strengthened me for the task, as I tremblingly observed every eye fixed upon me. I lifted my quivering hand, and then and there told what rum had done for me. I related how I was once respectable and happy, and had a home; but that now I was a houseless, miserable, scathed, diseased, and blighted outcast from society. I said, scarce a hope remained to me of ever becoming that which I once was; but having promised to sign the pledge, I had determined not to break my word, and would now affix my name to it. In my palsied hand I with difficulty grasped the pen and . . . signed the total abstinence pledge, and resolved to free myself from the inexorable tyrant—rum. Although still desponding and hopeless, I felt that I was relieved from part of my heavy load. . . . I had exerted a moral power, which had long remained lying by, perfectly useless. The very idea of what I had done strengthened and encouraged me. . . . [M]any who had witnessed my signing, and heard my simple statement, came forward kindly, grasped my hand, and expressed their satisfaction at the step I had taken. A new and better day seemed to have dawned upon me. (66-67)

The form of confession that occurs before Gough signed the temperance pledge acts as the ritual required for entrance into the public sphere. Gough inaugurates the crucial use of the past tense in separating the supposed old/sinful subject from the new/converted one; after he is greeted by Stratton and given permission to proceed with his confession, a split manifests itself into a "once respectable/now blighted outcast" binary. Michael Warner (239), in his discussion of embodiment and publicity, refers to such formations in terms of the self-abstraction that is required to enter into bourgeois public spheres; the principle of negativity that occurs in confession—when Gough renounces his former habits—operates to temper the working-class male by creating a relation of bad faith to his own positivity. In signing the pledge, then, the "demon" is rum, not the discursive and economic constraints that require the subject to abstract himself from a part of his context of living.

Gough does feel power and freedom here, though, for as Foucault theorizes, confession is a ritual "in which expression alone, independently of its external consequences, produces intrinsic modifications in the person who articulates it: it exonerates, redeems, and purifies him; it unburdens him of his wrongs, liberates him, and promises him salvation" (61-62). But in the context of temperance it is not the confession alone that exonerates Gough from his "sins" of intemperance. It is actually his signature on the temperance pledge that enters him into the public sphere and gives him full recognition from his peers. The experience, it seems, is not redemptive in itself, but with the addition of a signature as its telos, experience gets inscribed within a new set of moral and social parameters. This marks the confession in a rather significant way: the speech act ends with a contract, a public promise, one similar to that which would transpire in the marketplace. In signing the pledge, Washingtonians join the passion of intemperance in contest with the passion of economic interest in the hopes of triumphing against social backsliding and economic instability.

Thus far Gough's autobiography appears to be a classic immigrant's tale of personal ascendancy—a linear progression from itinerant stage actor to celebrity temperance orator. But Gough's "context of living," the material conditions of experience he also narrates, begins to increasingly chafe against the rhetorical packaging of experience in the representation of his experience speech (Hansen 189). In its exposure of the self-abstraction needed to function in the public sphere for those whose identities are marked as not normative, the larger narrative in which the speech is embedded complicates the theme of conversion. For example, before he makes his public confession to the Washingtonian audience assembled in the town hall, we are privy to Gough's countless attempts at earning a living as a performer and craftsman, and for providing for his family amid the temptations of the city. After strenuous efforts to remain temperate and gainfully employed, he expresses the profound frustration he feels over what he interprets as a constant social surveillance of his personal habits:

> What had I done to make me so shunned and execrated by my kind? . . . I drank! And in those two words lay the whole secret of my miserable condition. . . . This impression nettled me to the quick, and, ere long I began to feel indignant of the control exercised over me. I thought that as I had battled with the world, single-handed[ly], for twelve years, and had received nothing . . . but unkindness and misery, I had a right to do as I chose, without being watched over wherever I went. My proud spirit would not break this system of espionage. . . . (54)

Here Gough expresses the feeling that he and "his kind" are under an inescapable gaze, one meant to control and prescribe his actions and one that even works to counteract the positive efforts he has made on his own. With this kind of hyper-awareness of the gaze, Gough's social struggle is first cast as a frustrating search for a respectable audience. His desire to be on stage, his stories of boyhood dramatic performances, and the need to remake himself in a new country attest to his keen awareness of an exclusionary public gaze. His "conscience" realized that there was something illicit in him that was reflected in the theatrical stages where he performed—a persona that did not fit within the bourgeois public spheres to which he wished to gain access. His struggle to succeed is then cast in the discourse of intemperance, and to succeed he realizes he needs to satisfy the gaze of the "respectable" audience that he so forcefully feels upon him.

Toward these ends, overwhelming tropes of performativity pervade and even overtake Gough's narrative. Just after he speaks his testimonial, for example, he receives the gift of a new suit from a Washingtonian: "My new suit was fashionably cut, and as I put on the articles, one by one, I felt more awkwardness than, I verily believe, I even exhibited, before or since, in the course of my life. The pantaloons were strapped down, over feet which had long been used to freedom, and I feared to walk in my usual manner, lest they should go at the knee. I feared, too, lest a strap should give, and make me lopsided for life" (74). The metaphor of fashionable clothing signifies Gough's performative fashioning of his new public self. Descriptions of awkwardness give way to the pain of constriction that unnaturally perforces itself on Gough's body. This expression of constriction gives way to a paranoia over whether he will be able to perform within this new stricture, if rhetorical "strap[s] should give" in his attempt to fashion himself temperate.

The veil of truth-motivated confession slips further when we acknowledge that conquering alcoholism takes infinitely more than the offering of a public testimonial. Gough recalls of his detoxification, "Alone I encountered all the host of demoniac form which crowded my chamber. No one witnessed my agonies, or counted my woes, and yet I recovered; how, still remains a mystery to myself, and still more mysterious was the fact of my concealing my sufferings from every mortal eye" (71). The actual process of detoxification gets mystified and privatized in temperance narratives, and this concealment suggests that, within this discourse, intemperance is not something from which one physically recovers. His confession, his awareness of an inescapable gaze, and his obsession with performance each evince a painful splitting that has occurred within Gough's proletarian "context for living," where a part of his experience is reabsorbed into the public sphere of production and gives him access and legitimacy, and other very real experiences are disqualified and rendered, through discourse of pain and anxiety, as private (Negt and Kluge 18).

Gough does succeed in remaining temperate by fashioning himself a hugely successful public career as a temperance orator. But where he once was addicted to the consumption of liquor, Gough is now addicted to consuming publicity. In an amazing textual turn, by the time we arrive at the third and final section of the autobiography, Gough's own narrative is wholly displaced by reviews of his oratory from newspapers and temperance newsletters, along with excerpts from his appointment book that catalogue his engagements. The reader is privy to seemingly endless stories about the speeches he made and awards he received; we read excerpts of accolades from various local temperance chapters, marvel at the extensive travel he has enjoyed, and can easily picture the massive temperance parades for which he was grand marshal: "I found on my arrival," he recalls, "that a barouche and four white horses has been prepared to convey me into the city" (92). Temperance gave a celebrity status to Gough's talent for speech, one in which he moves past an interest in bourgeois codes of respectability and toward a representative publicity. The spectacle of his performance allowed an acceptable way to theatricalize his experience and use it to channel him into legitimate public spheres. At this point we recall E. L. Godkin's anxious analogy between the excesses of rhetorical performance and alcohol: that both, in extremes, can be addictive. Gough's temperance narrative, then, becomes intemperance, as he gets consumed by the spectacle, the event, the reportage, and the experience of his performance.

If a public sphere is a horizon for the organization of social experience, what is at stake here is "whether and to what extent experience is dis/organized from 'above'—by the exclusionary standards of high culture or in the interests of property—or from 'below,' by the experiencing subjects themselves, in the basis of their context of living" (Hansen 201-02). More subtle than the binary of "inauthentic," dominant publicity and a repressed, real-life context, the narratives that emerge from the experience of occupying such hybrid public spheres involves, as Miriam Hansen observes, "the dialectical interplay of the experience of re/production under alienated conditions; the systematic blockage of that experience as a horizon in its own right; and, as a response to that blockage, imaginative strategies grounded in the experience of alienated production—psychic balancing acts, a penchant for personalization, and creative reappropriations" (202). In narratives that focus on young working-class intemperate men, a rhetorically staged conversionary moment intended to express a "truth of experience borne of suffering" is exposed here as the requisite performance the working-class male staged to assume a non-threatening public identity. It offers readers an example of an intemperate conversion, demonstrating less of the kinds of coherently critical experiential discourse that one finds in proletarian public spheres. Still the ambivalence that surfaces in this kind of hybrid formation is striking in its revelation of the limits of the bourgeois public sphere for emancipatory social politics.

Notes

1. For a full account of Washingtonian temperance as a response to economic conditions, see Lawrence Blumberg, *Beware of the First Drink: The Washingtonian Temperance Movement and Alcoholics Anonymous* (Seattle: Glen Abbey, 1991) and Jack S. Blocker, *American Temperance Movements: Cycles of Reform* (Boston: Twayne, 1989). Along with its function for men in the public sphere, Washingtonianism, and temperance in general, provided women with access routes to public life and an agency that allowed them to negotiate the intimate connections between public and private spheres. See Ruth Bordin, *Woman and Temperance: The Quest for Power and Liberty, 1873-1900* (New Brunswick: Rutgers UP, 1981); Ruth M. Alexander, "'We are Engaged as a Band of Sisters': Class and Domesticity in the Washingtonian Temperance Movement, 1840-1850," *Journal of American History* (December 1988); Barbara Epstein, *The Politics of Domesticity: Women, Evangelism, and Temperance in Nineteenth-Century America* (Middletown, CT: Wesleyan UP, 1981); and Carol Mattingly, *Well-Tempered Women: Nineteenth-Century Temperance Rhetoric* (Carbondale: Southern Illinois UP, 1988).
2. For information on the role of reform societies in the rise of public spheres in antebellum America, see Mary P. Ryan, "Gender and Public Access: Women's Politics in Nineteenth-Century America," and Geoff Eley's "Nations, Publics, and Political Cultures: Placing Habermas in the Nineteenth Century," both in Craig Calhoun's edited collection, *Habermas and the Public Sphere* (Minneapolis: U of Minnesota P, 1993).
3. For a detailed description of the Washingtonian experiential meeting, see Ian Tyrrell, *Sobering Up: From Temperance to Prohibition in Antebellum America, 1800-1860* (Westport, CT: Greenwood P, 1979).
4. See Karen Halttunen, *Confidence Men and Painted Women: A Study of Middle-Class Culture in America, 1830-1870* (New Haven, CT: Yale UP, 1982).

Works Cited

Blocker, Jack S. *American Temperance Movements: Cycles of Reform*. Boston: Twayne, 1989.
Douglass, Frederick. "Principles of Temperance Reform: An Address Delivered in Rochester, New York, on 5 March 1848." *The Frederick Douglass Papers*. 5 vols. Ed. John W. Blassingame and John R. McKivigan. New Haven: Yale UP, 1979-92. 2: 106-07.
Foucault, Michel. *History of Sexuality: An Introduction*. Vol. 1. New York: Random, 1978.
Furnas, J. C. *The Life and Times of the Late Demon Rum*. London: Allen, 1965.

Gabler-Hover, Janet. *Truth in American Fiction: The Legacy of Rhetorical Idealism.* Athens: U of Georgia P, 1991.
Godkin, E. L. "Rhetorical Training." *The Nation* 20 (1875): 145-46.
Gough, John Bartholomew. *Life of J. B. Gough: An Autobiography.* Boston, 1850.
Hansen, Miriam. "Unstable Mixtures, Dilated Spheres: Negt and Kluge's *The Public Sphere and Experience*, Twenty Years Later." *Public Culture* 5 (Spring 1993): 179-212.
Hirschman, Albert O. *The Passions and the Interests: Political Arguments for Capitalism before Its Triumph.* Princeton: Princeton UP, 1977.
Negt, Oscar, and Alexander Kluge. *Public Sphere and Experience: Toward an Analysis of the Bourgeois and Proletarian Public Sphere.* Trans. Peter Labanyi et al. Minneapolis: U of Minnesota P, 1993.
Reynolds, David S. "Black Cats and Delirium Tremens: Temperance and the American Renaissance." *Serpent in the Cup: Temperance in American Literature.* Ed. David S. Reynolds and Debra J. Rosenthal. Amherst: U of Massachusetts P, 1997. 22-59.
Warner, Michael. "The Mass Public and the Mass Subject." *The Phantom Public Sphere.* Ed. Bruce Robbins. Minneapolis: U of Minnesota P, 1993. 234-56.

SHELLEY ALEY
Cottey College

Brave New World: How Alexander Bain's Educational Reforms Addressed Student Needs During the Industrial Age

Remember when you really thought you had something if your computer hardware included a 120-MB hard drive, with a 16-MHz operating system? Somehow the marvels of the past just do not work for us today. Life is complicated. As soon as your writing lab updates its software, you will find out that your computer's version of Microsoft Word is no longer compatible. Try as we might to assimilate into the new (i.e., to the improved) somehow we are never able to keep up.

In this brave new world of microchips, e-mail, and the Internet, what can we possibly learn from looking backward to the nineteenth century? What good is examining the contributions of nineteenth-century rhetorical practitioners and theorists when our world is so different from theirs? As we move closer to the twenty-first century, we will continue to be exposed to the explosion of innovations in computer and communication technology, and we must face how we are to deal with them in the classroom. Therefore, why should we turn to the past?

Like us, nineteenth-century rhetorical practitioners and theorists faced an unprecedented explosion in technology as a result of industrialization. They found themselves dealing with urgent issues, including urbanization and urban poverty, class restructuring, and education that could lead to a better life for those who could attend training schools and colleges. More and more people were forced into new jobs that required specialized training, or they faced poverty. The University of Aberdeen served its mostly regional students by providing an arts curriculum that was flexible enough for so-called private students to take one or two courses before entering a profession, while at the same time providing a degree for those who wished it. It even had a program for those students wanting to take the degree with honors. The opportunities the university provided grew out of its students' needs for that particular time. One had to assimilate into British culture, which was driven by industrialization. According to Aberdeen scholar R. D. Anderson, "new forces like the railways and the press were putting an end to regional distinctiveness everywhere in Britain, and a common middle-class culture was emerging" (116). Assimilation was the aim, and whether it was pressed on Scotland from within its boundaries or from its powerful neighbor to the south, assimilation was not a matter of easy choice. It was a matter of necessity. And those who dealt with students' needs in those days cannot really be judged for what they did based on our narrow understanding of their predicament, just as no one in a hundred years will be able to judge what we do today without taking our context in time and space into consideration.

Thomas P. Miller writes in *The Formation of College English* that,

> [f]ollowing the Universities Act of 1858, English studies became a formal part of the standard curriculum, and professorships in English Literature were widely instituted, often by renaming chairs of rhetoric and belles lettres or rhetoric and logic. Those chairs of rhetoric had been established by Scots who assumed that assimilation meant progress, but assimilationist pressures were now undermining those institutional features that had made the universities responsive to social change. (262-63)

Miller contends that the eighteenth-century provincials, due to an explosion in population and literacy, blurred the boundaries of the literate culture, leading to its restructuring. Assimilation into the dominant English culture was desirable. It was good for them. So Scots, Irish, Americans, and dissenters focused attention on the vernacular in order to master it and enable others to master it so that they could assimilate. Early attempts were made to "regulate" or control the literate masses. Stress, therefore, was placed on correct usage. The "essay of taste and manner" became all-important. After all, how can one tell if one is British? It can be boiled down to how well one speaks.

The message in this curriculum, clearly, was that it is possible to assimilate into the dominant culture, and to do so quite successfully. But, according to Miller, the process of assimilation had the effect of narrowing the definition of "literature" and reducing composition to criticism. Rhetoric became lost between the realms of science and the liberal arts. It was devalued as an academic subject because it did not suit the new language of the academy, the scientific discourse that, once it had a foothold, rapidly took over.

Miller includes Alexander Bain, chair of logic at the University of Aberdeen from 1860 to 1880, in the category of assimilation rhetoricians who were driven by the science of man, or psychology. In this way, he claims that Bain reduced "teaching and learning to sciences" (265). Miller states:

> Science and mechanical correctness had had a natural affinity from the beginnings of the "new" rhetoric, but when the need for efficiency in public education became a compelling factor, the combination of science and mechanics became a deadeningly efficient routine of drills to skills that divorced formal conventions from matters of public significance. (265)

Miller's assessment of Bain fits nicely with the way he has traditionally been viewed by rhetorical scholars from Kitzhaber (1953) to the present. Scholars have repeatedly defined Bain's contributions as reductive and prescriptive. Andrea Lunsford has pointed out that over the last forty years, many have labeled Bain the *bane* of modern composition studies, "a popular whipping boy, identified with a rigidly prescriptive, product-centered system" ("Alexander Bain's Contributions" 290). But, if Bain was misinterpreted for over forty years, then what did he really do? Lunsford's view is that in his English instruction, "[w]hat Bain constructed were patterns his students could use in analyzing writing and hence in exercising their intellectual judgment. It has been succeeding writers, including many of our contemporary authors, who turned Bain's analytic structure into a cage and twisted the key in the lock" ("Alexander Bain's Contributions" 299).

Lunsford has more recently noted that Bain's commitment to his students and to the cause of educational reform "should not be taken lightly" ("Alexander Bain and the Teaching of Composition" 222), and she calls for an understanding of his influence to be based on readings of his major works on psychology "as well as of his total plan for the education of students" (222). Bain wrote two major works in psychology, *The Senses and the Intellect* (1855) and *The Emotions and the Will* (1859). His works in rhetoric and English studies include the original and the enlarged editions of *English Composition and Rhetoric* (1866, 1886) and its teaching guide, *On Teaching English* (1887), among several other works on education, logic, and English grammar.

Kathryn T. Flannery's article on Bain in *Rhetoric Review* moves in the direction called for by Lunsford. Her examination of this nineteenth-century logician who was charged with teaching the first English class at the newly formed University of Aberdeen provides insight into his reformist pedagogy and a fresh way of looking at his contributions. Perhaps her insight will lead to a brave new critical view of Bain. Instead of perpetuating the time-worn issue of whether or not Bain led to prescriptive, product-centered "current traditional" rhetoric, she raises the question of how representational his rhetoric was. She states that "a number of revisionary historians have argued, the meaning of a given rhetoric or a given pedagogy is dependent on its location in time and space" (6). A representational pedagogy is one that is inclusive. By examining Bain's reformist ideas, she determines that indeed Bain's is a representational pedagogy. But, she points out that his pedagogy's

> efficacy ... is always contingent, local. How we read the rhetoric and the composition pedagogy that are associated with Bain necessarily will change, depending upon how we read the circumstances of their deployment. As a textbook put in the hands of an over-worked and underprepared teacher in late nineteenth-century America, Bain's

popular *English Composition and Rhetoric Manual* no doubt participated in a narrowly conceived normative discourse. (6)

His secular, content-neutral pedagogy, taken in its context at the University of Aberdeen, was something entirely different. Although Miller sees Bain's insistence in separating matter from form in his instruction as limiting, Flannery sees this as Bain's way of enhancing his student's access to education. By not having the students discuss a composition's matter, they were not in the position of buying into one particular belief system or another, which could easily be touted in an English classroom at that time. This is an important point. According to Anderson, life at the University of Aberdeen for the nineteenth- and early twentieth-century student was steeped in political and social turmoil. Bain, for his entire career, led the liberal side in campus debate. According to Anderson, Bain was the most "celebrated" of the university's professors and immensely popular (23). To this day, scholars at the University of Aberdeen refer to him, with pride, as Barbarian Bain. He won the 1881 election to the rectorship of the University of Aberdeen by a large majority. This is a position voted on by the students, which attests to both his popularity and the popularity of his views. He was again voted rector in 1884. Bain shares the honor of holding the rectorship at the University of Aberdeen with the likes of Thomas Henry Huxley, Andrew Carnegie, and Sir Winston Churchill. He is one of only a few to be elected into the position more than once. According to Anderson:

> As a philosopher, [Bain] was noted as a disciple of Mill and Comte and a religious agnostic. He avoided controversy in his lectures, but his general intellectual stance challenged the religious orthodoxy of the age, which was under attack simultaneously from Darwinism, following the publication of the *Origin of Species* in 1859 [the year before Bain's appointment], and from the new biblical criticism coming from Germany. (24)

Bain's agnosticism, one must remember, had kept him from achieving a teaching position for nearly twenty years. He was a friend of Darwin's, and he knew well that a person's beliefs, if publicized during this dramatic period of religious turmoil in Scotland,[1] limited possibilities. Keeping matter separated from form, and the focus of the English class on principles of rhetoric instead of religion, was one way to make his class more accessible to his students. However, Flannery sees irony in the success Bain's pedagogy achieved. Through no fault of Bain's, his approach, in its "very success, its very popularity," became less likely to "be enacted within the broad terms of a liberal education geared toward the individual's independence" (18). Instead, it became entrenched as the accepted "way" of the new establishment. By focusing on rhetoric and avoiding controversial topics that could have excluded some of his students, Bain dealt with Aberdeen's politically charged atmosphere. If the spirit of Bain's approach became lost, what Flannery finds extremely valuable in her study of Bain is that "both representational and universalist pedagogies can be put to use by students (even while each delimits what is possible within the particular pedagogical frame)" (19). And she insists that it is important to remember "no rhetoric in and of itself assures educational access. And there is nothing in either representational or universalist rhetorics, by themselves, that makes it more likely that students will achieve either independence of thought or a greater repertoire of literate strategies" (19).

Flannery's assertions open the door for scholars, freeing them from having to constantly measure one age against our own. Whereas this has been the practice over and over again in studies of Bain, Flannery calls for us to ask new questions and seek better answers to old questions.

One question concerns Bain's context in Aberdeen during the last half of the nineteenth century, and the kinds of students he instructed. Most of the facts about Bain's life can be found in his autobiography, published posthumously in 1904. Although Bain provides a session-by-session detail of his professional life, one has to look at other sources to see what life was like in Aberdeen and where the students in his English class came from.

Modern Scottish scholars consider the nineteenth century to be Aberdeen's golden age, one that can be divided into three nearly equal periods: two periods of growth, divided by one period of economic decline. According to R. E. H. Mellor and R. E. Tyson, textiles and shipbuilding dominated the first period of Aberdeen's nineteenth-century economy, the time when Bain's father, a young soldier, married and took up the trade of hand loom weaving. During this first boom, between the turn of the century and 1851, the population of Aberdeen nearly tripled from 27,000 to 72,000 (Tyson 19). However, during this time, the introduction of steam-powered ships destroyed shipbuilding in Aberdeen. There just were not the ready resources to meet the needs of this industry. Aberdeen suffered another great blow when the booming textile industry was destroyed—again, by lack of resources and by steam-powered looms that rapidly began replacing the workforce. Bain was born into a working-class family during this great period of decline in ship building and textile manufacturing in Aberdeen, a period that lasted until 1860, the year he returned to Aberdeen after an eighteen-year absence and was appointed chair of logic at the newly formed university.

Just as Bain had been forced to reinvent himself (after his dismissal as Professor Glennie's assistant at Marischal College in 1842 for changing and updating lecture notes) and wait for the right time to come into his own, so too did Aberdeen. In the eighteen years Bain was away from Aberdeen, he created a discipline, psychology, for which he had written the first textbooks. He was the first person to devote himself to the study of the mind, and the first who had been able to make the important link between the mind and the body, between psychology and physiology. The versatility of this self-disciplined, self-trained man made him the prime candidate for the chair of logic at Britain's newest university, yet he faced fierce opposition from the religious conservatives.

Despite the controversy over his appointment, Bain enjoyed his triumphant return to Aberdeen, which was emerging as one of Britain's fastest growing modern cities, a city of white granite with a commanding skyline against the backdrop of the North Sea. After a lull in growth during its period of decline, Aberdeen's population shot up again from the 1860s onward, until after the turn of the century. According to Tyson, "From 1880 onwards Aberdeen grew more rapidly than any other Scottish city, even Glasgow, and the immigrants who poured in still came from its hinterland" (34). The University of Aberdeen, Anderson states, "retained close links with the largely agricultural northeastern region of Scotland which it served, and the shared background of its students gave them a natural sense of community and identity" (1). The students, for the most part, lived at home or in lodging, and their lives were very different from the lives of students at Oxford and Cambridge. The numbers of students attending the University of Aberdeen rose steadily in the 1870s and peaked in 1890, followed by a decline in enrollment. Arts and divinity were based in Old Aberdeen at King's College, and law and medicine were based at Marischal College in the new town, about a mile away. Bain had graduated from Marischal College in 1840, twenty years before the fusion of the two institutions that created the University of Aberdeen. Upon his appointment as the chair of logic in 1860, he taught his English and logic courses at King's College.

In 1860, students ranged from 13 to more than 21 years old. Most were the sons of professionals and farmers. Only 26 of 343 students in the arts curriculum were from a working-class background, like Bain. Most, according to Anderson, "were the sons of farmers and ministers, solicitors and farm managers" (11). When they came to the university, "[m]ost Aberdeen students had a career clearly in mind, and since the class records have details of their later careers, it is possible to relate the origins of students to their 'destinations', and to see what social transformations a university education wrought" (11). Most went on to become ministers, doctors, and teachers, but tables also indicate the importance of overseas careers, due to Aberdeen's connection with the Indian Civil Service. Students also went abroad to America or Australia, or to other British provinces. Many who became ministers, doctors, and teachers spent their lives abroad. "Thus," according to Anderson, "the university made the North East [of Scotland] an exporter of talent" (11).

Students, for the most part, did not attend the university to obtain the degree. Anderson explained:

Some parents evidently used the arts classes as a form of liberal education before their sons went into the family firm, a practice which died out as secondary schools improved; others made use of the University mathematics and science classes as part of a business training. . . .

This was possible because of the flexibility of the system. Each year was self-contained, and so-called "private students" could take a single class in one subject. Studies could be interrupted and resumed later, at Aberdeen or elsewhere, and by no means all students took the full four-year course. (12)

Although Anderson broadly defines Aberdeen students as middle class, "many of them came from a background where the class divisions of modern industrial society had not fully developed, being brought up in villages and small towns, and educated at local schools used by a wide spread of classes" (13).

Thus were the youths Bain encountered in his English class, where over 40 students were seated in a tiered classroom. They were a rowdy bunch, conditioned by university tradition to express their acceptance or disapproval of their professors by stomping their feet (for approval) or shuffling them (for disapproval) during lectures. But class time involved more than lecture. Professors and their assistants examined students orally, encouraged discussions, and had the students complete a great deal of work in the classroom, with the professor going around the room to consult with individual students as they did their assignments. There was a great deal of interaction in Bain's class. And a look at the record he left of his students' performance indicates that he considered their merits in a variety of areas, from the way they accomplished class debates and oral examinations to the way they wrote. The diversity of approaches to learning is commendable, considering what we now know about different learning styles.

Diversity was also Aberdeen's answer to raising itself out of its depressed economy. As a sign of its recovery, between 1851 and 1911, "the labour force of Aberdeen grew by over 36,000, a clear demonstration that economic growth in the Victorian age was not dependent upon iron and coal. There is also evidence that it was accompanied by a rise in the standard of living more rapid than in many other areas of Britain" (Tyson 35). By 1911, Aberdeen's population had more than doubled since its earlier boom. Over 164,000 people called Aberdeen their home, more than six times as many as in 1801 (Tyson 20). How did Aberdeen achieve its great recovery from its depressed economy? According to Tyson, "Development was not to be built around a single industry, as in the case of jute in Dundee, for a surprising variety of industries thrived in Aberdeen, some of them small and highly specialized" (24). This specialization of industry continued to feed a steady stream of young men into the university to seek the powers of assimilation into the dominant culture. The fate of Aberdeen depended on its versatility and its diversity, its ability to recreate itself in the face of changing technology. Papermaking was introduced to Aberdeen, along with granite mining, and a rebirth of agriculture (especially livestock), which led to a whole range of subsidiary industries. Fishing, which surprisingly had not played a very important part in Aberdeen's economy, became a booming industry after 1880. "Within a decade Aberdeen became the largest white-fish port in Scotland, accounting for something like 20% of the total catch" (Tyson 27). Indeed, Aberdeen's most distinguishing feature was its diversity, with its reliance on local resources.

During his lifetime, Bain had risen from the working class to the middle class, assimilating into British culture through education. His success was in large part due to the opportunities made possible by reforms to the educational system, which made it more modern and relevant to his times. Through his own experience, Bain saw the need for a less classical educational system that would assist Aberdeen's youth in assimilating into the industrial age. Overall, this assimilation was quite successful.

The existence of Aberdeen's extensive middle class by 1880 demonstrates that it was a relatively wealthy city, comparing "more than favourably" with most English equivalents. As a measure of wealth, Tyson uses per capita Schedule D income tax (32), and points out that Aberdeen was the tenth wealthiest provincial town in Britain, comparing tax paid per head. But he says, perhaps the best indicator of its wealth was its "magnificent west end and the villas that stretched along the North Deeside Road" (32). An example of the kind of architecture that dominates the Aberdeen skyline, Marischal College, rebuilt and inaugurated in 1906, is one of the two largest granite buildings in the world, and Bain is one of those honored in the great stained glass commemorative window in Mitchell Hall.

Just as Bain in the nineteenth century, we face our own challenges today. Computer technology offers us more and more opportunities, as well as frustrations. Examining what Bain did in light of his circumstances demonstrates refreshingly that students do use what is offered them, and in surprising ways. The trick to meeting their needs lies in keeping our eyes open to our own time and space. As technology changed the lives of Bain's students—many of whom were entering new fields created by the industrial age—he grappled with what they needed and how he could most effectively provide it. His psychology-based innovations led to educational reform at the University of Aberdeen designed to address his students' needs as they prepared to enter a world that was changing as drastically for them as ours is for us today.

Note

1. See A. Allan MacLaren's "The Disruption of the 'Establishment': James Adam and the Aberdeen Clergy" (1988) for an account of the so-called Disruption of the Scottish church during the mid-nineteenth century. All Aberdeen churches were affected by the Disruption.

Works Cited

Anderson, R. D. *The Student Community at Aberdeen: 1860-1939*. Aberdeen, Scotland: Aberdeen UP, 1988.
Bain, Alexander. *Autobiography, with Supplementary Chapter*. Ed. William L. Davidson. London: Longmans, 1904.
—. *The Emotions and the Will*. London: J. W. Parker, 1859.
—. *English Composition and Rhetoric*. London: Longmans, 1866, 1886.
—. *On Teaching English*. London: Longmans, 1887.
—. *The Senses and the Intellect*. London: J. W. Parker, 1855.
Flannery, Kathryn T. "The Challenge of Access: Rethinking Alexander Bain's Reformist Pedagogy." *Rhetoric Review* 14.1 (1995): 5-22.
Kitzhaber, Albert Raymond. *Nineteenth-Century Rhetoric in North America*. Carbondale: Southern Illinois UP, 1953.
Lunsford, Andrea A. "Alexander Bain and the Teaching of Composition in North America." *Scottish Rhetoric and Its Influences*. Ed. Lynee Lewis Gaillet. Mahwah, NJ: Erlbaum, 1998. 219-27.
—. "Alexander Bain's Contributions to Discourse Theory." *College English* 44 (1982): 290-300.
—. "Essay Writing and Teachers' Responses in Nineteenth-Century Scottish Universities." *College Composition and Communication* 32 (1981): 434-43.
MacLaren, A. Allen. "The Disruption of the 'Establishment': James Adam and the Aberdeen Clergy." *Aberdeen in the Nineteenth Century: The Making of the Modern City*. Ed. John S. Smith and David Stevenson. Aberdeen, Scotland: Aberdeen UP, 1988. 106-20.
Mellor, R. E. H. "Aberdeen—the Great Century." *Aberdeen in the Nineteenth Century: The Making of the Modern City*. Ed. John S. Smith and David Stevenson. Aberdeen, Scotland: Aberdeen UP, 1988. 1-18.
Miller, Thomas P. *The Formation of College English: Rhetoric and Belles Lettres in the British Cultural Provinces*. Pittsburgh: U of Pittsburgh P, 1997.
Tyson, Robert E. "The Economy of Aberdeen." *Aberdeen in the Nineteenth Century: The Making of the Modern City*. Ed. John S. Smith and David Stevenson. Aberdeen, Scotland: Aberdeen UP, 1988. 19-36.

PEGEEN REICHERT POWELL
Miami University

Facing the Audience: Reconsidering "Audience" through the Chinese Concept of "Face"

This chapter considers how the concept of "face" can inform discussions of audience in the fields of rhetoric and composition studies. Face is a primary concern in verbal interaction, but an understanding of face productively expands and complicates issues of audience in written communication as well. As I will argue, the concept of face provides a locally situated and dynamic understanding of audience, but one that sees each particular interaction, each text, as explicitly and intricately connected to the way the world works.

The Audience Dilemma

For the sake of brevity and clarity, I will use Lisa Ede and Andrea Lunsford's "Audience Addressed/Audience Invoked" and their later "Representing Audience" to outline the ways that audience has been talked about in composition and rhetoric. The outline will necessarily be rough and perhaps oversimplified so that the focus of this chapter is the discussion of how face can inform these understandings of audience. In "Audience Addressed/Audience Invoked," Ede and Lunsford consider two strains of theories of audience. The first, what they call "audience addressed," views audience as the real people who exist outside the text, and whose attitudes, beliefs, and demographics can and must be known. In this model, the audience is paramount as the writer constructs the text. Their second model, "audience invoked," stresses the writer's role in creating the audience. The proponents of this view, of whom Walter Ong is the most prominent, hold that it is impossible to know one's audience as they exist in the material world. Instead, in Ede and Lunsford's words, the "writer uses the semantic and syntactic resources of language to provide cues to the reader—cues which help to define the role or roles the writer wishes the reader to adopt in responding to the text" (160).

Ede and Lunsford argue that either position, to assume a knowable audience or to assume an entirely constructed audience, is too simple. Rather, they argue for a synthesis of the two. Their both/and approach to audience, "audience addressed/audience invoked," does indeed resolve, to some extent, the dilemma of audience. Yet, even the typography of their title suggests that there is a persistent dichotomy that must be negotiated in this understanding of audience. In "Representing Audience," Lunsford and Ede do not dispute the argument they make in "Audience Addressed/Audience Invoked"; rather, they read their earlier model of audience in light of institutional and discursive demands (e.g., their imbrication in codes of educational success) that they now recognize were (and are) operating on their own writing. This reading enables them to further complicate their understanding of audience, and in some ways, move beyond the apparently opposed conceptions of audience as addressed or invoked. Commenting on the earlier piece, Lunsford and Ede admit that

> we do not pursue the multiple ways in which the student writer's agency and identity may be shaped and constrained not only by immediate audiences but also, and even more forcefully, by the ways in which both she and those audiences are positioned within larger institutional and discursive frameworks. Nor do we consider the powerful effects of ideology working through genres, such as those inscribed in academic essayist literacy, to call forth and thus to control and constrain writers and audiences. (170-71)

In this later piece, Lunsford and Ede explore how the institution, discourse, and genre that surround the writing situation shape and constrain reader, writer, and text, exigencies that did not occur to them as they wrote the earlier article.

In "Representing Audience," Lunsford and Ede argue that their previous inability to see what is absent in "Audience Addressed/Audience Invoked" was in part due to their reliance on traditional rhetoric. Specifically, they recognize the influence of "the tradition's insistent impulse toward successful communication on the one hand and exclusion on the other" (173). Regarding the former, the "impulse toward successful communication," they argue that successful rhetoric has been traditionally synonymous with persuasion. Regarding the second limitation of traditional rhetoric, Lunsford and Ede remark on how "the ways in which the exclusionary tendencies of the rhetorical tradition are tied to a view of the human subject as coherent, autonomous, and unified. Such a view assumes that writers and readers have no options but to be either in—or out of—a particular rhetorical situation" (174).

Face concerns, as I will explain, are not about persuasion, but about maintaining one's self in social relationships; moreover, the concept of face explicitly and necessarily resists the notion of self as "coherent, autonomous, and unified." Face is other-directed, so it demands an understanding of self as always in relation to other people and the institutions and discourses that shape the social network. Thus, reading issues of audience through the concept of face enables a complex but more thoroughly integrated understanding of audience that resists dichotomous terms and accounts for the exigencies that Ede and Lunsford have come to see as integral to concerns about audience.

Facing the Audience

David Ho defines face this way[1]:

> Face is the respectability and/or deference which a person can claim for himself from others, by virtue of the relative position he occupies in his social network and the degree to which he is judged to have functioned adequately in that position as well as acceptably in his general conduct; the face extended to a person by others is a function of the degree of congruence between judgments of his total condition in life . . . and the social expectations that others have placed upon him. (883)

There are a couple of important points worth highlighting in Ho's concept of face. First, according to Ho, an individual's face is not a self-image, but an image of the self that is given to an individual through the actions of others, namely through an extension of respectability and/or deference. Second, an individual's face is handled according to the degree to which the individual fulfills the expectations others have for her, and these expectations are determined by the person's relative position in society.

Finally, the notion of self that is implicit in Ho's concept of face is significant. He acknowledges that his definition of face may be difficult to reconcile with a Western ideology of individualism. However, he argues that the individual under the ideology of individualism is an ideal: "It does not reflect the true state of affairs—namely, that much of the time man is subject to the impact of social actions beyond his control and responsibility and that his subjective volitions are constrained by the necessity of having to meet the social expectations of others" (882). Although Ho does not acknowledge the extent to which people's expectations of each other in Anglo-American culture are conditioned by the ideology of individualism, he does remind readers that when people communicate, there are always constraints placed on the communicative event that are external to the individuals' desires or intentions. Ho's definition of face is located in the concept's Chinese origins, but he asserts that "the presentation of self vis-à-vis others is a basic problem that no one, in any society, can avoid" (881). To put it simply, Ho's model of face is other-oriented.

Erving Goffman's concept of face is an important complement to Ho's, because there are nuances to his understanding that arise from his perspective as a Westerner, specifically an Anglo-American. For Goffman, a "line" is "a pattern of verbal and nonverbal acts," through which a person indicates the stance she assumes in relation to the conversation and the other conversationalists (5), and face is "the positive social value a person effectively claims for himself by the line others assume he has taken during a particular contact" (5). Whereas Ho asserts that an individual's face comprises the actions or attitudes others perform (especially extensions of deference and/or respectability), Goffman asserts that an individual's face comprises the actions or attitudes others assume the individual has performed through the line she has taken. In either case, what is significant is that in both definitions an individual's face depends on others. Even for Goffman, the line an individual takes is not as important as the line that others assume the individual has taken and others' response to this line. Moreover, in order to choose an appropriate line, the individual must be discerning about her relationships with the other conversationalists and even with people not present. Like Ho's, then, Goffman's concept of face is other-directed. Three aspects of face, which are especially relevant to the issues of audience in rhetoric, emerge from Ho's and Goffman's discussions of face: face in the social structure, face in interaction, and face as "rules of the group." I separate these three aspects for ease of discussion, but they are profoundly interrelated.

Face in the Social Structure

The first aspect of face that is central to Goffman's and Ho's discussion and relevant to the issue of audience in rhetoric is that individuals' faces are intimately tied to their positions in the larger social structure that exists outside the interaction. Goffman says that "while concern for face focuses the attention of the person on the current activity, he must, to maintain face in this activity, take into consideration his place in the social world beyond it" (7). In other words, individuals will lose face if others assume they have taken a line in a particular interaction that does not correspond to their positions in the wider social structure. Ho makes a similar claim in his definition (quoted earlier) when he says that face is the respect and/or deference an individual can expect "by virtue of the relative position he [she] occupies in his social network and the degree to which he [she] is judged to have functioned adequately in that position."

When communication is mediated, as in the case of a written text, interactants do consider each other's positions in the world outside the text, thus attending to this aspect of face. In one very limited respect, this is similar to Ede and Lunsford's "audience addressed": writers should know their audiences as they exist in the "real" world. Understood in terms of face, though, one acknowledges a much more complex interaction between writer and reader. Not only must writers consider the material circumstances of audiences outside their texts, but they must also take into account their own relationships to those audiences. Such an approach shifts the burden away from attempting to know the specific demographics of an audience, including its attitudes and beliefs, a knowledge that will never be complete and is usually impossible. Rather, writers attempt to know their relative positions in the hierarchies surrounding their discourses—whether they be the hierarchies of a corporation, a discipline, a society, or a classroom. Based on these relationships, the writer can begin answering questions: "To what extent can I expect deference or respect from my audience?" "What face will they extend to me?" "What face must I extend to my readers?" A student writing for a teacher must answer these questions differently than an academic writing for colleagues. The questions are not necessarily easier to answer than those in a traditional "audience analysis" (e.g., What is the average age of my audience? What will they think about socialized health care?). But questions about face take into account the complexities of a rhetorical situation in ways that the traditional analysis does not, including the implications of where authority and power lie.

Face in Interaction

Whereas the face of writer and reader are intimately connected to the individuals' relative positions in the social world outside of the text, their faces should be understood to exist only in interaction. So, the second aspect of face that is significant to a discussion about audience, as Goffman asserts, is that "the person's face clearly is something that is not lodged in or on his body, but rather something that is diffusely located in the flow of events in the encounter and becomes manifest only when these events are read and interpreted for the appraisals expressed in them" (7). Echoing Goffman, Ho says that "face is never a purely individual thing. It does not make sense to speak of the face of an individual as something lodged within his person" (882). Face cannot be fully understood outside of interactions with others.

In this way, face incorporates Ede and Lunsford's second half of the "audience addressed/audience invoked" model. A reader's role is invoked in the text through choices in topic, tone, and word choice, among other things. However, reading through the concept of face, one cannot think of the reader's role as constructed solely by cues in the writer's text. Instead, it is more useful to understand the reader's role as being constructed through a dynamic interaction that is the text. And, the interaction creates a role for the writer as well. The reader will extend a face to the writer depending on whether or not the writer has assumed an appropriate line. Careful face work, or in Goffman's words, "the actions taken by a person to make whatever he is doing consistent with face," is necessary to maintain face for both reader and writer (12); to say that the text creates a role for the reader is a model that is too static to account for these dynamics.

Face and the "Rules of the Group"

Finally, the third aspect of face relevant to a discussion of audience is captured in Ho's emphasis on "social expectations," and more important, the individual's ability to meet these expectations. Perhaps Goffman is more useful here, though. In his words, "one's own face and the face of others are constructs of the same order; it is the rules of the group and the definition of the situation which determine how much feeling one is to have for face and how this feeling is to be distributed among the faces involved" (6). Individuals cannot know how to attend to others' face in interaction unless they are familiar with the "rules" that govern that interaction. Moreover, the "rules of the group" do not exclude anyone; in fact, as Ho argues, "the concern for face exerts a mutually restrictive, even coercive, power upon each member of the social network" (873). Although the concern for face exerts itself equally on all involved, this is not to say that the face available to everyone is of equal value. Rather, what this aspect of face recognizes is that the same "rules of the group" are brought to bear on the face concerns of everyone in a given interaction—no one is exempt.

Face, because it is other-directed, demands an understanding of self as always in relation to other people and the institutions and discourses that shape the social network. In the context of writing, this means an understanding of the writer's and reader's selves as they are constructed in discourses that are shaped by genre conventions, disciplinary definitions of argument and evidence, and notions of successful language use. These are the "rules," or "constraints," that Ede and Lunsford discuss in "Representing Audience," the exigencies they failed to account for in their earlier piece.

Conclusions

I have separated three aspects of face for ease of discussion. The third aspect reintegrates them nicely. The "rules of the group" overlap with the rules that determine one's roles in the social network outside the interaction that must be considered when attending to face in interaction, which I discussed as the first aspect of face. And, it is the rules of the group that determine the course of interaction and, as I explained regarding the second aspect, face is something that is diffusely located in that course of interaction. Thus, what is admittedly only vaguely referred to here as "the rules of the group" is of primary interest when attempting to understand face or audience.

In order to illustrate further what might be considered the "rules of the group," I turn to James Porter's notion of forums and forum analysis. Porter defines a forum as a

> concrete, local manifestation of the operation of a discourse community.... Forums provide well-defined speaking and writing roles for its members, who are, in turn defined by these roles. A forum shares assumptions about what objects are appropriate for examination and discussion, what operating functions are performed on those objects, what constitutes evidence and validity, and what formal conventions are followed. (107)

Forums might be read as the specific interactions or series of interactions of a particular group. Forum analysis, the pedagogy suggested by this understanding of audience, requires that students attempt to understand the assumptions and conventions—what one might call the "rules of the group"—of a forum in order to successfully communicate within that forum.

However, forum analysis differs from face in that the former "assumes that audience is defined by the texts (oral and written) it produces and that the writer needs to systematically explore this textual field in order to produce acceptable discourse within it" (Porter 112). Face, on the other hand, although located within the texts (oral and written) that comprise interactions, takes into account "rules" that circulate within and surround the interactions as well. Thus an analysis of face must look carefully at the details of a given interaction, a given text, but it must connect these details to the institutional and social discourses and hierarchies that surround the interaction as well. The concept of face provides a locally situated and dynamic understanding of audience, but one that sees each particular interaction, each text, as explicitly and intricately connected to the way the world works. As Ho says, "Face is a concept of central importance because of the pervasiveness with which it asserts its influence in social intercourse. It is virtually impossible to think of a facet of social life to which the question of face is irrelevant" (883).

Perhaps the most fruitful ramification of this approach to audience, then, is that it lends itself to a writing pedagogy that absolutely must introduce questions about the "rules of the group," whether that group be an academic discipline, a local community, or a national audience. Students must consider what the rules are, who knows the rules, and who does not and why, which are all issues that—when taken seriously—should lead to a discussion of ethics. And, if we teach audience through the concept of face, then we must become a new kind of audience for our students' writing. We must recognize and be honest with our students about the fact that our relative positions in the social world outside the text entail unequal amounts of power. We must open ourselves to the realization that we are representatives of the institutions that, in many ways, constrain our students' writing. We must acknowledge that discourses and genres are not simply transparent mediums for an individual's thought, but that inherent in them is a network of rules that we need to teach. And perhaps most important, we must allow ourselves to truly interact with our students' work.[2]

Notes

1. Both Ho and Erving Goffman, who I will discuss later, use masculine pronouns throughout their work. Quoting their texts reminds me of the need to bring explicitly feminist perspectives to the study of face. Unfortunately, doing so is beyond the scope of this present work.

2. I would like to thank LuMing Mao for his guidance on this project.

Works Cited

Ede, Lisa, and Andrea Lunsford. "Audience Addressed/Audience Invoked: The Role of Audience in Composition Theory and Pedagogy." *CCC* 35.2 (1984): 155-71.

Goffman, Erving. *Interaction Ritual: Essays on Face-to-face Behavior.* New York: Pantheon, 1967.

Ho, David Yau-fai. "On the Concept of Face." *American Journal of Sociology* 81.4 (1976): 867-84.

Lunsford, Andrea A., and Lisa Ede. "Representing Audience: 'Successful' Discourse and Disciplinary Critique." *CCC* 47.2 (1996): 167-79.

Porter, James E. *Audience and Rhetoric: An Archaeological Composition of the Discourse Community.* Englewood Cliffs, NJ: Prentice, 1992.

SCOTT RICHARD LYONS
Miami University

The Incorporation of the Indian Body: Peyotism and the Pan-Indian Public, 1911-23

In his primary campaign speech for president of the Southwest Regional Indian Youth Council in 1960, 21-year-old Ponca activist Clyde Warrior countered his opponent's standard line of the day—Indians' need for education and professionalism—with a short speech that prefigured the revolutionary rhetoric of the coming Indian movement of the sixties and seventies and signaled a turn in Native discourses of politics, publics, and the body. Strolling up to the podium with his cowboy hat pushed casually back on his head, Warrior looked at the audience of young Indian people, rolled up his sleeves, held out his arms, and said only two lines: "This is all I have to offer. The sewage of Europe does not flow through these veins" (Smith and Warrior 42). Clyde Warrior won the election by a landslide that day, thus marking a shift in the Indian public from a politics and rhetoric of assimilation and accommodation to one of nationalism and essentialism. The rhetorical effectivity of his short speech assumes a number of political notions of Native identity. Warrior addressed his audience pantribally, as "Indians" opposed to "Europe," illustrating that distinction through the concept of blood, and then using blood and body (specifically, his own) to symbolize Indian culture and nationhood, a linkage that would continue to resonate in the Indian movement from Alcatraz to the Longest Walk to Wounded Knee II.

The construction of the pan-Indian public is a twentieth-century development elaborated in its modern sense in a less radical but no less political location: the strained but crucial relationship between the Society of American Indians (SAI) and the peyote church during the first few decades of this century. Historians and theorists of Native American rhetoric should pay attention to this interesting, important site for its complex interplay of three related developments we find at work in the formation of Indian political movements. First, the site witnessed for the first time the successful development of a pan-Indian public identity. Second, this "Indian" identity was inscribed onto—and into—the body. Third, the logic of pan-Indian movements and factions during that time and beyond points to what I think is a dialectic at work in the construction of American Indian political activity—between Native American publics and what I call metis spaces, or mixed blood sites where culture is created from multiple sources and ethnicity deployed as a process responsive to domination. Rethinking the dialectics of "blood" and culture, publics and metis spaces, and the construction of the "Indian" body can help us better understand the trajectory and logic of Native American political movements.

Fashioning the Pan-Indian Public

Non-Indians have had little problem lumping the hundreds of different tribes, languages, and cultures on the American continent under a single rubric, "the Indian," ever since Columbus arrived on these shores and announced "Indios!" and then later designated the group a "race" (Berkhofer 5-7, 57). But how did this same diverse collection of Native tribes and peoples arrive at such an understanding of themselves at the turn of the century? The easy answer is that they were simply responding to representations of themselves presented by their oppressors, exhibiting the consciousness of the colonized, which is certainly true to an extent. However, to read this development more complexly requires us to take into account government policies and the pressures they engendered in addition to the cultural upheaval everyone knows about. A materialist reading of pan-Indian self-fashioning might uncover a more slippery political response to a "New World" marked by colonization, imperialism, and racism, as well as trouble usually unproblematically fixed terms like "assimilation." For example, although usually identified with an assimilationist agenda, the Society of American Indians was nonetheless an indigenous attempt to recover power for Native peoples through the formation of a pan-Indian public committed to political action. Although there were certainly other attempts at forging pan-Indian groups by such leaders as Pontiac (Delaware), Joseph Brant (Mohawk), and Tecumseh (Shawnee), not to mention Wovoka (Paiute) and the Ghost Dance movement of the 1890s, SAI was the first to engage in publicity as "Americans," as an "Indian" yet "internal" public; and they did it by mastering the master's tools. This was a metis group in the fullest sense of the term, and although the organization was beleaguered, short-lived, and generally unsuccessful at accomplishing its objectives, it must be recognized that SAI in no small way paved the road for later groups such as the American Indian Movement (AIM) by presenting its members as political, public Indians.

Ironically founded in Columbus in 1911 and disbanded in 1923, SAI was a group committed to "the honor of the race and the good of the country" (Hertzberg 80). Like other reform organizations of the time (and back then, wherever two or more white liberals and a Carlisle Indian were gathered, there was reform) SAI utilized the mechanisms of public formation available to them: annual conferences, a headquarters in Washington, the issuing of programmatic statements, applied political pressure for remedial legislation, the publication of an authorized *Quarterly Journal* (later renamed *American Indian Magazine*) and even a dissenting, "unauthorized" publication attacking the authorized one, Carlos Montezuma's *Wassaja*. White reform groups like the Lake Mohonk Conference and the Indian Rights Association shared a concern for educational reform, universal citizenship for Natives, the establishment of an American Indian Day, and many other goals with SAI, but the latter pursued these objectives using mainstream methods of organization and communication, and effectively constituted itself as a public interest group for 12 years.

Primarily composed of middle-class, highly educated professionals, intellectuals, anthropologists, and writers (e.g., the famous Charles Alexander Eastman, Sioux; Gertrude Bonnin, Sioux; Dr. Carlos Montezuma, Yavapai; Thomas Sloan, Omaha; and Arthur C. Parker, Seneca), SAI's leaders were mostly "assimilated" Christians from mixed blood, non-reservation families; and most importantly, they were almost to the number graduates from General Richard Henry Pratt's Carlisle Indian Industrial School. Pratt, "the father of Indian education," was responsible for boarding schools: institutions designed to turn children against their culture, language, and family through mental and physical means, including beatings. The schools themselves were only part of a fuller U.S. assimilationist policy coming on the heels of the General Allotment Act (Dawes Act) of 1887. Indeed, Pratt's influence was so strong that it is tempting to suggest that his infamous dictum, "Kill the Indian, save the man," was a primary goal of the organization. SAI almost always discussed the most effective methods of Indian assimilation, generally believed in doing away with special programs for Natives, and strongly suggested that the best thing for Indians to do was to internalize the norms of white society (Hertzberg 164).

The assimilationism of SAI, however, is a complicated affair, owing itself not only to the disorder of Indian life and culture—which Eastman, Bonnin, and the others knew all too well, having been witness to the transition to reservation life—but also to the disorder and decay of white society. As Robert Warrior (Osage) explains, "Natives within SAI failed to understand that they were caught up in a battle of community values versus individualistic chaos, rather than a conflict between one set of cohesive, livable values and another" (237). In other words, one of the reasons for the assimilative thrust of SAI is the fact that they did not quite know where the mainstream was going, because as Vine Deloria (Sioux) puts it, "the only alternative that white society had to offer was a chaotic and extreme individualism" (qtd. in Warrior 237). Unable to enlist the support of reservation Indians, or even to agree on long-term visions among themselves, the members of SAI ultimately failed at their assimilationist agenda, and in fact most of them gave it up as a goal entirely; even Eastman and Montezuma died in tipis, returning "back to the blanket" themselves after the collapse of their public sphere.

Taken as a cultural formation, SAI can seem sadly conceived, but seen as a public, they were impressively astute. SAI's attempt to form a public was remarked on in the opening address of their founding conference in Columbus, when Robert G. Valentine, commissioner of Indian Affairs, remarked,

"We need an All-Indian public opinion" (Hertzberg 60). This fledgling, "All-Indian" public allowed only people of Native descent a right to vote and at times even to speak. On what foundation did they, could they, stand together? It certainly was not consensus or the bracketing of status attributes, as Habermas finds in the eighteenth-century bourgeois public sphere, and it was not "Indian" language or culture. Instead, as Hazel Hertzberg has noted, the common organizing principle at work in this public sphere was a biological definition of "the Indian race." It was so strong that the Columbus conference proceedings show that in the discourse on SAI goals and identity, references to race proliferated whereas other "available terms were conspicuous by their absence. 'Culture' was one of these . . . another was 'nation'" (Hertzberg 73). On the one hand, this emphasis on "race" was on a par with the dominant ideology of the day. According to Robert Berkhofer, in nineteenth-century white discourse on Indians, "the word *race* replaced . . . the word *nation*" (55-56), whereas up until that time, "[n]ations, races, and cultures were all basically seen as one interchangeable category for the understanding of peoples" (25). Berkhofer attributes the ideological shift to post-Darwinian racial science, later picked up by armchair anthropologists like Lewis Henry Morgan. On the other hand, although this is certainly true with non-Indian ideologies, to understand the Indian use of the concept, we must also make a frankly literal reading of the Abolition of Treaty Making Act of 1871, which states that "hereafter no Indian nation or tribe within the territory of the United States shall be acknowledged or recognized as an independent nation" (Prucha 136). That is, the Indians of SAI were not only ideologically but legally stripped of their nationalities. Without recognition as a nation and without universal U.S. citizenship, Indians at that time had little else to turn to: "race" was one possibility, "culture" was another. Considering the historical moment and educational backgrounds of participants, "race" seemed more plausible than culture (to which no serious public attention would be paid), and so SAI formed a public based on biology.

Small wonder, then, that citizenship was one of their major goals. It was also the only stated objective they actually achieved, in 1924, one year after the demise of SAI. When the Indian Citizenship Bill was passed, Chief Joseph Strong Wolf (Ojibwe) celebrated it in an editorial that reflected a racial understanding of Indian identity in the spirit of SAI: "The hardest part of the work is now to come, and that is to arouse a feeling of racial consciousness in the breast of every Indian, whether full blood or not, in our country, and to teach him to take his place in our civilization . . ." (qtd. in Hertzberg 225). Strong Wolf's call for "racial consciousness," civic duty, and Indian pride in "our civilization," a call to action written eloquently in a newspaper editorial, captures well the labors of the Society of American Indians during their short tenure, despite all their assimilationist rhetoric and ultimate failure to achieve emancipatory results as a public. Overall, SAI's "All-Indian" public formed in response to exigencies we might call imperialism and its fallout, what they termed "Indian issues," in the face of a state power that recognized their right to exist as neither nations nor citizens. In no small part due to SAI, Native people from various tribes became "Indian," and Indians went public. Ironically, the pan-Indian public SAI worked so hard to forge eventually collapsed over a larger, more powerful pan-Indian movement based not on "race" but on "culture" in the metis spaces of reservations: the peyote religion.

Peyotism and the Pan-Indian Body

Peyotism is a pan-Indian religious movement that uses the hallucinogenic cactus, peyote, as a sacrament. Some groups have incorporated peyote into traditional practices, but by now most resemble Christian ceremonies and employ some degree of Christian cosmology—in no small part as a defensive measure against legislation that would outlaw peyotism. Although an ancient practice among Indians in Mexico, the use of peyote first appeared among the Mescalero Apaches around 1870. It quickly spread throughout Indian country in the late nineteenth and early twentieth centuries, causing alarm not only with white reformers and aghast Christians but conservative traditionals as well—it being, after all, yet another foreign practice on most reservations (Hertzberg 240). Its main prophets were John Wilson (Delaware/Caddo) and Quanah Parker (Comanche), and its earliest enthusiasts were typically young, educated, and Christianized, much like the constituency of the Society of American Indians (Hertzberg 243, 246).

Peyote was the most divisive issue among SAI's leadership, and it alone might be blamed for dealing the final death blow to an already faltering organization. As if factionalism and personal dislikes were not enough, in 1918 various leaders of SAI found themselves testifying against one another on opposite sides of the Hayden Bill (HR 2614), which sought to outlaw peyote as an intoxicant unprotected by religious freedom laws. Charles Alexander Eastman and Gertrude Bonnin testified against peyote, the former calling it "not an Indian idea, nor . . . an Indian practice," the latter alleging that peyote "excited the baser passions," "creat[ing] false notions in the mind of the users," which caused them to "reject the teachings of the church" (Hertzberg 263, 256). In their view, peyotism was not authentically Indian (Eastman), and it was not to be trusted for its effects on the body, and subsequently, the mind and spirit (Bonnin). By contrast, both Thomas L. Sloan (Omaha) and Francis LaFlesche (Omaha) testified that peyotism was helping people beat alcoholism and find new enthusiasm for life. As LaFlesche explained, "The Indians who have taken the new religion strive to live moral, upright lives and I think their morality can be favorably compared with any community of a like number in the country" (Hertzberg 267). For supporters among the SAI, peyotism was a panacea to the ills of reservation life; it had the power to heal a community.

At stake in these debates seems to be peyote's tangible power over both body and mind, and specifically its ability to keep them together in the pursuit of spiritual contact. "The white man goes into his church house and talks *about* Jesus," Quanah Parker was fond of saying, "but the Indian goes into his tipi and talks *to* Jesus" (qtd. in Hertzberg 243). In this saying, which practically became a mantra for peyotists, we can see that in addition to combining both Indian and non-Indian elements and fostering yet another pan-Indian identity, peyote also creates in the body of the Indian unmediated religious experience, a direct connection to the divine:

> The belief is that God put some of his Holy Spirit into peyote, which he gave to the Indians. And by eating the sacramental peyote the Indian absorbs God's Spirit. . . . For the Peyotist, this occurs because he has put himself in a receptive spiritual mood and has absorbed enough of God's power to make him able to reach God. (LaBarre et al. 582-83)

The ability to achieve unmediated religious experience in the body, and the pan-Indian body in particular, is a theme that has resonated in Native discourse ever since, perhaps most notably in Vine Deloria's classic work, *God Is Red* (1972), which accuses Christianity's "time-centered" theologies of creating a Western mind/body split unfathomable to indigenous Americans' "place-centered" beliefs. Certainly, in the peyote church, body and mind are kept intact in ceremonies emphasizing dancing, singing, rattling, eating, drinking, quiet contemplation, and the seeking of visions. As the Menominee anthropologist (and peyotist) J. S. Slotkin wrote in 1956, the peyotist "always prays in his or her own Indian language, even if the rest of the rite is conducted in English. Also, the Indian spoken prayer is spontaneous, 'from the heart.' By contrast, among the Whites some smart man writes down a prayer which is then printed, and others simply look in a book and repeat the prayer with their lips" (73). In resisting a mind/body split, peyotism invokes through its creative fusions of different elements a new pan-Indian body, one based not on "race," as was the public body forged by SAI, but on culture—belief, ceremony, and unmediated religious experience made in metis space. In this space, the Indian body is constructed through the communal, ritualized ingestion of the holy herb, an incorporation of tribal, extratribal, and non-Indian elements (i.e., natural, cultural, human) with a hope of healing, fusing body and mind, engaging and disengaging domination, making "Indian" identity and calling it all "tradition."

Of course, the practice was offensive to Enlightenment-bound SAI members who were perhaps more invested in Reason than we might think. At any rate, the differences between these two pan-Indian bodies—SAI's "racial" body public, and peyotism's cultural body of believers—should not be overemphasized; remember, there is a lot of overlap between the two. Still, peyotism thrives today, whereas SAI lasted little more than a decade. Why? Slotkin suggests that "the Peyote Religion's program of accommodation . . . was the basic reason for [its] success" (21); that is, although it was "an Indian defense against consequences of White domination," it was not militant (7). It survived, but did not conquer, white imperialism. The Society of American Indians did neither, but started a trajectory of Indian public formation.

For these reasons, I would like to suggest that the two sites—the public, the metis space—work dialectically and have ever since in the history of American Indian political movements. As a public formed in the midst of a truly heavy assimilationist political atmosphere, the Society of American Indians tried to define itself "racially," keeping culture out of public view, yet never denounced it completely. Far from it: embedded in the ostensibly assimilationist writings of Eastman and Bonnin is a critique of white individualism and Christian hypocrisy that is undeniable. By the time of Clyde Warrior, and still later in the public work of AIM, pan-Indian publics would bring culture into full view, wearing feathers and braids and denouncing assimilation at the top of their lungs, in addition to drawing on the discourses of "race"; those movements were both critical and militant. What remains to be seen is how the dialectics of culture and "race," metis spaces and public movements, political discourse, and the Indian body will develop in our political, pan-Indian pursuit of social justice.

Works Cited

Berkhofer, Robert F., Jr. *The White Man's Indian*. New York: Vintage, 1978.
Deloria, Vine, Jr. *God Is Red: A Native View of Religion*. 2nd ed. Golden, CO: Fulcrum, 1994.
Hertzberg, Hazel W. *The Search for an American Indian Identity: Modern Pan-Indian Movements*. Syracuse: Syracuse UP, 1971.
Labarre, Weston, David P. McAllester, J. S. Slotkin, Omer Stewart, and Sol Tax. "Statement on Peyote." *Science* 114 (1951): 582-92.
Prucha, Francis Paul, ed. *Documents of United States Indian Policy*. 2nd ed. Lincoln: U of Nebraska P, 1990.
Slotkin, J. S. *The Peyote Religion*. Glencoe, IL: Free, 1956.
Smith, Paul Chaat, and Robert Allen Warrior. *Like a Hurricane: The Indian Movement from Alcatraz to Wounded Knee*. New York: New, 1996.
Warrior, Robert Allen. *Tribal Secrets: Recovering American Indian Intellectual Traditions*. Minneapolis: U of Minnesota P, 1995.

JANE DONAWERTH
University of Maryland, College Park

Hannah More, Lydia Sigourney, and the Creation of a Women's Tradition of Rhetoric

Women have taught and written rhetorical theory from its beginnings, as far back as Aspasia, a fifth-century Athenian sophist, and Pan Chao, a first-century contemporary of Quintilian, who taught eloquence to the Empress of China (see Bizzell; Bizzell and Herzberg; Donawerth, "Transforming"; Glenn; Levine and Sullivan; Lunsford; and Wertheimer). Not until the nineteenth century, however, did a tradition of women's rhetoric exist. It was a transatlantic EuroAmerican tradition. This chapter examines the ways that women constructed a women's tradition of rhetoric: Hannah More, who erects a proper sphere for women's rhetoric by demonizing the work and style of *précieuses* like Madeleine de Scudéry; Lydia Sigourney, who eulogizes the work of Hannah More as foremother and Eliza Farrar as sister; and Eliza Farrar, who copies materials freely from Hannah More and Lydia Sigourney because she takes for granted the field of women's rhetoric. These women are not the radical end of the spectrum of women's rhetorical theory, but instead, co-opt, as a means to make room for rhetorical theory by women, the movement to delineate a women's sphere.

Hannah More lived in England from 1745 to 1833, was a member of the circle around Dr. Johnson, helped to establish a famous girls' school, wrote plays that David Garrick and his wife produced, helped to found the Sunday School Movement and wrote dozens of moral tracts for it, and also published pieces on education and rhetorical theory. Here I concentrate on her poem, "The Bas Bleu" (1783-86)—not her only work on conversation—in which More defines a salon rhetoric of conversation and distinguishes it from other kinds. "The Bas Bleu" is a mock-heroic poem, in the manner of Pope's versified "Essay on Criticism." More's poem celebrates the famed Bluestockings salons, especially that of Elizabeth Vesey, and praises a conversation rhetoric based on good sense, female facilitators, education, and high moral purpose.

More begins her poem on salon conversation, after brief reference to the Greek salon of Aspasia and Pericles, with a history of the growth of the British salon out of parties that emphasized card games and dancing. She cites "*Good sense*, of faculties the best," as the regulator of proper conversation (362), treating it as a national British characteristic. In praising good sense, she attacks the seventeenth-century French salon made famous by Mme Rambouillet (whom she names) and Madeleine de Scudéry (whom she does not name) and, following Moliére, mocks *précieuses ridicules* (362). She blames French salons and conversation for rigid precision in grammar (where "mood ... banished ease"), for use of "stiff antithesis," for puns that "distorted every word they spoke," and for "forced conceit" (extended metaphors) (363). More attacks the old style French salon—demonizes it—in order to defuse potential anxieties about women's role in the current salon in England.

More's portrayal of French *précieuse* style and conversation is especially interesting when compared with de Scudéry's own works on conversation. De Scudéry published two dialogue essays on conversation, and others on wit, invention, and letter writing, and also a book of orations by women with a preface defending women's education (Donawerth, "As Becomes"). More is right in arguing that antithesis and precise grammar are characteristic of the *précieuses* and of de Scudéry, but incorrect on puns and conceits—*précieuses* avoided extended metaphor and puns as old fashioned and vulgar. The characteristics that More further sets out as defining good salon conversation would seem quite agreeable to de Scudéry, except for the emphasis on women being good listeners. Thus More performs a classic underclass maneuver in her criticism of the French salon: she blames other women (foreign, dangerous ones) in order to claim privileges for her own elite group of British women.

More shares with de Scudéry an admiration for female facilitators who manage the environment for conversation. In de Scudéry's *Conversations*, the facilitator who helps the group reach consensus is often a woman. More praises Mrs. Vesey for instituting the custom of conversational groups in England (365-66), for breaking up the circle at the edge of a room that watches the dancing and gossips about the courtships—the circle we have seen in so many Jane Austen movies. But this arrangement of conversational groups is actually characteristically French: in a frontispiece to a 1685 volume of de Scudéry's *Conversations Nouvelles* in the Folger Shakespeare Library, men and women stand in small groups around a long hall, and the hall furniture is arranged to facilitate this grouping, with a small table here and a portrait gallery there to attract groups. More concludes her poem by praising good listening skills, "attention, / Mute angel," and "The silence of intelligence" (371). In this poem, More does not assign listening a gender, although her description of "silent flattery" that "soothes our spirit" (371) may make one suspicious. In her other works, however, she is quite precise about who is to do the listening: because girls have received poor educations in comparison to boys, and because women are required to place themselves in submission to men, women must do the listening (More, *Strictures* 47-50). Masculinity may not be marred by thoughtless wit, but femininity may.

Besides seeing women as managers of conversation, More also sees education as intellectual capital (based on wit, taste, and science) that must circulate in commerce with others. In her mock-heroic praise of conversation, education is thus the "moral mint" and conversation is "commerce" ("Bas

Bleu" 368). These metaphors taken from trade expose one goal of the salon and of More: the inclusion into society of the middle class, the class defined by trade. This is a goal of the seventeenth-century French salon as well, according to Carolyn Lougee.

Finally, conversation must be based on high moral purpose so that it is civilizing. Here again More is drawing on a tradition of salon rhetoric that extends back to de Scudéry. In this tradition, the discourse of the salon sphere, not quite public, is still a discourse of power, and its practitioners establish their status by contrasting their "high" discourse with the "low" discourse of the businesses of government, marketplace, or courthouse, because these institutions are meant not for pleasure but only for utility. The purpose of such rhetoric is to establish status and to create a beneficial society—in More's terms, to allow women of a certain class and education to join intellectual society, which More calls "th'elect" ("Bas Bleu" 370). For this joining, she uses a telling metaphor of marriage and romantic love. In good conversation, "kindred souls demand alliance; / Each in the other joys to find / the image answering to his mind" (370). Because "The flash of intellect expires, / Unless it meet congenial fires" (370), women must be educated and admitted to conversation, and they must also be good receptors of men's ideas. More wants the men to stay for conversation after dinner, instead of going off for port in the library, but she has decided that the only way to persuade her society to allow such behavior is to retain the separate spheres of masculine and feminine talents in the drawing room.

Lydia Huntley Sigourney lived from 1791 to 1865 in the United States, helped establish a school for girls, published sixty-five volumes of poetry and prose over her lifetime, and battled publicly for causes such as humane treatment of the insane and protection of Native Americans from persecution. She also published rhetorical theory: advice on conversation, letter writing, and parlor elocution. It is the natural vocation of females to teach, she explains (11) in *Letters to Young Ladies* (1833), which went through over fifteen editions. Sigourney urges a republican ideal for women, stressing industry (14), which she interprets to mean self-education. Using the platform of "teacher-as-public-servant" to authorize her speaking out, Sigourney advocates a separate spheres conception of rhetoric that yet allows women public voice through republican motherhood and teaching.

Sigourney co-opts the social institution of women's gendered sphere by analyzing women's means to power through that sphere: teaching, conversation, reading aloud as part of parlor entertainment, and letter writing. Sigourney's contemporaries, the early female abolitionists, also used these strategies: when they were denied public speaking, they used teaching and conversation, letter campaigns, and parlor speaking to all-women audiences. Sigourney also shapes her writings to address the women of that gendered sphere, constructing a tradition of rhetorical theory by women through her citations of Hannah More and other female rhetoricians.

The sisterhood that Sigourney creates through her citation is not a liberated one. On the title page of *Letters to Young Ladies*, Sigourney cites More in pride of place: "Every sort of useful knowledge should be imparted to the young, not merely for its own sake, but for the sake of its subserviency to higher things." This seems a conservative claim: frivolous, irrelevant things should be left out, and the young should only be taught what is useful to spiritual or moral goals. But this is a quotation of an expert in girls' education, on the cover of a book addressed to schoolgirls, by another expert in girls' education. So this quotation is actually an argument for women's education, which in the mid-nineteenth century was unfortunately still in need of defense.

Sigourney cites More four other times in *Letters to Young Ladies*: on the weakness of girls' education in its emphasis on appearance, on speaking or writing unclearly (a passage also cited by Sigourney in *Letters to My Pupils*), on the dangers of reading romance novels, and on conversation. In these instances, too, Sigourney aims at a progressive goal by appropriating a conservative argument: to argue against stressing appearance in girls' education is also to argue against the beauty myth and in favor of stressing intellect and character, for girls as well as boys (110); to argue against timid, soft speech or unclear handwriting for girls is to argue in favor of girls' speaking out and having more training (115); and to argue against girls' reading novels is to argue for their reading philosophy and science (150).

Especially telling is Sigourney's use of More to navigate the idea of conversation as a woman's art, and the demonization of that art as gossip. Sigourney quotes More on the need for self-restraint in speech. She then explains, "Women, acting in a narrower sphere, examine with extreme ardour, whatever . . . enters into competition with them" (192). This is surely a warning against women allowing themselves to be placed by societal expectations into competition with each other. Sigourney ends her expansive warning against the feminine dangers of character demolition through gossip by explaining that women have better things to talk about: "The wide circle of the sciences, the whole range of literature, the boundless world of books, open for you sources of conversation, as innumerable as they are sublime. Subjects to which your mothers were strangers, are as familiar to 'your lips as household words'" (195). Asking girls to be kind and polite in their speech places Sigourney squarely in a conservative camp protecting gendered spheres; her conclusion, asking girls to read, study, and talk insistently about intelligent subjects, places her just as squarely in resistance to those spheres as they were gendered in the nineteenth century. Once we finish the recovery of the history of nineteenth-century parlor entertainment by women, I predict we will have a similar history of compliance and resistance, of accepting the domestic sphere, but using it as a powerful weapon on public issues (as Anne Ruggles Gere has argued women deployed their club activities).

Sigourney similarly moves from a restrictive to a liberated position on women's roles when she cites her contemporary, Eliza Farrar, on letter writing. Sigourney is, first of all, establishing "private" forms of communication, especially conversation and letter writing, as appropriate for women. By providing a theory for this communication, and by citing other women who have theorized it, she is also constructing a tradition of rhetorical theory by women. Sigourney's point that good letter writing is like conversation is quite common in theories of letter writing by the mid-nineteenth century, but also central to both Madeleine de Scudéry's seventeenth-century dialogue on letter writing, and to Hannah More's eighteenth-century poems and treatises.

In the discussion of letter writing in *Letters to Young Ladies*, Sigourney begins with the appearances of letters, the art appropriate to ladies: handwriting, paper, ink, folding, and sealing. She then cites Eliza Farrar's work, *The Youth's Letter-Writer* (1840), and Farrar's advice that even small tasks are worth doing well (obviously, Sigourney had revised her 1833 book by the time of the 1851 edition I use, to include reference to Farrar's 1840 book). At this point, Sigourney raises the ante: "Our sex," she claims, "have been complimented as the possessors of a natural taste for epistolary composition" (*Letters to Young Ladies* 116). This stereotyping was not a compliment, as scholars on seventeenth-century French epistolary works have demonstrated, because it granted women talent only to take it away (it was only a natural talent, not one acquired by art). Sigourney then reminds her audience that she is not stepping out of bounds (although she is), by explaining that letter writing "admits the language of the heart which we understand, and rejects the elaborate and profound science in which we are usually deficient." We are back in conservative territory here, with women expressing emotion and nature rather than reason and art. But she ends this passage by explaining that "Ease and truth to nature" are the qualities of good letter writing, qualities that Cicero claimed. Surely this is double-voiced discourse with a vengeance.

Eliza Ware Rotch Farrar (1791-1870) grew up in Wales and as an adult lived in the United States with her husband, a Harvard professor. She was a noted author of educational treatises, circulated in the Boston transcendentalist salons, and knew Margaret Fuller. Farrar treated conversation and education for girls in rhetoric and composition in *The Young Lady's Friend* (1836), and set out in great detail prescriptions for letter writing in *The Youth's Letter Writer or The Epistolary Art* (1840). Both books are designed for self-education, especially for families tutoring their children at home or for girls and young women who have left school for family responsibilities.

Whereas More established a proper British women's rhetoric through demonizing French salon rhetoric, and Sigourney cited other women to promote a women's rhetoric, Farrar demonstrated the popularity of this field of women's conduct book rhetoric by simply plagiarizing. Farrar sometimes cites More and Sigourney. She cites by name "Mrs. Sigourney, in her excellent letter on Conversation" (*Young Lady's* 300), for example, when she discusses proper conversation with a young man. At other times, Farrar lifts whole passages by paraphrase from the books by More or Sigourney. In giving prescriptions for subject matter in conversation, Farrar advises, "One of the great uses of reading is, that it furnishes you with interesting and safe topics of conversation with your young friends. . . . You cannot turn your advantages of education to better account, than by inducing your female friends to read with you, and to exchange the frivolous gossip of the day for communion with the mighty spirits of the dead" (258). This passage from *The Young Lady's Friend* paraphrases, without acknowledgement, a passage in Sigourney's *Letters to Young Ladies* that I have already quoted. It is significant, though, that Farrar cites Sigourney in a passage where she is citing More. Farrar's plagiarism results from the development of the field of women's rhetoric to the point that assumptions are shared, general public knowledge, and so are no longer attached to specific individuals.

I do not mean to imply that Farrar is unoriginal and that her work is only copies of others' materials. In *The Young Lady's Friend*, Farrar adds a great deal to the tradition of women's rhetoric, treating delivery under "self-possession" (362-63), discussing the classical rhetorical exercise of paraphrase to develop memory in her plan for girls' continuing education in the home (426), and making a self-conscious argument for conversation as an art like reasoning and composition (385). Her book on letter writing, *The Youth's Letter Writer*, is an inventive narrative, in the style of Maria Edgeworth's children's textbooks, the story of a boy's visit to relatives and the consequent necessity of learning how to write letters to his family. Many of the elements set out in de Scudéry or More, borrowed with proper credit by Sigourney, paraphrased by Farrar without documentation, are so much a part of the conduct and education literature for women by Farrar's time that sources do not need to be acknowledged. The selfless listener, the faults of conversation to be avoided, and the agreeable as the goal of women's speech—even the precision of grammar and presentation that More inveighs against in the *précieuses*—are the grounds of women's rhetoric, no longer attributable to individuals, but part of the field.

The rhetorical theory of de Scudéry, More, Sigourney, and Farrar, then, centers on conversation (domestic discourse), letter writing, and reading aloud and elocution as parlor entertainment. In order to justify a place for women in the conversation, More, Sigourney, and Farrar promote firmly bounded gender spheres, with women often occupying the role of good listener. Nevertheless, these women did by this means write rhetorical theory, and established a transatlantic rhetoric for women published in conduct literature. Their theory ventures into areas men's theory did not often treat, making art of conversation, and an art not performative but collaborative. Their theory is extremely influential. Jennie Willing's "Talking," a chapter in her WCTU (Women's Christian Temperance Union) handbook for working girls, *The Potential Woman* (1887), for example, is a radical activist revision of women's rhetoric from the conduct literature.

This "women's rhetoric" disappears about 1900, when women were admitted into college. By this time women have won the right to speak publicly in the long activism against slavery, and then in support of women's rights. Once women attend colleges, they also are allowed to write and publish textbooks on speaking and writing. We can still see vestiges of this women's sphere of rhetoric, however, in a textbook like Mary Augusta Jordan's treatise on *Correct Writing and Speaking* (1904). Published in a series called the "Woman's Home Library," Jordan's textbook includes very gendered advice on conversation, letter writing, and conversing with servants, side-by-side with distinctly equal rights advice on composition, correct English, and public speaking (Donawerth "Textbooks").

Works Cited

Bizzell, Patricia. "Opportunities for Feminist Research in the History of Rhetoric." *Rhetoric Review* 11.1 (1992): 50-58.
Bizzell, Patricia, and Bruce Herzberg, eds. *The Rhetorical Tradition: Readings from Classical Times to Present*. Boston: Bedford, 1990.
Donawerth, Jane. "'As Becomes a Rational woman to Speak': Madeleine de Scudéry's Rhetoric of Conversation." Wertheimer 305-19.
—. "Textbooks for New Audiences: Women's Revisions of Rhetorical Theory at the Turn of the Century." Wertheimer 337-56.
—. "Transforming the History of Rhetorical Theory." *Feminist Teacher* 7 (1992): 35-39.
Farrar, Eliza. *The Young Lady's Friend*. 1836. New York: Arno, 1974.
—. *The Youth's Letter-Writer*. New York: H. & S. Raynor, 1840.
Gere, Anne Ruggles. *Intimate Practices: Literacy and Cultural Work in U.S. Women's Clubs, 1880-1920*. Urbana: U of Illinois P, 1994.
Glenn, Cheryl. "sex, lies, and manuscript: Refiguring Aspasia in the History of Rhetoric." *CCC* 45.2 (1994): 180-99.
Jordan, Mary Augusta. *Correct Writing and Speaking*. The Woman's Home Library 6. New York: A. S. Barnes, 1904.
Levine, Carole, and Patricia Sullivan, eds. *Political Rhetoric, Power, and Renaissance Women*. Albany: State U of New York P, 1995.
Lougee, Carolyn. *Le Paradis des Femmes: Women, Salons, and Social Stratification in Seventeenth-Century France*. Princeton: Princeton UP, 1976.
Lunsford, Andrea, ed. *Reclaiming Rhetoric: Women in the Rhetorical Tradition*. Pittsburgh: U of Pittsburgh P, 1995.
More, Hannah. "The Bas Bleu, or, Conversation (1783-86)." *The Works of Hannah More*. Vol. 5. New York: Harper & Brothers, 1855. 359-71. 7 vols.
—. *Strictures on the Modern System of Female Education*. 1799. 2 vols. Philadelphia, 1800.
Scudéry, Madeleine de. *Conversations Nouvelles sur Divers Sujets, Dedie'es Au Roy*. 2 vols. La Haye, 1685.

Sigourney, Lydia. *Letters to My Pupils: With Narrative and Biographical Sketches.* New York: Robert and Carter and Brothers, 1851.
—. *Letters to Young Ladies.* 1833. New York: Harper & Brothers, 1852.
Wertheimer, Molly, ed. *Listening to Their Voices: The Rhetorical Activities of Historical Women.* Columbia: U of South Carolina P, 1997.
Willing, Jennie. *The Potential Woman.* 1881. Boston: McDonald & Gill, 1887.

MELISSA J. FIESTA
University of Arizona

Reconstructing Home in Early Feminist Rhetorics: The Religious Discourses of Protestantism and Transcendentalism as Sites of Production for Sarah Grimké and Margaret Fuller

Surprisingly little work has been done by rhetoricians on Sarah Grimké and Margaret Fuller, considering that these first-wave feminist rhetors published the first widely circulated feminist rhetorics in America (see Bartlett, Conrad, Lerner, and Urbanski).[1] One reason for this oversight may be that Grimké and Fuller used religious discourses as sites of production for their rhetorics.[2] Grimké and Fuller developed the religious discourses of Protestantism and transcendentalism into *Letters on the Equality of the Sexes* and *Woman in the Nineteenth Century*, respectively. Protestantism and transcendentalism offered much more empowering discourses for Grimké and Fuller than the dominant discourses available to them as women in nineteenth-century America. Ironically, the discourses of Protestantism and transcendentalism that have predominantly been associated with men enabled Grimké and Fuller to recover serious rhetorics of women's issues from previous trivializations in the popular press, publishing their views as scholarly texts.

In addition, the rhetorics of Grimké and Fuller substantively differ from the rhetoric of the women's suffrage movement that followed in the late nineteenth century. Unlike the suffragettes, Grimké and Fuller explicitly identified the oppression of women within the home as the source of their oppression in society. Ellen DuBois attributes the failure of the nineteenth-century suffragette movement to a rhetorical strategy that Grimké and Fuller deliberately reject, one that "bypassed women's oppression within the family, or private sphere, and demanded instead her admission to citizenship, and through it admission to the public arena" (63). Through the discourses of Protestantism and transcendentalism, Grimké and Fuller effectively link the roles of women in the private sphere to their roles in the public sphere.

This chapter first briefly outlines the most pervasive commonplaces about women in nineteenth-century America. I then foreground Protestantism and transcendentalism as religious discourses and consider how their distinct conventions affected the rhetorical strategies of Grimké and Fuller independently from one another in order to show how different traditions for feminist rhetoric arose from the separate influences of Protestantism and transcendentalism by the same methodological procedure. I finally will use Grimké and Fuller's texts as examples of how access to these privileged discourses not only helped to create a home for the first wave of feminist rhetoric in America but also enabled Grimké and Fuller to write persuasively about women's oppression in the home, a rhetorical purpose that would not be attempted again by feminists in the first wave of feminism until the Women's Christian Temperance Union (WCTU) in the late nineteenth century (DuBois).

Writing "Home" before Feminist Rhetoric in America

Much has been written to reconstruct the commonplaces associated with True Womanhood, which dominated discourses on women in nineteenth-century America. Historian Barbara Welter first defines the term *True Womanhood* as a woman's demonstration of "four cardinal virtues—piety, purity, submissiveness, and domesticity" through her family identities—"all together ... they spelled mother, daughter, sister, wife—woman" ("True Womanhood" 152). True women were true in the sense that they performed the appropriate roles for women. In historian Nancy C. Cott's words, "'Womanhood' itself summed up the vocation" (99). But women also were presumed to be true in the sense that they were thought to be inherently more virtuous than men (Welter, "Cult of True Womanhood"). For example, in *Letters*, Grimké references this commonplace in her argument for the equality of women, quoting the more conservative Lydia Maria Child (a fellow abolitionist, Quaker, and later women's rights advocate), who pointed out that "'we find a strong tendency to believe that women were in more immediate connection with heaven than men'" (37). Grimké, however, undercuts this commonplace to argue for women's equality: "If there be any truth in this tradition, I am at a loss to imagine in what the superior of man consists" (37). Intending to argue for equality and not supremacy of either sex, Grimké suggests that if women are superior in some ways then men must be superior in other ways.

Grimké's contemporaries, on the other hand, use True Womanhood to legitimize a separate sphere for women that would preserve their sanctity while providing their fathers, brothers, husbands, and sons with sanctuary from "the cruel and competitive world of work and the marketplace" (Bartlett 12). In less euphemistic terms, True Womanhood constituted woman as "the hostage in the home" (Welter, "True Womanhood" 151). As Cott finds, "The contradistinction of home to world had roots in religious motives and rhetoric" (65). But, a paragraph later, Cott leaves behind rhetoric, "The rhetorical origins of the contrast between home and world demand less interpretation than the canon of domesticity built upon it," suggesting that the canon of domesticity existed independently from rhetoric (66). In this chapter, I use Grimké and Fuller to demonstrate an early nineteenth-century awareness that the canon of domesticity did not exist independently from rhetoric. I further contend that the reconnection of home to world also had its roots in religious rhetoric.

Indeed, religious rhetoric constituted and reconstituted True Womanhood. In an 1845 review of Fuller's *Woman*, Charles F. Briggs writes, "The true position of woman is not a disputable point; the universal sentiment of mankind has determined it; God himself has said 'her desire shall be unto her husband, and he shall rule over her'" (qtd. in Myerson, *Critical Essays* 14). Another of Fuller's critics, Orestes A. Brownson goes beyond "the universal sentiment of mankind," leaving even less room for disputing women's proper sphere: "Their appropriate spheres are allotted to man and woman by their Creator, and all they have to do is to submit, as quietly, and with as good a grace, as they can" (qtd. in Myerson, *Critical Essays* 22). Indeed, rhetors who relied on True Womanhood had religious "truth" on their side. Thus, as rhetors of feminism's first generation in America, Grimké and Fuller had the extremely arduous project of demonstrating that True Womanhood relied on rhetoric rather than on religious truth. In producing the first American feminist rhetorics, Grimké and Fuller successfully fulfilled this rhetorical purpose, using the discourses of Protestantism and transcendentalism to reconstitute religious truth into religious belief.

In an 1844 article, Lydia Maria Child identifies a common religious underpinning in Quakerism and transcendentalism that informs the shared rhetorical purpose of Grimké and Fuller: "This idea of an inwardly revealing faculty, *transcending* mere intellectual perception, will naturally remind many of the 'inward voice,' believed in by the Society of Friends" (93). Indeed, significant similarities exist in these first American feminist rhetorics despite their adoption of different religious traditions. Both Grimké and Fuller apply the intuitive and experiential knowledge of women to scriptural and historical sources in order to subvert nineteenth-century commonplaces on women (Conrad; Dickenson). Even more significantly, both Grimké and Fuller turned to respected religious traditions to construct their *ethos*—a claim that I only have time to note here. (I allude to another work-in-progress considering how both used religious commonplaces to establish ethical pisteis for future feminist rhetors in America.)

Protestantism as a Site of Production for Grimké

I chose Protestantism rather than Quakerism as a site of production for Grimké for several key reasons. Grimké was influenced by several different strands of Protestantism, including Episcopalianism, Methodism, and Unitarianism; she chose Quakerism because it allowed for the greatest articulation of her feminist ideas (Lerner). Furthermore, Grimké did not consider herself to be sectarian: "I feel that I have no sectarian views to advance; for although among the Quakers, Methodists, and Christians, women are permitted to preach the glad tidings of peace and salvation, yet I know of no religious body, who entertain the Scripture doctrine of the perfect equality of man and woman, which is the fundamental principle of my argument . . ." (85). And unfortunately, the radical implications of her feminist rhetoric even led to her excommunication from Quakerism (see Birney). Whereas earlier feminists had turned to the Bible for proofs of women's equality—"a prime example of their subversion and transformation of patriarchal doctrine"—Grimké was not aware of her English predecessors Margaret Fell and Mary Astell, among others (Lerner 138, 159, 162).

The thrust of Grimké's argument against True Womanhood originates in biblical support for women's inclusion in the public sphere. She defines her primary task as reconstructing the commonly held biblical beliefs of her audience in order to recast the woman question in new terms through scriptural hermeneutics: "I solely depend on the Bible to designate the sphere of woman, because I believe almost every thing that has been written on this subject, has been the result of a misconception of the simple truths revealed in the Scriptures, in consequence of the false translation of many passages of Holy Writ" (31). She begins with the Protestant premise that each individual has a moral responsibility to interpret the Bible: "I believe it to be the solemn duty of every individual to search the Scriptures for themselves, with the aid of the Holy Spirit, and not be governed by the views of any man, or set of men" (32). Grimké extends this premise to include women not only in her diction "not be governed by the view of any man, or set of men," but also in her symbolic action of putting forth her scriptural interpretation to argue for the equality of women.

A second premise on which Grimké's argument rests is that men have assumed sole responsibility for reading and interpreting the Bible to a mass audience. Grimké proceeds with her counterargument against "the traditions of men" that have misinterpreted the Bible and conveyed their fallacies to women: "I am aware that I have the prejudices of education and custom to combat, both in my own and the other sex, as well as 'the traditions of men,' which are taught for the commandments of God" (85). Well aware of the commonplaces about women—"corrupt public opinion"—that she must subvert, Grimké attempts to demonstrate that King James's translators were prejudiced by their own cultural practices: "[T]hey are the opinions of interested judges, and I have no particular reverence for them, *merely* because they have been regarded with veneration from generation to generation" (81). The translations do not deserve veneration because their spiritual meanings rest on oppressive secular agendas, "opinions based on the false construction of those passages" (81). She also rejects "what seems to me an irresistible conclusion from the literal interpretation of St. Paul, without reference to the context, and the peculiar circumstances and abuses which drew forth the expressions, 'I suffer not a woman to teach'—'Let your woman keep silence in the church,' [I Cor. 14:34]" (97). Implicitly, Grimké questions the *ethos* of the scriptures, both on grounds that the translators and protagonists cannot be read outside of their earthly contexts. If, on the other hand, women had access to the original scriptures as translators of God's will, then more versions of divine truth would be offered: "I am inclined to think, when we are admitted the honor of studying Greek and Hebrew, we shall produce some various readings of the Bible a little different from those we now have" (38).

In Grimké's readings, she finds no religious basis for True Womanhood. In her view, the "traditions of men" have artificially associated certain virtues with women that differ from those associated with men. As a result, women have been prevented from participating "in the sphere which her Creator has assigned her" and women "having been displaced from that sphere has introduced confusion into the world" (38). Grimké places the moral characters of men and women on equal terms, urging women to take responsibility for their own consciences in the public sphere: "I am persuaded woman can do much in this way to elevate her own character. And that we may become duly sensible of the dignity of our nature (103). Challenging another of True Womanhood's misguided commonplaces that women involved with social ills lose their virtuosity, Grimké finds that socially responsible women become "more elevated and refined in her feelings and views" (43). Grimké most pointedly questions the consciences of middle-class women who "would shrink from duty in this exigency, . . . retiring within her own domestic circle":

> Shall woman disregard the situation of thousands of her fellow creatures, who are the victims of intemperance and licentiousness, and retreating to the privacy for her own comfortable home, be satisfied that her whole duty is performed. . . . Shall she, because "her house is her *home*," refuse her sympathy to the down trodden slave, to the poor unhappy outcasts who are deprived of those blessings which she so highly prizes? (53)

And Grimké later asks, "Can any American woman look at these scenes of shocking licentiousness and cruelty, and fold her hands in apathy and say, 'I have nothing to do with slavery'?" (61). To which Grimké responds on behalf of middle-class women: "*She cannot and be guiltless*" (61). Thus, Grimké revises the commonplaces associated with womanhood, finally arguing that religious women cannot separate themselves from the public sphere in good conscience.

Transcendentalism as a Site of Production for Fuller

Like Protestantism in Germany, transcendentalism in the United States arose in response to religious debate. Also a byproduct of Germany, transcendental philosophy originated with German philosopher Immanuel Kant's 1781

Critique of Pure Reason, but Americans imported and changed Kant's philosophy to address a particular rhetorical situation in New England religious and intellectual circles. As the last Fuller biographer to know both the movement and Fuller personally found, "The intellectual and spiritual excitement, popularly called 'Transcendentalism,' had at least one merit, that, whatever else it was, it was indigenous" (Higginson 130). Thus, transcendentalism more immediately grew out of Unitarianism. The discourse of Unitarianism, which emphasized "the primacy of reason in the interpretation of the Scriptures; "the unity and moral perfection" of God; and "the spiritual leadership" of Jesus, found its most powerful voice in William Ellery Channing and surrounded Margaret Fuller, first as a child in her father's home and later as a lifelong friend to men who studied at Harvard to become Unitarian ministers—William Henry Channing, James Freeman Clarke, Ralph Waldo Emerson (Von Mehren 39). Transcendentalism principally departed from Unitarianism in its emphasis on intuitive understanding as a means of interpretation, "the unity and moral perfection" of humankind, and "the spiritual leadership" of each individual (Von Mehren 39). Simply put, transcendentalists reassigned what had been deemed God's province to mankind. This premise in itself caused conservative religious critics to charge transcendentalists with blasphemy even before Fuller extended this province to womankind.

Anne C. Rose refers to the transcendentalists as "the philosophers of evangelical Unitarianism who stopped to consider the intellectual issues raised by the movement itself" (38). Considering the intellectual issues raised by the movement itself eventually led next-generation Unitarian ministers like Emerson to move far enough away from sanctioned tenets to be considered transcendental. In his scandalous "Divinity School Address" delivered in 1838 to a senior class at his alma mater Harvard, Emerson reveals his antipathy toward his Unitarian ministerial training and practices: "Meantime, whilst the doors of the temple stand open, night and day, before every man, and the oracles of truth cease never, it is guarded by one stern condition; this, namely; it is an intuition. It cannot be received at second hand. Truly speaking, it is not instruction, but provocation, that I can receive from another soul" (127). Emerson criticizes Unitarian preaching primarily on the grounds that ministers impede the intuitive and passionate spirituality of individuals by attempting to speak for God and to persuade parishioners on the basis of past miracles. Furthermore, Emerson implicitly castigates the elitism of Unitarianism as an undemocratic religion, which tells individuals not only what to think but also what to believe. Emerson seeks a religious society firmly rooted in the beliefs of individuals and urges these future ministers "to go alone; to refuse the good models, even those which are sacred in the imagination of men, and dare to love God without mediator or veil" (145).

Much important scholarship has already been done considering how transcendentalism as a social, intellectual, and literary movement impacted Fuller (e.g., Conrad; Douglas; Rose; Urbanski's *Margaret Fuller's Woman*). Significantly, this existing scholarship does not treat transcendentalism as a religious movement that directly impacted Fuller.³ Ironically, most of the transcendentalists themselves reinforced the commonplace associated with True Womanhood that women "represented the highest and best parts of man" (Welter, *Dimity Convictions* 95). To my knowledge, no one has yet noted that Fuller uses the religious tenets of transcendentalism to challenge the commonplaces of True Womanhood, so I will begin to establish this claim here.

It even disappointed Fuller that only one of her contemporary reviewers, Charles Lane, responded to the religious tenor of *Woman* (Von Mehren 197). In the same year of *Woman*'s publication, Fuller reviewed *The Narrative of the Life of Frederick Douglass, an American Slave* for her column in *The New York Tribune*. Steven Mailloux finds that Fuller's focus on "'the subject of Religion'" is not a misreading of Douglass but rather a carefully crafted rhetorical response to the Bible politics associated with abolition in 1845 (17). Fuller also conceived of transcendentalism not only as intellectual and social movement but also as a religious and political movement. At the age of twenty-one during a time in her life when she shared most of her intellectual and religious insights with Unitarian minister-in-training William Henry Channing, Fuller experienced a religious awakening that greatly influenced how transcendentalism came to her and how she used its religious matter for her own rhetorical purposes in *Woman*. Like Emerson, Fuller reacted against Unitarianism preaching in her most thorough religious disclosure written in a letter almost seven years, October 21, 1838, after the occurrence she describes here:

> It was Thanksgiving day, (Nov., 1831), and I was obliged to go to church, or exceedingly displease my father. I almost always suffered much in church from a feeling of disunion with the hearers and dissent from the preacher; but to-day, more than ever before, the service jarred upon me from their grateful and joyful tone. I was wearied out with mental conflicts, and in a mood of most childish, child-like sadness. I felt within myself great power, and generosity, and tenderness; but it seemed to me as if they were all unrecognized, and as if it were impossible that they should be used in life.... But when I could bear myself no longer, I walked many hours, till the anguish was wearied out, and I returned in a state of prayer.... I saw how long it must be before the soul can learn to act under [earthly] limitations of time and space, and human nature; but I saw, also that it MUST do it,—and that it must make all this false true,—and sow new and immortal plants in the garden of God, before it could return again. I saw there was no self; that selfishness was all folly, and the result of circumstance; that it was only because I thought self real that I suffered; that I had only to

live in the idea of the ALL. . . . I was for that hour taken up into God. In that true ray most of the relations of earth seemed mere films, phenomena. (qtd. in Emerson et al. 139-41)

Because of her transcendental religious beliefs, Fuller particularly concerns herself with the problem of selfishness on the part of both women and men in *Woman*: "[T]he growth of the individual, is continually obstructing the holy work that is to make the earth a part of heaven" (3). Unlike Emerson, who champions self-reliance and human perfection, Fuller seeks to balance self-reliance with interdependence and spiritual harmony on earth (112).

Fuller also uses her transcendental religious beliefs to conceive of "the garden of God" from where the soul originates and to where the soul returns as "home": "What woman needs is not as a woman to act or rule, but as a nature to grow, as an intellect to discern, as a soul to live freely and unimpeded, to unfold such powers as were given her when we left our common home" (20). Thus, she extends the province of home not only into the public sphere (as Grimké does before her) but also into the spiritual realm. Further, Fuller's association of "our common home" with the domestic sphere also transcends True Womanhood's premise that women inhabit a naturally more virtuous space, because women are no more likely to be spiritual than men. Rather, also like Grimké, Fuller puts women and men on equal terms: It is "our common home." When women and men "left our common home," they left with the same "powers" to further develop—"a nature," "an intellect," and "a soul." As Fuller suggests, then, earthly commonplaces, such as those associated with True Womanhood, prevent both women and men from realizing spiritual homes on earth. To realize their spiritual homes on earth, the "arbitrary barrier" between home and world must be removed (20). In Fuller's words, "Such divisions are only important when they are never to be transcended" (50). She finally transcends the commonplaces associated with True Womanhood by claiming an "infinite scope" for not only the home but also women and men who reside in the home (61).

Writing "Home" after Feminist Rhetoric in America

Cott suggests that women "cross[ed] the boundaries from 'woman's sphere' to 'woman's rights'" most often as a "variation on or escape from the containment of conventional evangelical Protestantism—whether through Quakerism, Unitarianism," and other sects (204). But historians have not considered how the first American feminists reconnected the woman's sphere to woman's rights through rhetoric. As I have briefly outlined here, Grimké and Fuller reconstituted the commonplaces about home through religious rhetoric that extended the private sphere into the public sphere. Implicitly, these first feminist rhetors also reconstituted religious "truth" into religious belief that ultimately depended on an individual's conscience in communion with social reform.

Notes

1. The most notable publications considering Grimké as a significant first-wave feminist rhetor are Karlyn Kohrs Campbell's *Man Cannot Speak for Her* (1989) and "The Sound of Women's Voices" (1989). The most notable publications considering Fuller as a significant first-wave feminist rhetor are Kolodny's work recovering Whately as a rhetorical source for Fuller's *Woman* and Rouse's work with Fuller's public discourse as a site for rhetorical scholarship.

2. Similarly, Mattingly finds that rhetoricians have overlooked the contributions of WCTU members to first-wave feminist rhetoric as a result of the "temperance women's religious/evangelical associations" (58).

3. Habich and Myerson touch on the impact of transcendentalism as a religious movement on Fuller in relation to the Unitarian and transcendental journals—*The Western Messenger* and *The Dial*, respectively.

Works Cited

Bartlett, Elizabeth Ann. Introduction. *Letters on the Equality of the Sexes*. New Haven: Yale UP, 1988. 1-29.
Birney, Catherine H. 1885. *Sarah and Angelina Grimké: The First American Women Advocates of Abolition and Woman's Rights*. St. Clair Shores, MI: Scholarly, 1970.
Campbell, Karlyn Kohrs. *A Critical Study of Early Feminist Rhetoric*. Westport, CT: Greenwood, 1989. Vol. 1 of *Man Cannot Speak for Her*. 2 vols.
—. "The Sound of Women's Voices." *Quarterly Journal of Speech* 75 (1989): 212-58.
Child, Lydia Maria. "Transcendentalism." 1844. *Critical Essays on American Transcendentalism*. Ed. Gura Myerson. Boston: G. K. Hall, 1982. 92-95.
Conrad, Susan Phinney. *Perish the Thought: Intellectual Women in Romantic America, 1830-1860*. New York: Oxford UP, 1976.
Cott, Nancy F. *The Bonds of Womanhood: "Woman's Sphere" in New England, 1780-1835*. New Haven: Yale UP, 1977.
Dickenson, Donna. *Margaret Fuller: Writing a Woman's Life*. London: Macmillan, 1993.
Douglas, Ann C. *The Feminization of American Culture*. New York: Knopf, 1977.
DuBois, Ellen. "The Radicalism of the Woman Suffrage Movement: Notes Toward the Reconstruction of Nineteenth Century Feminism." *Feminist Studies* 3 (1975): 63-71.
Emerson, Ralph Waldo. "Divinity School Address." 1838. *Nature: Addresses and Lectures*. Boston: Houghton Mifflin, 1902. 117-52.
Emerson, Ralph Waldo, James Freeman Clarke, and William Henry Channing. *Memoirs of Margaret Fuller Ossoli*. Vol. 1. Boston: Phillips, Samson, 1852.
Fuller, Margaret. *Woman in the Nineteenth Century*. 1845. Ed. Donna Dickenson. New York: Oxford UP, 1994.
Grimké, Sarah. *Letters on the Equality of the Sexes*. 1838. Ed. Elizabeth Ann Bartlett. New Haven: Yale UP, 1988.
Habich, Robert D. *Transcendentalism and the Western Messenger: A History of the Magazine and Its Contributors, 1835-1841*. Rutherford, NJ: Fairleigh Dickinson UP, 1985.
Higginson, Thomas Wentworth. *Margaret Fuller Ossoli*. Boston: Houghton Mifflin, 1884.
Kolodny, Annette. "Inventing a Feminist Discourse: Rhetoric and Resistance in Margaret Fuller's *Woman in the Nineteenth Century*." *Reclaiming Rhetorica: Women in the Rhetorical Tradition*. Ed. Andrea A. Lunsford. Pittsburgh: U of Pittsburgh P, 1995. 137-66.
Lerner, Gerda. *The Creation of Feminist Consciousness*. New York: Oxford UP, 1993.

Mailloux, Stephen. "Misreading as a Historical Act: Cultural Rhetoric, Bible Politics, and Fuller's 1845 Review of Douglass's *Narrative*." *Readers in History: Nineteenth-Century American Literature and the Contexts of Response*. Ed. James L. Machor. Baltimore: Johns Hopkins UP, 1993. 3-31.

Mattingly, Carol. "Woman-Tempered Rhetoric: Public Presentation and the WCTU." *Rhetoric Review* 14 (1995): 44-61.

Myerson, Joel, ed. *Critical Essays on Margaret Fuller*. Boston: G. K. Hall, 1980.

—. *The New England Transcendentalists and the Dial*. Cranbury, NJ: Associated UP, 1980.

Rose, Anne C. *Transcendentalism as a Social Movement, 1830-1850*. New Haven: Yale UP, 1981.

Rouse, P. Joy. "Margaret Fuller: A Rhetoric of Citizenship in Nineteenth-Century America." *Oratorical Culture in Nineteenth-Century America*. Ed. Gregory Clark and S. Michael Halloran. Carbondale: Southern Illinois UP, 1993. 110-36.

Urbanski, Marie O. *Margaret Fuller's Woman in the Nineteenth Century: A Literary Study of Form and Content, of Sources and Influence*. Westport, CT: Greenwood, 1980.

—. "Margaret Fuller's *Woman in the Nineteenth Century*: The Feminist Manifesto." *Nineteenth-Century Women Writers of the English-Speaking World*. Ed. Rhoda B. Nathan. Westport, CT: Greenwood, 1986. 201-07.

Von Mehren, Joan. *Minerva and the Muse: A Life of Margaret Fuller*. Amherst: U of Massachusetts P, 1994.

Welter, Barbara. "The Cult of True Womanhood: 1820-1860." *American Quarterly* 18 (1966): 151-74.

—. *Dimity Convictions: The American Woman in the Nineteenth Century*. Athens: Ohio UP, 1976.

Part III

Rhetoric Tech: Defining Rhetorics in Modern Media and Electronic Discourses

SUSAN GIESEMANN NORTH
University of Tennessee, Knoxville

Are the Barbarians of Technology Knocking at the Gate? Vico and Scientism in Twentieth-Century Culture

Imagine a dark, decaying city in which you encounter a woman so desiccated and apathetic she cannot summon the energy to brush an insect from her cheek. Now, cut to an image of a two-story white house in a pastoral setting. The birds are singing. The sun is shining. God seems to be in his heaven and all's right with the world. These scenes are not part of a grim, postapocalyptic science fiction film but are from a recent television commercial touting the benefits of a certain brand of home computer. If you buy this computer, then one assumes that you can do all your work at home and avoid personal interaction with the denizens of that dreadful city. A consistent theme of the computer age seems to celebrate an ability to communicate with each other from a distance, even to the extent that we isolate ourselves and avoid all human contact. As students of rhetoric, we should be asking the following question: Have we created the new communications technology in order to contact and keep in touch with people who are very distant from us, or has the new communications technology developed in response to an increasing desire to keep our distance from one another? In other words, to mix some of President Clinton's favorite metaphors, is the information superhighway a bridge or a moat?

In his introduction to Giambattista Vico's *On the Study Methods of Our Time*, Elio Gianturco describes our twentieth-century world as "a Cartesian world, a world of scientific research, technology, and gadgets, which invade and condition our lives" (xxi). Gianturco has chosen his words carefully. He does not see scientific progress as an unmitigated good, but suggests that it has come at the expense of similar progress in the humanities. He uses the conflict between scientism and humanism, which he traces to the Enlightenment Quarrel of the Ancients and Moderns, as the context for his discussion of Vico's discourse. Vico, an eighteenth-century professor of rhetoric at the University of Naples, was tremendously concerned about how an emphasis on scientific studies would affect human society. Writing in 1729 to Francesco Saverio Estevan, Vico lamented the effects of Cartesian metaphysics, which he believed led to a solipsistic skepticism that puts "in doubt the truth that unites men, disposes them to follow their own sense [*senso propio*] . . . and thus recalls them from civil community to the state of solitude . . . of huge fierce [animals] which live scattered and alone in their dens and lairs" (qtd. in Mooney 101). This quotation may seem eerily to predict the alienation of a postmodern technological world in which the quarrel between the Ancients and Moderns, or between scientism and humanism, continues to thrive. On the one hand are theoretical scientists who believe, with all the fervor of the deeply religious, that rigorous research will ultimately unlock the secrets of the universe. On the other hand, the neo-Luddite perspective suggests that the technological fruits of positivist science are inherently destructive to human existence. We can gain a sense of how our society values these different perspectives if we consider that the individuals with whom we identify the scientistic and neo-Luddite positions are, respectively, Stephen Hawking and Unabomber Theodore Kaczynski. What has been lost in the centuries between the early modern era and our own is a rhetorical sensibility that would allow us to negotiate between these positions. This chapter employs Vico's critique of the Cartesian paradigm as a context for examining the popular discourse about twentieth-century technology. I want to examine, not only instances of popular rhetoric that echo the Cartesian and anti-Cartesian positions, but others indicating that it is possible to negotiate between these extreme views.

It is important to begin with a clear understanding of the nature of Vico's quarrel with Cartesianism, because it is not Descartes' method per se that he found objectionable. Rather, he was opposed to the reduction of education to training in "philosophical criticism" (Vico's term for the Cartesian method) at the expense of rhetoric. One of the clearest statements of Vico's views on Cartesian skepticism is found in his *De nostri temporis studiorum ratione* (*On the Study Methods of Our Time*). *De nostri* was published in 1709 as an expanded version of Vico's inaugural oration solemnizing the opening of the 1708 school year at the University of Naples, and is the only one of his annual inaugural orations deemed worthy of publication during his lifetime. In *De nostri*, Vico undertakes what is ostensibly a comparison of the state of learning in ancient and contemporary times, but might accurately be described as a critique of contemporary pedagogical practices, particularly those of the Port Royal logicians (Vico 17-20). The gist of Vico's long and complex argument is that limiting instruction to philosophical criticism failed to prepare young students for the "incertitude" of which "nature and life are full" or to equip them for their roles in society (15). Vico's objections to philosophical criticism were both teleological and ontological. The final purpose of philosophical criticism, as Vico saw it, was "to cleanse its fundamental truths not only of all falsity, but also of the mere suspicion of error, plac[ing] on the same plane of falsity not only false thinking, but also those secondary verities and ideas which are based on probability alone" (13). But for Vico such a goal was insufficient, because he felt the discovery of "truth" should be only one step toward the real aim of any art: right action. He says, "[T]he foremost, indeed, the only aim of our 'arts' is to assure us that we have acted rightly" (15). Knowledge, then, is meaningless unless it leads to right action.

If Vico saw the aim of philosophical criticism as flawed, then he was even more seriously concerned about the ontological limitations resulting from this inadequate purpose. The ultimate danger of Cartesian skepticism was that it failed to equip students to take their places within the human community. Vico suggests that philosophical criticism led to "excessive attention" to physical phenomena "because their nature seems unambiguous" (33). The cost of this limited focus was a failure to "inquire into human nature which, because of the freedom of man's will, is difficult to determine" (33). The result is that "our young men . . . are unable to engage in the life of the community, to conduct themselves with sufficient wisdom and prudence" (33). It is the concern with abstract concepts at the expense of "prudential behavior in life" (34) that leads Vico to conclude in his letter to Estevan that "the reflective wisdom of the educated, which is supposed to guide the vulgar wisdom of the masses, gives them instead the cruelest shove so that they rush headlong forward and perish" (qtd. in Mooney 101). This vision of a headlong rush to destruction recalls Vico's cyclical view of human history and we might suspect that he sees Cartesian solipsism as the instrument by which humankind will be pushed from the ultimate phase of the historical cycle back to its barbaric beginnings.

The purpose here is not to cast Vico as some sort of rhetorical Nostradamus, or to argue over whether his predictions of doom are about to come true. We may or may not believe that we are now living in the last days of the technological era. As we approach the eve of the new millennium, we are increasingly invited to speculate on the possibility. Rather, my goal is to suggest that the humanistic and scientistic positions held by Vico and the Cartesians, respectively, are still current at the end of the twentieth century and can be discovered in the rhetoric of popular culture. To that end, the rest of this chapter examines some examples of that popular culture in advertising campaigns and the literature of science fiction.

There is little argument that Gianturco is right in his assertion that we live in a Cartesian world. And if we accept Vico's argument that an emphasis on philosophical criticism leads to solipsism, then it seems not too great a step to consider the contemporary cult of the individual as evidence of such solipsism. Apple Computer company's recent successful advertising campaign is a case in point. This campaign features very simple print ads that consist primarily of a full-page photograph of a famous individual known for taking a different path. Among these individuals, who represent both sciences and the arts, are Albert Einstein, Amelia Earhart, and Bob Dylan. Superimposed on the photograph is the slogan, "Think different." Grammatical considerations aside, the logical construct behind this advertising slogan seems to be that if you are a unique individual who thinks differently from the crowd, you will buy an Apple computer. Or, if you want to be the sort of individual who "thinks different," then using an Apple computer will help you accomplish this goal. Because this company has recently shown a profit for the first time in several quarters, we might surmise that this campaign has been successful. We can speculate that the ads are successful because they tap into commonly held cultural values about individuality and creativity, and because they exploit the *ethos* of widely recognized cultural icons in its appeal. But consider the logical implications of this thinking "different." If all Apple users truly do "think different," and if the machine enhances that difference, then what will serve to facilitate communication, cooperation, or a sense of community between and among all these differently thinking individuals? Thus, when carried to its logical extreme, this advertising campaign seems to represent the kind of Cartesian solipsism that Vico describes.

Not all visions of our contemporary cultural world are so positive as the one in the Apple computer ads. In his novel *Virtual Light*, science fiction writer William Gibson gives us a vision of a world that most closely conforms to that predicted by Vico. The novel is set in San Francisco in the year 2005. The world of Gibson's fiction is a dystopian, technological nightmare filled with pollution, violence, and disease. The technological wonders of the culture are more than offset by the hazards of postmodern life. In this novel, the mainstream society is in a state of decay, divided between the rich and the poor, old and young, men and women, the sacred and the profane. It is an out-of-control world run by multinational corporations where virtual reality beats the real thing any day of the week. What is most striking about this world is the almost universal lack of any real human contact or sense of community. Gibson has vividly symbolized postmodern technological alienation in his use of the automobile. The novel opens in a car wash where we meet Rydell, an ex-cop with an uncomplicated sense of ethics and a propensity for trouble. Though Rydell is on a downward career spiral from cop to private security guard to man on the run, he remains a valuable commodity because of his skill at handling automotive technology's answer to the crime problem: a totally enclosed vehicle in which the driver can see what is outside only through a system of closed circuit cameras. Gibson evokes several recurrent themes of the postmodern era. The first is the notion of the automobile as a symbol of technological isolation. The second is the idea that increasingly complex technology leads to greater degrees of specialization and corresponding fragmentation. Finally, Rydell's situation powerfully dramatizes the subjugation of human to machine in an increasingly automated culture.

The only community of any significance in this fractured and dangerous society is called "The Bridge," which consists of a group of makeshift dwellings perched on the towers and cables of San Francisco's Golden Gate Bridge. This community is inhabited by misfits, people whom the rest of the society describe, at best, as homeless, and at worst, as "anarchists, antichrists, cannibal[s]" (165). But the view the mainstream society has of the Bridge is at odds with Gibson's description of what goes on there, because it is in the community of the Bridge that people watch out for each other, help each other, and bear each other's burdens.

Gibson seems to sum up his ideas about postmodern culture in one of the few lyrical passages in the book. It is a description of the Bridge from the perspective of Yamazaki, a Japanese graduate student in sociology who is writing a dissertation on the social phenomenon of the Bridge. He has just heard from Skinner, one of the original "settlers," the story of how the Bridge came to be appropriated by the homeless and destitute. He sees the Bridge through new eyes:

> Yamazaki rode Skinner's lift down to where stairs began.... All around him, now, the rattle of an evening's commerce, and from a darkened doorway came the slap of cards, a woman's laughter, voices raised in Spanish.... Boys in ragged leather crouched above a game whose counters were painted pebbles.
>
> Yamazaki stopped.... Skinner's story seemed to radiate out ... like concentric rings of sound from some secret bell, pitched too low for the foreign, wishful ear.
>
> *We are come not only past the century's closing,* he thought, *the millennium's turning, but to the end of something else? Era? Paradigm? Everywhere, the signs of closure.*
>
> Modernity was ending.
>
> Here on the bridge, it long since had. (105; emphasis in original)

In this passage, which is as clear a statement as any of the themes of the novel, Gibson seems to echo Vico's notions about the incompatibility of modernity and community and to show us a vision of what the world might be like once the Vichian cycle has been completed and our complex society returns to barbarism.

Finally, I want to examine another television advertisement that seems to represent a more realistic view of both the possibilities and problems of the communications technology. This commercial, advertising IBM's Lotus Notes computer software, is a brief vignette of an interaction between a corporate executive and the computer technician who has just installed the software on the executive's laptop computer. Hanging on the wall behind them are a series of photographs of the executive with various world leaders and other important individuals. Unimpressed, the computer technician explains that this new software will allow the executive to communicate much more efficiently with people all over the world and will eliminate the need for so much travel. He says, "I guess we'll be seeing a lot more of you around here." The final image is of the executive alone with his photographs and his laptop computer, seemingly uncertain about what to make of this new development. This advertisement very tidily sums up the dilemma of the information age. The executive is presented with the opportunity to swap personal interaction with a worldwide community for personal interaction with the home community of his business. He must make a choice between one or the other. This advertisement lacks the unmitigated optimism of the Apple ad and the grim pessimism of Gibson. Rather, it seems to recognize the potential for both good and ill from the technological revolution, although it offers no guidance about how to insure either outcome.

In 1993, Howard Rheingold popularized the term "virtual community" in a book by that name. He describes the history of his participation in the electronic community that has come to call itself "the WELL," an acronym for Whole Earth 'Lectronic Link:

> It became clear to me during the first few months . . . that I was participating in the self-design of a new kind of culture. I watched the community's social contracts stretch and change as the people who discovered and started building the WELL in its first year or two were joined by so many others. Norms were established, challenged, changed, reestablished, rechallenged, in a kind of speeded-up social evolution. (2)

Rheingold celebrates the many ways in which the new communications technology can benefit millions of ordinary citizens, but he is not unaware of the potential for problems with this new technology. He says, "Virtual communities could help citizens revitalize democracy, or they could be luring us into an attractively packaged substitute for democratic discourse" (276). He recognizes that the technology is ripe for abuse by the politically powerful, that censorship is a real danger, and that the technology can easily be commodified. Nevertheless, Rheingold believes that "this technology, if properly understood and defended by enough citizens, does have democratizing potential in the way that alphabets and printing presses had democratizing potential" (279). Thus, it is not the technology itself, but the use to which the technology is put that is at issue for Rheingold.

Like Vico, Rheingold reminds us that knowledge, or a technology, is not an end in itself. The use of that technology to benefit society is the ultimate goal. He suggests that we pay attention to what historians and social scientists have to tell us about previous technological revolutions in order to insure reaching this goal:

> [I]t's best to continue to listen to those who understand the limits, even as we continue to explore technologies' positive capabilities ... actively questioning and examining social assumptions about the effects of new technologies, reminding ourselves that electronic communication has powerful illusory capabilities.... Armed with knowledge, guided by a clear, human-centered vision, governed by a commitment to civil discourse, we the citizens hold the key levers at a pivotal time. What happens next is largely up to us. (300)

Rheingold's call for community action in determining the future of the new technology echoes Vico's description of a pedagogy that offers more than philosophical criticism.

> [Y]oung men [sic] should be taught the totality of sciences and arts, and their intellectual powers should be developed to the full.... Were this done, young students, I think, would become exact in science, clever in practical matters, fluent in eloquence, imaginative in understanding poetry or painting, and strong in memorizing what they have learned in their legal studies. (19)

For Vico, the way to prolong the golden days of Renaissance humanism and keep the barbarians from the gate was not to replace the traditional, rhetoric-based pedagogy, but to expand it to include the Cartesian method. Vico's notion of rhetoric offers the means by which to discover "right action" to preserve a human community in the unexplored terrain of the new technological world.

Works Cited

Gianturco, Elio. "Translator's Introduction." *On the Study Methods of Our Time*. By Giambattista Vico. Ed. Donald Philip Verene. Ithaca: Cornell UP, 1990.

Gibson, William. *Virtual Light*. New York: Bantam-Spectra, 1994.

Mooney, Michael. *Vico in the Tradition of Rhetoric*. Davis: Hermagoras, 1994.

Rheingold, Howard. *The Virtual Community: Homesteading on the Electronic Frontier*. Reading: Addison-Wesley, 1993.

Vico, Giambattista. *On the Study Methods of Our Time*. Trans. Elio Gianturco. Ed. Donald Philip Verene. Ithaca: Cornell UP, 1990.

S. MICHAEL HALLORAN AND GREGORY CLARK
Rensselaer Polytechnic Institute and Brigham Young University

It's a Great Place to Visit, but I Wouldn't Want to Live There: Virtual American Landscapes of the Nineteenth Century

As the United States was busily engaged in transforming itself from an agrarian republic into an urban and eventually metropolitan nation, improved technologies of inscription (e.g., steel engraving, lithography, steam-driven printing presses) made possible the production and wide dissemination of elaborate landscape representations that anticipate more recent developments in electronic media. Most typically, landscape paintings and prints of the nineteenth century portrayed the sublime wilderness or the pastoral countryside, suggesting that this was the true America, and attributing moral and political significance to the act of gazing on such scenes. *The Home Book of the Picturesque*, for example, makes this claim explicit in its introduction: "To our mind, this book on American Scenery has an import of the highest order. The diversified landscapes of our country exert no slight influence in creating our character as individuals, and in confirming our destiny as a nation" (Deakin 3). Problematically, such representations address an audience for whom the idealized wilderness and idyllic pastoral countryside exist only as places to visit—and virtual rather than actual places at that. That is, these scenes of American culture that so intensely engage the moral citizenship of the viewer depict places where the people who view them do not (and for the most part, cannot) actually live.

This chapter argues that such nineteenth-century visual representations of the American landscape are important instances of civic discourse in the early United States. Our focus is to theorize the process that enabled visual representations of the American landscape to shape emerging notions of national identity. Specifically, we suggest that these nineteenth-century landscape representations functioned rhetorically by casting the people who receive and contemplate them in the role of a typified American perceiver whose way of seeing becomes an idealized and normative way of national being. In other words, these aesthetized images of America prompted Americans who read and viewed them to identify themselves with the values and attitudes presented there. Such landscapes thus function as instances of civic discourse, but in ways that exemplify what Kenneth Burke called a "new" rather than an "old" rhetoric ("Rhetoric—Old and New")—using the essentially aesthetic appeal of identification to prompt people to "make themselves over in the image of the imagery" (*Philosophy of Literary Form* 281) presented them. We will illustrate this rhetorical process with examples of visual landscape representation in different media that appeal to different audiences and in this way bring into focus some issues that divided nineteenth-century Americans as they attempted to unite themselves.

I

Among the best-known visual representations of the landscape that survive from nineteenth-century America are the paintings of the so-called Hudson River School. Artists such as Frederick Church, Jasper Cropsey, and Asher Durand worked in the medium of oil paint on canvas, producing objects whose value lies partly in their extreme rarity. They are unique objects, though in the case of Thomas Cole's *Voyage of Life* series there are two virtually identical sets of the four canvas series. Cole chose to paint a duplicate of the series when the patron owner of the original set died and his heirs considered selling the individual paintings separately. The narrative told in the series (a moral allegory representing infancy, childhood, manhood, and old age as the voyage of a lone individual down a river from its source to its outlet at the ocean of eternity) was of sufficient importance to Cole that he chose to duplicate the entire series at his own personal expense rather than allow the story to be erased through the separation of the four panels.

There are, then, two distinguishable kinds of value located in the painted images: their commodity value, which was no doubt diminished significantly by Cole's production of a duplicate set; and their moral value as the representation of a socially significant narrative. Commodity value gives any painting, like any other rare object, the potential to mark an individual's status in the socioeconomic hierarchy. To possess and display an oil painting in one's home is to signify one's standing as a member of the elite. In doing so, however, such a commodity value may limit the reach of the image's moral value. If the painting serves as a status marker in a private residence, then its narrative will be told only to those few who are privileged to inhabit or to visit in that residence. Some recognition of this paradox was probably at work in Cole's decision to duplicate the *Voyage of Life* series. He depended for his living on the commodity value of his paintings, but was also deeply invested in their moral value and wanted to make it publicly available. And so when it seemed that the moral value of the *Voyage of Life* was to be not only privatized but largely vitiated by the breakup of the series, he set about producing a duplicate set whose commodity value he must have known would be seriously diminished by the fact that they were duplicates.

Like some other paintings of the Hudson River School artists, Cole's *Voyage of Life* series was eventually duplicated more widely by the process of steel engraving. The sets of prints of the series produced by this process obviously had considerably less commodity value than the original oil paintings, and for that very reason the technology extended the reach of their moral value. The same narrative that Cole created to adorn the residence and edify the soul of a wealthy patron could now hang in the more modest homes of hundreds of middle-class Americans. Still, the process by which the steel-engraved prints were produced was a carefully supervised one that preserved much of the detail in the originals, and the prints as a consequence were significantly more expensive than the lithographic prints that were produced by the thousands by Currier and Ives and other firms, though far less expensive than oil paintings.

What we are suggesting here is a continuum of processes for the production and reproduction of visual images in the nineteenth century, from the making of unique objects of high commodity value at one end of the scale, to the mass production of objects of low commodity value at the other end. The nineteenth-century audiences for these images ranged similarly from the socioeconomic elite who could buy oil paintings to the middle and lower classes to whom Currier and Ives marketed their lithographic prints. These mass-produced, mass-audience prints were often reproductions, more or less faithful, of paintings originally made for the elite. There are, for example, Currier and Ives prints of John Trumbull's paintings of *The Battle of Bunker Hill* and *The Signing of the Declaration of Independence*, although these lithographic reproductions have nowhere near the degree of detail that can be found in the steel engraved reproductions of those same paintings, of Cole's *Voyage of Life* series, or of Frederick Church's *The Heart of the Andes*. There are also Currier and Ives prints that emulate, in a more general way, the thematics and style of Hudson River School paintings of wilderness and pastoral scenes. The rhetorical function of these mass reproduced images was to extend the moral reach of the original painted images. Engraved and lithographed prints made available to a mass audience the edifying narratives told originally by painters such as Trumbull and Cole to their elite patrons. In so doing, the prints helped to create a sense of national identity that could be shared across at least some of the boundaries of social class.

Importantly, these mass-produced reproductions of the paintings were by no means exact. Subtle but crucially important shifts of content can be observed as we move from one end of the continuum to the other: from the one-of-a-kind images made by Trumbull, Cole, and others for the socioeconomic elite to the mass-produced prints marketed by Currier and Ives to the middle and lower classes. Apart from the obvious contrasts in finish and detail, the most noticeable difference has to do with the relative scale and prominence of humans and human artifacts on the one hand and the works of nature on the other. Hudson River School paintings tend to focus primarily on the landscape itself, and when people and objects made by people appear in them, they are typically dwarfed by sky, trees, hills, bodies of water, and other natural phenomena. Engraved reproductions of paintings by Hudson River School artists tend to remain absolutely faithful to the composition, and hence to the scale, of the originals. However, those Currier and Ives prints that are thematically related to Hudson River School art tend to focus more heavily on people and their artifacts rather than on the landscape itself. We will return to this contrast later.

II

In the first retrospective history of the six-decade career of Currier and Ives, Russel Crouse, writing in 1930, introduced them as "romanticists" who "supplemented the gaunt and annoyingly accurate chronicles of the historians with a vision less constrained" (1): one that attempted to document the collective experience of the majority of the people who lived in the nineteenth-century United States—at least those whose racial and cultural ancestry is European.[1] Their images, in other words, attempted to identify the collective vision of what they identified as the cultural mainstream. Hundreds of different images were mass-produced and mass-marketed throughout the country and even in Europe. And Crouse makes the undocumented claim that "in the middle of the Nineteenth Century almost every American home had at least one of their pictures" (3). It is undocumented, but probably more valid than not. This is why the first major collector of their prints, Harry T. Peters, could title the first book that reproduced a significant number of them, *Currier and Ives: Printmakers to the American People*. Interestingly, on the sign that hung over the door of their Manhattan store, Currier and Ives identified themselves as "Engravers for the People." This often-reproduced sign is a misnomer, as Peters's alteration of it in his book's title seems to recognize. Currier and Ives were not engravers but lithographers. Perhaps they were attempting to claim for their products some of the prestige of the more established, expensive, and technically exacting medium of engraving. If so, the title "Engravers for the People" can be read as an oxymoron reflecting a deep ambivalence about class status that was then and remains now a part of the American ethos. In that single phrase, Currier and Ives manage to both claim and repudiate their proletarian orientation. They are "for the people," but they will not admit to being humble lithographers.

Currier and Ives was, despite any pretensions we might find in their self-descriptive sign, an aggressively commercial enterprise. Their explicit goal was to keep the commodity value of their product low in order to maximize sales volume. The prints they produced were those projected to sell well: those that did were continued indefinitely and those that did not were discontinued and the stones from which they were printed were ground down and reused for other prints. Their moral value was linked intimately to their commodity value: unlike a painting, which could express a morality acceptable to that handful of people who could consider it an accessible commodity, a Currier and Ives print had to express attitudes and interests acceptable to the broad spectrum of the American public who were its potential buyers. And with average retail costs of twenty to fifty cents for a print, many Americans were potential buyers. Consequently, in terms of what we are calling their moral value, Currier and Ives prints attribute to the Americans who would buy and hang them a common identity that they express in the shared tragedies and triumphs, and the shared ideals and agendas that they so vividly portray. Essentially, the mass production and mass marketing of these prints, which kept their commodity value deliberately low, necessitated that they express a kind of shared American experience, a national identity, that would be recognizable and acceptable to the American masses. In this case, choices made about commodity value—fundamentally, choices about the class of Americans to address—determine to a large degree the moral value, and the dogmas of collective identity it conveyed, that these images attributed to the individual Americans who acquired and displayed them.

The primary subject matter of Currier and Ives prints is the American landscape, a term that includes, for us, scenery of both nature and culture. And we find instructive a comparison of the moral values displayed in illustrations of high commodity value (like landscape painting) and those of low commodity value (like Currier and Ives prints of American scenes) as we try to understand how perceptions of a national identity were prompted and promoted in the nineteenth century by images of the American landscape. Consider the Hudson River, for example. Throughout that century, scenes of the Hudson River were reproduced as cultural icons: as typifications of American experience set in what was treated as a paradigmatic American landscape. This is demonstrated by the prominence through the century of the Hudson River School, as well as the number of Currier and Ives prints with Hudson River scenes as their subject. But a direct comparison of the content of painted and lithographic representations of that landscape shows important differences that inform our understanding of conflicts between classes about the shared expectations and desires of American citizens. (Reproductions of the paintings and prints discussed here may be accessed electronically at the following Web address: www.english.byu.edu/faculty/clarkg/landscapes.)

In 1860, Jasper Cropsey painted a massive rendering (60" x 108") of the Highlands of the Hudson, titled "Autumn on the Hudson River." It is an intricately composed and carefully detailed scene painted from an elevated and distanced point of view found in many Hudson River School landscapes. In the foreground are the trees and topography of the forest, and in the distance there is the river and a late afternoon sun obscured by developing storm clouds. Cropsey's representation carefully attends to the complexities of light present at the moment of the composition, and to the details of autumn color.

It is a painting about the overwhelming beauty of the pristine American nature (and, of course, a stunning display of the artist's skill in representing it) in which any signs of human activity or habitation are conspicuously absent.

Currier and Ives produced at least two prints depicting the same Hudson Highlands. They were probably done around mid-century, but because they did not date many of their prints it is hard to know, except for the kinds of boats they show working on the river. One, "The Entrance to the Highlands," shows the cliffs and hills of the steep shoreline in the immediate background, but the foreground is dominated by sail and steam traffic. And the point of view is almost at water level: the viewer is close to the action in a landscape that displays not the sublimity of nature but the potency of human activity. A second print, "A Night on the Hudson," has precisely the same vantage point on the Highlands as the first, and the foreground here is dominated by two steamboats, billowing smoke under a full moon and ablaze with light as they run parallel upriver. Both, of course, are unsigned, and were probably designed by a team of artists—one specializing on the scenic background, one on the boats, one on the sky. Unlike the Cropsey painting, which removes the viewer to a contemplative distance from a scene from which all evidence of human culture is removed, the Currier and Ives prints place the viewer at the near edge of a landscape that is the setting for intense human action. But both instruct the viewer in attitudes and actions regarding this particular landscape: Cropsey in aesthetic contemplation of a sublime wilderness, Currier and Ives in celebration of an essentially commercial use of the land. In terms of national identity, Cropsey's American is the figure of the isolated philosopher/aesthete and the American of Currier and Ives, by contrast, is the figure of the active participant in the dynamic economy of the new republic.

Contrasting identities can be read more directly in a pairing of two narrative series that echo each other thematically: Cole's *Voyage of Life*, originally painted in the late 1830s; and Currier and Ives's *The Four Seasons of Life*, dated 1868. Cole represents life as a river voyage through a wilderness landscape undertaken by a solitary male attended only by a guardian angel who stands with the voyager in the childhood picture, then withdraws to a watchful distance in the stages of boyhood and adulthood, and finally rejoins the voyager in old age when he has reached the sublime bay of eternity. Currier and Ives's *Four Seasons* do not correspond exactly with Cole's stages: they give us childhood in "The Season of Joy," in which a group of children are at play in a field; youth in "The Season of Love," in which a young man courts a young woman; middle-age in "The Season of Strength," in which a father is greeted at home by wife and children; and old age in "The Season of Rest," in which an elderly couple sits at a cozy hearth with a granddaughter at the old man's feet. Where Cole's life narrative is one of male solitude in an idealized American wilderness, Currier and Ives's narrative is one of sociality in the context of family life and pastoral scenery. Thematically, Cole shows us ambition in his boyhood image, where the young voyager seems literally to be chasing a castlelike cloud formation; but in the manhood image, the theme changes to risk and the voyager responds to the danger of approaching rapids by abandoning the helm and supplicating for heavenly assistance. In Currier and Ives, ambition and achievement are represented both more subtly and more consistently: the youth image represents courtship and the middle-age image represents the fruits of successful courtship, as the father returns to an apparently happy and prosperous family in a home setting that seems noticeably more grand than the modest farmstead of the childhood scene.

Cole's life narrative, told originally for an elite audience who could afford oil paintings and then reproduced for those who could afford fine steel engravings, is one of individual endurance and spiritual fidelity in the setting of a sublime landscape. The setting and other objects represented by Cole are clearly to be interpreted symbolically; the castle-in-air of the youth image, for example, might represent some material goal, but in the context of the whole series should probably be read as a temptation to be resisted rather than as some worthy life goal. Cole's narrative is fundamentally religious and allegorical, representing the inner life of a solitary soul. For its elite audience, it was a celebration of individual spiritual worth and an inspiration to continued fidelity. By contrast, Currier and Ives seem to tell a more literal narrative of social and material advancement in which children who grow up on a prosperous but relatively modest farm move on to better things. The home of the middle-age picture looks more like a country villa than a farmstead, and the returning husband less like a farmer than an urban merchant whose material success enables him to maintain his family home in the countryside. The setting of the old-age image is a comfortable and well-appointed Victorian parlor, perhaps in that same grand country villa, and through the window we can see arriving visitors, perhaps the adult children of the elderly couple. For the middle-class audience to whom Currier and Ives marketed their prints, the narrative would serve as a celebration of the ideology of success and an inspiration to continued striving for material improvement and domestic satisfaction. Significantly, the growing commercial metropolis that was the actual setting for this striving and success is in these prints only hinted at. It is the place from which people arrive at the idyllic pastoral scene in which the family enjoys the fruits of their success—where the prints invite Americans to *imagine* themselves at home.

Interestingly, then, although essentially opposite in their commodity value, and divided in many aspects of the moral narratives they convey, these nineteenth-century representations of the American landscape converge in a common theme: the daily reality of city life is seemingly absent in the land—at least in the land as it is idealized by many Americans from across a variety of classes. Whether one displayed in one's home a landscape in oil, or an engraved print, or a Currier and Ives lithograph, the image of the homeland that was presented to Americans was of a place where most of them did not, and could not, actually live. Then, as perhaps is still true now, the landscape representations available through a variety of media that help to enculturate Americans—or at least the classes of Americans those media can address—in shared ideals and expectations are more idealized and idyllic than they are real. The claim of the editors of *The Home Book of the Picturesque* that "[t]he diversified landscapes of our country exert no slight influence in creating our character as individuals, and in confirming our destiny as a nation" seems to stand. And, despite the differences in the character of their classes, Americans seem united in our insistence on imagining themselves together in places that are clearly not the places where they actually live.

Note

1. This exclusion is evident without subtlety in the popular Currier and Ives "Darktown" prints that render the experience of black Americans as a cartoon version of national civic life, and in the many prints that celebrated western expansion as a process of displacing native Americans.

Works Cited

Burke, Kenneth. *The Philosophy of Literary Form.* 3rd ed. Berkeley: U of California P, 1973.
—. "Rhetoric—Old and New." *Journal of General Education* 6 (1951): 202-09.
Crouse, Russel. *Mr. Currier and Mr. Ives : A Note on Their Lives and Times.* Garden City, NY: Garden City Publishing, 1936.
Deakin, Motley F. Introduction. *The Home Book of the Picturesque, or American Scenery, Art and Literature, Comprising a Series of Essays by Washington Irving, W. C. Bryant, Fenimore Cooper, and Others.* New York: G.P. Putnam, 1852.
Peters, Harry T. *Currier and Ives: Printmakers to the American People.* New York: Doubleday, Doran, 1942.

KRISTIE S. FLECKENSTEIN
University of Missouri, Kansas City

CyberEthos: *Ethos* as a Cybernetic System

Ethos, the means of persuasion within Aristotle's *Rhetoric* that receives the briefest treatment, ostensibly appears to be the most straightforward of any of the three proofs. But *ethos*—the art of an individual speaker giving the "right impression of himself [*sic*]" and "evinc[ing] a certain character" (Aristotle II.2.1) by means of intelligence and good will—turns out to be the most mutable proof of all, defying neat categorization or characterization (Baumlin). The concept of *ethos* slips and slides in and out of focus in three ways. First, the malleability of ethos manifests itself in what scholars, in their various translations and commentaries on the *Rhetoric*, say that Aristotle says. Thus, Lane Cooper gives *ethos* a practical twist, William M. A. Grimaldi a philosophical spin, and George A. Kennedy a sophistical one (Myers). Second, *ethos* transforms itself in response to the evocation of particular historical-cultural milieus (Alcorn; Johnson). As Marshall W. Alcorn argues, "[I]f both language and the self undergo historical change, then it must follow that *ethos* also undergoes historical change . . . assuming many shapes as those structures change over time" (7). Thus, within specific times and places, *ethos* evolves in ways that are manifested by and reflected in the social-intellectual predispositions of an era. Third, the malleability of ethos is shown by its elusive discursive position. Within both Aristotle's *Rhetoric* and individual historical epochs, the placement of *ethos* itself (i.e., the locus of "good character") shifts its point of origin from rhetor to audience, from in the speech to by/through the speech (see II.2.1; see Yoos for *ethos* as audience based; see Reynolds for *ethos* as position).

Thus, *ethos* slips in and out of the textual, historical, and situational gaps. What I wish to argue in this essay is that an examination of *ethos* as a cybernetic system, or as CyberEthos, enables us to understand the difficulty of locating *ethos* in any definition (either that dictated by text, time, or discourse situation) or within a single element of a speech act (language, subject matter, rhetor, audience, or place). Through a cybernetic lens, we can see that the slippage and transformations that mark *ethos* are, in fact, its defining characteristics. *Ethos* is that which materializes within and because of textual, temporal, and situational gaps. The "what" of *ethos* is also the "why." From this cybernetic perspective, *ethos* is composed of and by permeable boundaries, subject to the limits of both time and space, resisting allocation to anything but its constituent context and the constancy of its own relationships. Framed cybernetically, *ethos* evolves into CyberEthos, guided by the dual logics of adaptation and survival, yet again molding itself to (forming itself out of) the constraints and demands of an age, in this case, the cybernetic age of virtual reality, digital processing, and information networking.

I begin by defining cybernetics, focusing on the constitution of a cybernetic system through and by the flow of information. As I describe the properties of cybernetic information, I also investigate its implications for a reconceptualization of *ethos*, building a theory of CyberEthos as a system that redraws its boundaries according to pathways of information inflected by the constraints of place and time. I conclude by suggesting a CyberEthos that, in Donna J. Haraway's words, is an "argument for *pleasure* in the confusion of boundaries and for *responsibility* in their construction" (150).

Cybernetics, a term coined in 1948 by MIT mathematician Norbert Wiener to describe his new probabilistic theory of messages, is a science devoted to investigating questions of control and communication via a theory of messages. "It is the purpose of Cybernetics [*sic*] to develop a language and techniques that will enable us indeed to attack the problem of control and communication in general, but also to find the proper repertory of ideas and techniques to classify their particular manifestation under certain concepts" (Wiener 17). Derived from the Greek term *kubernetes*, meaning steersman, cybernetics serves as the underpinning to human interactions (Wiener 15). "Society," Wiener argues, "can only be understood through the study of the messages and the communication facilities which belong to it; and that in the future development of these messages and communication facilities, messages between man and machines, between machines and man, and between machine and machine, are destined to play an ever increasing part" (16). A complex science that stands at the cross-roads of many disciplines, cybernetics interweaves elements drawn from anthropology, engineering, neurology, and mathematics. Briefly, cybernetics is the theory that an entity—machine, human being, society—is constituted and reconstituted by means of the flow of information throughout transacting and circular pathways by which messages communicate (and control) content about the system and about the ambient environment. Information is core to the system's evolution and survival.

A system (biological, mechanical, and rhetorical) is created out of the flow of messages along its constituent pathways. The key to this concept of information flow is the definition of information. Cultural anthropologist Gregory Bateson, who applied cybernetics to evolution, epigenesis, and thought, defines information in his 1970 Korzybski Memorial Lecture as a "difference that makes a difference" (*Steps* 459). Information is not a thing or a content, ideas are not reifications, and a map is never the territory. Bats, coconuts, and candles do not exist in the mind; ideas about bats, coconuts, and candles exist in the mind. An idea, however, is descriptively real only within a system in which sign, object, and system are coexisting and co-constitutive. "[B]oth grammar and biological structure," Bateson explains, "are products of communicational and organizational processes.... The tissues of a plant could not 'read' the genotypic instructions carried in chromosomes of every cell unless cell and tissue exist, at that given moment, in a contextual structure" (*Steps* 154). What becomes "signable," and what to a certain extent becomes the system (and a part of the system simultaneously), are the differences that matter to the system.

Consider the concept of meaning making, either in writing or reading, from this cybernetic perspective. Meaning, or information, cannot be located in either the black marks of ink on a white page or on the page itself. Instead, meaning is the result of the differences between the black ink and the white page that matter to "readers" who are themselves constituted by the differences they evoke from within those gaps. Reader, ink, and page are created (and constrained) by the recognition, thus the transformation, of that difference, a theory of "reading" or "writing" the world analogous to that delineated by Louise Rosenblatt in which text and writer/reader are mutually evoked within the limits of a specific environment. Meaning exists only as long as the relationships exist, only as long as the differences are significant to the constituting and constitutive system. Meaning is not substance; it is pattern (Bateson, *Steps* 455). An individual does not "understand" or "evoke" a text: a system does.

What evolves from this ensemble performance of information flow is an ecology of the mind, in which meaning exists of and through relationships. We cannot point to any one part of the system and say here lies meaning because it is an emergent property of the entire configuration, traceable back to no single causal force. Thus, to a literate member of a literate society who is plugged into an ink-page textual system, ink and page constitute a difference that makes a difference (even if the language is foreign and the ink purple). But ask that same literate society member to read the iconography of the chicken coop as a means to gather breakfast eggs, and the reading would be a misreading because the system constituting coop, intruder, and hens is unable to recognize and transform the differences that make a difference. Rather than evoking a meaningful text, the now "illiterate" city dweller runs afoul of the rooster, outrages the hens, and escapes from the chicken coop with no eggs and no dignity. The system fails—or goes hungry or dies—because it is unable to transform the differences that make a difference; it is all chicken scratches. This ecology of the mind is what I call CyberEthos.

What evolves and survives from this systemic synchronization of information flow is not just the integrity of a thought, an utterance, an individual, a species, or a culture; it is the integrity of an entire system with its complement of subsystems all in action. Survival, Bateson explains, means "that certain descriptive statements about some living system continue to be true through some period of time" (339). To ensure survival of these descriptive statements, the system continually engages in a process of reciprocal adaptation, privileging not one element of the system but instead the constituting relations among those elements. CyberEthos, as an emergent property of that steady state system, results from the constancy of relations constantly changing as a means of maintaining equilibrium; CyberEthos is the process/product of the movement of adaptation dancing to the tune of survival. This contextual dance of adaptation can be illustrated by Bateson's ideas about evolution. Breaking from the traditional evolutionary focus on the single reproducing organism or single family line, Bateson argues that evolution is a contextual process involving a flexible organism in a flexible environment reciprocally interwoven through feedback and feedforward loops communicating information throughout the entire organism-in-its-environment. For example, the horse did not evolve in response to the changing constraints of its environment (with environment dictating change). Instead, the evolution of the turf was vegetation's response to the evolution of the horse. Horse and turf created themselves coterminously—adapting to changes in the other as a means of maintaining the constancy of relationships that welded them in their systemic identity. The horse did not evolve; the turf did not evolve; the context evolved (Bateson, *Steps* 153-55).

Similarly, CyberEthos exists and survives (i.e., is rendered ethical or remains descriptively true) by means of the same process. An utterance, like horse and grass, is dependent on a context that is dependent on an utterance. Members of a discourse situation cannot "read" each other unless they exist at that moment as part of the same system, as part of the same language game. Thus, a rhetorical act—rhetor's intent, audience's predisposition, location's design, language's variety, content's appropriateness—does not construct itself in response to the changing environment or to the dictates of a solitary displaced actor. No single element composes itself individually in isolation. Instead, the context evolves on the basis of the flow of information—on the basis of the flow of the differences that make a difference—enabling rhetor, audience, space, language, and subject matter to mutually create each other through the establishment of relationships, adapting to one another as a means of maintaining the constancy of those relationships. Like life, CyberEthos is a contextual process of continual adaptation. Through the flow of information, elements adjust their "constitution" to the shifts within their shared sphere, joined in an effort to uphold the equivalencies that constitute the *ethos* or the good character of the entire context. CyberEthos results from and requires this constant, improvised choreography.

On the basis of its composition through information flow, CyberEthos allows us to extend our approaches to *ethos* in productive ways. For one, it provides a theoretical frame by which we can begin to tease out the systemic transactions in play between the creation of individual and group *ethoi*. R. Allan Harris examines the development of the *ethos* of the early generative semanticists in which the "group's *ethos* became more distinctive, and more deeply entrenched, until, in fact, the group was defined almost entirely by its spirit" (129). From the perspective of CyberEthos, we can conceptualize group *ethos* as that which is composed of mutually transacting, thus mutually constitutive, subsystems connected through a series of homeostatic feedback and feedforward loops. Harris uses the powerful analogy of the constitution of a dialect "by lots of overlapping idiolects" to illustrate the reciprocity of individual and group *ethoi* (126), and it works well for him. The limitation of this analogy is that it treats group *ethos* as an additive or a summation of the various idiolects comprising the dialect. Dialect constrains idiolects, whereas idiolects alter those constraints, but the *ethos* that evolves is essentially traceable back to discrete elements of the system.

CyberEthos, however, as an emergent process of a steady state system—as the manifestation of that steady state—cannot be traced back to any concatenation of discrete elements. Like information, it exists as a constancy of relationships, not as an addition of relationships. It is pattern, not substance. Therefore, CyberEthos requires us to approach the idea of group (and individual) *ethos* from a different angle. Initial questions that would concern us include (1) ways in which the map—the fluid superordinate systemic sign-reality—is constituted, (2) the means by which certain differences from the territory—ambient environment in all its various configurations—get recognized and transformed into the map, and (3) the "key" by which the map can be read by its initiates. Furthermore, we can investigate the adaptive controls (feedback/feedforward loops) created by the system to maintain its CyberEthos, which is itself a transformation of the array of Cyberethoi created by the subsystems.

A final consideration offered by CyberEthos—and especially apropos in the case of generative semantics, which Harris tells us was "spectacularly successful, and then, even more spectacularly [wasn't]" (129), the movement (and its *ethos*) "collapsing like a bad lung" (129)—concerns the ways in which a system poisons itself. Through considerations of the flow of differences that make a difference, we can ask how a system becomes pathological, creating a CyberEthos that becomes toxic to its own existence as a system. On one level, a CyberEthos generates its own identity, strives after its own homeostasis through the constant dance of its constituent elements. What serves that balance, serves the system, and thus is ethical (i.e., remains descriptively true). What is pathological—or unethical—is that which threatens the existence of the system. However, systems do not exist in isolation. What is good for CyberEthos at one level can become toxic for the system at another. Lewis Carroll's bread and butterflies drink weak tea in order to survive, but by sipping weak tea, they destroy their sugar cube bodies, consumed by that which they consume. Similarly, in his 1974 speech for the Governor's Prayer Breakfast, Bateson tells the story of a group of Native Americans who were under siege to discontinue the use of peyote in their religious ceremonies (*Angels Fear* 71-74). Sol Tax, a leading anthropologist, proposed to the tribe that he film their ceremonies as a means to demonstrate the religious nature of the drug use. The Native Americans refused, believing that such an intrusion would destroy the integrity of the ceremony they wished to preserve. Survival and evolution, Bateson points out, function according to different time grains, dancing to the tune of different logics (*Steps* 339). The survival of the system—the maintenance of CyberEthos—may in certain instances require that the system itself does not survive. Evolution demands the revision, the rewriting, of a system's descriptively true statements, in effect, changing the identity of the system. Therefore, the question arises, is it at some point better to die as a system as a means of maintaining the integrity of that system? "In the story," Bateson says, "the Indians perceive that it is nonsense to sacrifice integrity in order to save a religion whose only validity—whose point and purpose—is the cultivation of integrity" (*Angels Fear* 75). Is this, then, what happened in generative semantics, a collision of the logic of survival with the logic of adaptation? A "steady state," Bateson explains, "which in one sense is so beautifully balanced may in a wider context contribute to the death of the system" (*Sacred* 112-13). From this perspective, the group *ethos* of generative semantics can be productively investigated as a question of the survival of CyberEthos when that survival requires adaptive measures that will in effect destroy that CyberEthos.

Perhaps the greatest value that CyberEthos offers us in this information age where international and personal boundaries are reconfigured by the ebb and flow of information in a virtual space is the freedom it opens to us and the demands it imposes on us. There is a pleasure in the freedom of constantly shifting boundaries, Haraway points out, and we should revel in that freedom of systemic self-creation, self-generation, and self-adaptation. But, simultaneously, that pleasure requires that we take responsibility for the boundaries we inevitably make and strive to maintain. Nothing is more monstrous, Bateson says, than the attempt to separate the mind from the body, the external mind from the internal mind (*Steps* 470). CyberEthos may be the way in which we can unite ourselves, reconfirming/recreating our identity and connectedness within the systems that offer us life. Perhaps good character, good will, and practical wisdom ultimately translate into global, as well as communal and individual, survival.

Works Cited

Alcorn, Marshall W., Jr. "Self-Structure as a Rhetorical Device: Modern *Ethos* and the Divisiveness of the Self." *Ethos: New Essays in Rhetorical and Critical Theory.* Ed. James S. Baumlin and Tita French Baumlin. Dallas: Southern Methodist UP, 1994. 3-36.

Aristotle. *The Rhetoric of Aristotle.* Trans. Lane Cooper. Englewood Cliffs, NJ: Prentice-Hall, 1960.

Bateson, Gregory. *A Sacred Unity: Further Steps to an Ecology of the Mind.* Ed. Rodney E.

Donaldson. New York: HaperCollins, 1991.
—. *Steps to an Ecology of the Mind: Collected Essays in Anthropology, Psychiatry, Evolution, and Epistemology*. Northvale: Aronson, 1987.
Bateson, Gregory, and Mary Catherine Bateson. *Angels Fear: Toward an Epistemology of the Sacred*. New York: Macmillan, 1987.
Baumlin, James S. "Introduction: Positioning *Ethos* in Historical and Contemporary Theory." *Ethos: New Essays in Rhetorical and Critical Theory*. Dallas: Southern Methodist UP, 1994. xi-xxxi.
Cooper, Lane. "Introduction." *The Rhetoric of Aristotle*. Trans. Lane Cooper. Englewood Cliffs, NJ: Prentice-Hall, 1960. xvii-xxxvi.
Grimaldi, William M. A. "Rhetoric and the Philosophy of Aristotle's *Rhetoric*." *Classical Journal* 53 (1957-58): 371-75.
Haraway, Donna J. *Simians, Cyborgs, and Women: The Reinvention of Nature*. New York: Routledge, 1991.
Harris, R. Allan. "Generative Semantics: Secret Handshakes, Anarchy Notes, and the Implosion of *Ethos*." *Rhetoric Review* 12 (1993): 124-59.
Johnson, Nan. "*Ethos* and the Aims of Rhetoric." *Essays on Classical Rhetoric and Modern Discourse*. Ed. Robert J. Connors, Lisa S. Ede, and Andrea A. Lunsford. Carbondale: Southern Illinois UP, 1984. 98-114.
Myers, Nancy A. "Whose Aristotle? A Dialogic Reading of Aristotle's Rhetoric in Rhetoric and Composition Studies." Diss. Texas Christian U, 1997.
Reynolds, Nedra. "Ethos as Location: New Sites for Understanding Discursive Authority." *Rhetoric Review* 11 (1993): 325-38.
Rosenblatt, Louise. *The Reader, the Text, the Poem: Transactional Theory of the Literary Work*. Carbondale: Southern Illinois UP, 1978.
Wiener, Norbert. *The Human Use of Human Beings: Cybernetics and Society*. Garden City: Doubleday, 1954.
Yoos, George E. "Rational Appeal and the Ethics of Advocacy." *Essays on Classical Rhetoric and Modern Discourse*. Ed. Robert J. Connors, Lisa S. Ede, and Andrea A. Lunsford. Carbondale: Southern Illinois UP, 1984. 82-97.

SALLY GILL
Rensselaer Polytechnic Institute

And Now a Word About Our Sponsors: Advertising and Ethos in the Age of the Global Village

The 1998 Rhetoric Society of America (RSA) conference engaged us in a lot of different conversations about mass media, global communication, and how a new communication environment is prompting us to redefine our notions of rhetoric, the polis, the village, and the relationships between rhetors and their audiences. Whether those conversations were about television, radio, or the World Wide Web, it is likely that little, if any, serious attention was given to the one ubiquitous entity we find in each of those media: advertising.

Although I would wager that most of us prefer to ignore the majority of the advertising that we encounter every day, I would like to direct our attention for the next few minutes, not toward any one ad or campaign in particular, but rather, in the spirit of this conference, toward redefining some of our notions of advertising. In particular I would like to question some commonly held assumptions about those who create the ads, how their beliefs and opinions are revealed in those ads, and what sort of relationship they attempt to develop or response they hope to elicit from their audience. In other words, I would like to talk about advertising and *ethos* in the age of the global village.

There are several different ways of conceiving of *ethos*, but the one that provides the best framework for this discussion comes from Gerard Hauser, who describes *ethos* as "the dynamic interaction between a communicator and an audience" (104) and "as a judgment that is caused by the speech itself. If you regularly meet your listeners' needs by being informed, interesting, succinct, and focused on their concerns, you will encourage them to perceive you as someone worth listening to" (100). Although from this perspective the emphasis of *ethos* is not on the rhetor's character, a rhetor's character is an element, nonetheless. And it is an element that is revealed within the speech. Because ad agency copywriters, art directors, and creative directors are the ones who compose the "speeches" of advertising aimed at meeting the needs and concerns of the audience, I think an important question to ask is, who are these people? How do their cultural frames of reference and categories of meaning shape and/or reflect our own? What motivates them to create the images and narratives they do? How do they define the relationship between themselves, their work, and the audience?

One of the reasons I pose these questions is because I worked as a copywriter at a major ad agency in San Francisco during the 1980s. Last fall, as a graduate student in communication and rhetoric, I began to do research helping to develop an undergraduate course on advertising and culture. Reading the academic literature, I became aware of many assumptions about advertising and its creators that did not always mesh with what I had learned to be true from my experience: Theodor Adorno and Max Horkheimer wrote in "The Culture Industry: Enlightenment as Mass Deception" that in advertising "the object is to overpower the customer, who is conceived as absent-minded or resistant" (Adorno and Horkheimer 163). Critiques in the popular press, such as the Media Foundation's *Adbusters*, also tended to paint the people who create the ads as manipulators skilled in the practice of brainwashing. Consider this quotation from a recent issue:

> Today's advertisers cannot "break down" their subjects' resistance with thorazine or acid. They cannot paralyze them with curare poison. They can and do use a kind of hypnosis—the seductive glow and flicker of television light—but for the most part, their tools are simply the ads themselves, which must be sharp enough to puncture a subject's consciousness and arresting enough to keep said subject from squirming as the payload is delivered. ("You have no confidence in yourself. You are weak and inadequate. Try these jeans.") (Grierson 20)

It sounds terribly sinister. As far as I could tell, however, none of the writers and art directors with whom I worked approached their work with the aim of wearing down resistance and hypnotizing people. In fact we looked down our noses at anyone or any campaign that tried to operate on that level. We worked with the assumption that people are skeptical about advertising, bored by most of it (with good reason), and that our job was (to quote the owner of the agency) "to go beyond accomplishing our sales purpose" (Riney 48) and give the audience something better: ads that were crafted with "taste and style" (48). Although I would not say this exact approach is embraced by all ad agencies, I would like to suggest that many commonly held assumptions about those who create advertising, and "the patterns of interaction that occur in the actual rhetorical event" (Hauser 94) (i.e., the ethos they seek to establish) may not be accurate. If one of our goals is to redefine the relations between ancient and modern rhetoric and the mass media, then I believe we should begin the task with a set of accurate assumptions.

In this chapter, then, I will attempt to do the following: (1) to examine several common assumptions about the people who create advertising and establish why those assumptions may be outdated and/or inaccurate; (2) to offer alternate (and what I hope are more accurate) characterizations; and

(3) to suggest we begin to think about advertising less in terms of its business and marketing appeal, and examine it from the perspective of the ethos that is often developed between agency creatives and the audience.

Common Assumptions: Hucksters, Buffoons, and Manipulators

In 1947, MGM released a motion picture, *The Hucksters*, based on Frederic Wakeman's novel about an advertising man. In one of the film's most memorable scenes, the Beautee Soap client—a despicable character played to perfection by Sidney Greenstreet—is seated at the head of a conference table, around which sit several Beautee Soap marketing people and two men from the advertising agency (played by Clark Gable and Adolphe Menjou). Assured that all eyes are on him, Greenstreet begins the meeting by spitting on the table. No one else says a word or makes a move. Addressing the men from the advertising agency he says, "You have just seen me do a disgusting thing, but you'll always remember what I just did." He then delivers a lesson on what makes effective advertising and ends by pounding his fist, droning "irritate, irritate, irritate!"

This particular depiction of people who work in advertising as cowering yes-men and women whose goal in life is to placate tyrannical clients and irritate the rest of us with drivel was created over fifty years ago, and continued to inform the popular imagination for decades. Similar scenarios (minus the spitting) popped up in other contexts, such as the 1960s TV show *Bewitched*. Less a cynical portrayal than broad caricature, *Bewitched* gave us Darrin Stevens and Larry Tate, two buffoonish admen who repeatedly needed Samantha's witchcraft to bail them out of trouble with clients.

Vance Packard's *The Hidden Persuaders* (1957) introduced a chilling version of advertising professionals as manipulators par excellence who used electrical signals and sophisticated techniques borrowed from psychoanalysis to "channel our unthinking habits, our purchasing decisions and our thought processes" (Fox 185). Focusing on motivation research, a form of research that had a brief heyday during the 1950s, Packard declared, "'No one, literally no one, evidently is to be spared from the all-seeing, Big Brotherish eye of the motivational analyst if a merchandising opportunity seems to beckon'" (Fox 185).

The academic literature has contributed its own brand of hyperbole on the subject. In *Advertising and Culture: Theoretical Perspectives* (1996), Mary Cross stated that advertising "asks us not to think, closing off the universe of discourse through one-dimensional words and a one-way communication that leave us panting, but passive, allowed to participate in the system only as consumers. Pandering to our base appetites or desires, advertising in the pornography of its excess eroticizes words into images and collapses individual consciousness into equations of money and psyche" (2). Robin Andersen, in *Consumer Culture and TV Programming*, asserts that "advertising's habitual equation . . . promises that products can solve problems and that emotional happiness and well-being in general can be found within the sphere of consumption" (66). Naomi Wolf claims that advertisers "are threatened by the possible effects on women's minds of too much excellence in women's journalism" (71). The underlying assumptions made by these authors seem to be that readers and viewers of advertising are passive yet gullible, helpless before an advertising onslaught, and that advertisers also believe this to be true.

Whereas such depictions may succeed in selling books, movie tickets, and television shows by appealing to the sentiment that advertisers are the people we all love to hate, they exemplify two common, inaccurate representations. First, little or no distinction is made between the "creatives" (copywriters, art directors, and creative directors, the ones I refer to here as the "rhetors" of advertising) and the "suits" (clients and account executives). Anyone who has worked at an advertising agency knows what a big difference there is, and what kinds of conflicts can often arise between the two. James Twitchell points to this in *Adcult USA*:

> [T]here is a continual tension not just between the agency's research and the client's research but between the agency's creative types and the agency's scientific types. As the English ad man John Ward observes, "Advertising is a craft executed by people who aspire to be artists, but assessed by those who aspire to be scientists. I cannot imagine any human relationship more perfectly designed to produce total mayhem." (126)

In other words, the people paying for the advertising and the people who create it do not always see themselves engaged in the same activity or seeking to fulfill the same goals.

The second inaccuracy is the assumption that the creatives believe the public is gullible, and that they use their talents as tools to exploit that gullibility. A closer look at some of the people whose art and craft is advertising reveals a different story.

An Alternate View of "The Creatives"

Why is it important to differentiate between the creatives and the suits? If we are to believe Judith Williamson, the people who create ads "are unknown and faceless, the ad in any case does not claim to speak from them, it is not their speech" (14). I am inclined, however, toward an alternate point of view offered by Stephen Fox in *The Mirror Makers*: "Ads and commercials reflect to a greater extent than most business products, the quirks and personalities of the people behind them" (6). For example, some of you might recall the eye-patch-wearing Hathaway Shirt Man and Schweppes-drinking Commander Whitehead of the late fifties and sixties. Both were created by David Ogilvy and were, in Ogilvy's own words, "All Walter Mitty Ogilvy" (Fox 245). When we looked at the Bartles & Jaymes TV spots of the 1980s, we were hearing the speech and seeing the quirks and personality of Hal Riney. (Rural denizens sitting on the porch making comments that were often thinly disguised critiques of Los Angeles, MBAs, and market research were common themes in Riney's work.)

We also heard the speech and saw the personality of Rosser Reeves, master of the hard sell, in the Anacin commercials of the 1950s. (You might recall the silhouette of a man's head within which three boxes were animated by hammers, coiled springs, and tension lines. If you did not have a headache to begin with, these commercials could give you one.) "I never tried to make *interesting* commercials" (Fox 188) Reeves once said. He felt that "the most dangerous word of all in advertising [is] *originality*" (193) and that an advertisement, "like a diesel motor, must be judged on whether it performs what it was designed to do" (188).

Reeves's style of advertising—the hard sell and repetition of the Unique Selling Proposition—was influential during the 1950s, but fell out of favor in the 1960s, when people such as Bill Bernbach, Robert Gage, Helmut Krone, Julian Koenig, and George Lois spurred what was called the "creative revolution." Bernbach, whose agency Doyle Dane Bernbach created campaigns for Volkswagen and Avis Rental Cars, believed "the art of making ads . . . drew on the same gifts of intuition and inspiration, creative leaps and flashes, as any other art form" (Fox 251). The Bernbach way emphasized respect for the audience, whom he believed were intelligent, bored by repetition, and who appreciated innovative ads that told the truth.

Firm believers in this kind of advertising, the DDB creative team, Helmut Krone and Julian Koenig, revealed their personal approach (or in Williamson's words, "speech") in the "Think Small" ad for VW. The ad pictured the VW beetle, surrounded by plenty of white space. The copy read:

> Our little car isn't so much of a novelty any more. A couple of dozen college kids don't try to squeeze inside it. The guy at the gas station doesn't ask where the gas goes. Nobody even stares at our shape. In fact, some people who drive our little flivver don't even think 32 miles to the gallon is going any great guns. Or using five pints of oil instead of five quarts. Or never needing anti-freeze. Or racking up 40,000 miles on a set of tires. That's because once you get used to some of our economies, you don't even think about them any more. Except when you squeeze into a small parking spot. Or renew your small insurance. Or pay a small repair bill. Or trade in your old VW for a new one. Think it over. (Ogilvy 13)

I wager that if Rosser Reeves's agency, Ted Bates, had been awarded the Volkswagen account, we would have seen a very different campaign.

Like many of the revolutions of the 1960s, the creative revolution in advertising has been tempered and diffused, expressing itself during the 1980s and 1990s in smaller agencies that are not necessarily located on Madison Avenue literally or figuratively. In the April 27, 1998 issue of *Advertising Age*, the cover story featured Jeff Goodby, Rich Silverstein, Dan Wieden, and Lee Clow under the headline, "These Creatives Set the Standards." Working three thousand miles from Madison Avenue, these four creative directors head three West Coast agencies: Goodby Silverstein & Partners in San Francisco; Wieden & Kennedy in Portland, Oregon; TBWA Chiat/Day in Venice, California. They are described as "the creative leaders of the '90s [who] are concerned with producing work that doesn't insult consumers, but treats them with respect" (Vagnoni 24); and as "masters of pop culture . . . [n]one adhere to formulas; nor are they believers in hard-sell" (20).

Goodby believes that advertising is "about treating people at their best" (20). Rich Silverstein, his partner, described their goal when they first opened their shop, "We wanted to do intelligent work that the public likes to see" (20). This philosophy, plus their work for the California Milk Processor Advisory Board (the "Got Milk" campaign), has prompted some in the advertising industry to draw comparisons between the Goodby Silverstein & Partners agency of the nineties and the Doyle Dane Bernbach agency of the sixties. What I mean to suggest with these examples is that the people who create the advertising that fills the literal and virtual spaces in the global village (and especially those who are in the position of influencing the rest of the industry) are not necessarily functioning according to the model set forth by films like *The Hucksters* ("irritate, irritate, irritate!") or assumed by scholars like Michael Geis, who described advertising as a practice where "everything claimed is false" (Cook 206).

I disagree with Judith Williamson's claim that an ad is not the speech of the creator. I put forward the idea that ads do reflect the people who create them, their voices, their perceptions of our culture, and their perceived relationship to the audience. This view is shared by Guy Cook in *The Discourse of Advertising*, who points to Bakhtin's theory that "no meaning can be divorced from people: the study of a text must always be of words and participants together. To treat language as an impersonal object is to simplify and misrepresent" (Cook 181). I believe that if we take the time to study the creatives and the relationship they are hoping to create with their audience—the concept of *ethos* as "an interpretation that is the product of speaker-audience interaction" (Hauser 93)—we might better understand the role that advertising plays in contemporary culture.

Ethos and Audience

To assume that today's audiences are passive, vulnerable, or easily manipulated is to assume that audiences do not flip channels, turn pages, talk back, and ridicule advertising. The creative directors I described a moment ago, the ones *Advertising Age* proclaims are setting the standards for the industry, do not assume the audience is gullible. Nor do they try to trick or outmaneuver what they recognize and respect as a savvy public. It is probably fair to say that their success and influence is largely due to respect for the audience, mixed with an innate ability to tap into pop culture, to "marshal its appeals, attitudes and icons and turn them into potent and potentially enduring branding messages" (Vagnoni 20).

If advertising is no longer being crafted as a series of humorless monological messages coercing naive consumers to buy (I'm thinking of the Rosser Reeves Anacin commercial now), what function does it serve today? The commercial aspect of serving client needs is clearly still advertising's raison d'etre, but might it provide the audience with something noncommercial as well? Thinking back to Hauser's analysis that rhetors are perceived as worth listening to when they focus on the needs and concerns of the audience, we might conclude that successful creative directors, writers, and art directors realize and appreciate the fact that viewers' needs may not have anything to do with the product being advertised at the moment the commercial is seen; what they know is when an audience needs a good laugh, or a 30-second escape to an ideal world of beauty and harmony. Guy Cook suggests that advertising often answers "a need for play and display in contemporary society" (Cook, back cover). This theory is given credence when we look at the number of ads that end up as poster art (e.g., Absolut vodka), or employ humor, poke fun at, and even parody advertising itself.

In the parody category, a recent fast-food commercial illustrates the trend toward self-parody. It begins like many designer perfume spots: black-and-white cinematography, skinny, bored-looking models complaining of life's emptiness and lack, when suddenly a man (in color) bursts on the scene and cries, "Then eat something!" and hands everybody burgers and fries. The Energizer campaign a few years ago also created parody spots that began like typical (boring) ads for other products only to have the drum-beating little bunny march by, completely disrupting the scene.

The hard sell world of *The Hucksters* and adpeople like Rosser Reeves no longer rules the industry the way it did fifty years ago. The strict division between selling and entertaining has blurred. Do we call it postmodernity? Or do we call it carnival culture? I am reminded of Bakhtin's description of the end of the medieval period and the beginning of the Renaissance: "The shoots of a new world outlook were sprouting . . . [and] in order to achieve this growth and flowering, laughter had to enter the world of great literature.

By the end of the Middle Ages a gradual disappearance of the dividing line between humor and great literature can be observed" (Bakhtin, *Rabelais* 96) so that by the time of the Renaissance, "the culture of laughter [had broken] through the narrow walls of festivities and [entered] into all spheres of ideological life" (Bakhtin, *Rabelais* 97). At this point literature became a possible site of contestation, where the struggle between our own words and the words of others could be played out by entering "into interanimating relationships with new contexts" (Bakhtin, "Discourse" 785).

Could the advertising being created by some of today's writers and art directors be providing us with a "culture of laughter" and "sites of contestation" where images of our cultural character are open to interpretation and judgment? The fact that we see advertising parodying advertising suggests that the answer could be yes. The fast-food spot urging anorexic models to eat might provoke people in living rooms around the country to talk about everything from media representations of women to nutrition to the nature of parody—or advertising—itself.

Marshall McLuhan has been amply quoted among the RSA conference papers. If you can stand one more, here is what he had to say about advertising in *Understanding Media* in 1964: "The ads are by far the best part of any magazine or newspaper. More pain and thought, more wit and art, go into the making of an ad than into any prose feature of press or magazine. Ads are news" (qtd. in Benedetti and DeHart 163). If you watch the Superbowl every year you have probably become aware of how the commercials aired during the show have begun to receive as much (or more) media attention as the game itself. I think we can clearly see that there is something going on here that is more than the simple delivery of messages coercing an audience to buy. I believe that by using their ability to entertain, create evocative images and poke fun, copywriters and art directors seek to establish a positive *ethos* for an audience with whom they realize they share similar habits, customs, and ideals.

A Few Final Words

Before I conclude, I would like to make it clear that it is not my intent to romanticize the creatives or excuse the excesses of the advertising industry. I agree that there is too much advertising and most of it is annoying. Some of it is not just annoying, but harmful, such as the cigarette ads geared at adolescents and fashion advertising that glorifies the kind of female shape that is usually possible only through bulimia and plastic surgery. But as much as I deplore what I think of as "bad" advertising, I also have a strong impulse to speak out against the tendency to look for scapegoats. And while doing research about advertising and culture last year, I encountered an abundance of literature where advertising was held up as the scapegoat for the ills of contemporary life.

The points I have made here suggest an ongoing project. My purpose here has been to pose hypotheses that I hope will stimulate further study. My own research plans include doing an ethnography at an advertising agency and I encourage others who are interested in this topic to conduct similar inquiries. It is my belief that the creative departments of advertising agencies are rich sites for investigating how rhetors today can—and do—connect with an audience, affirm their values, address their concerns, and satisfy certain needs in 30 seconds or less. I believe they might offer us insights into how *ethos* is established with an audience in the age of the global village.

Works Cited

Adorno, Theodor, and Max Horkheimer. "The Culture Industry: Enlightenment as Mass Deception." *Dialectic of Enlightenment*. New York: Continuum, 1972.
Andersen, Robin. *Consumer Culture and TV Programming*. Boulder, CO: Westview, 1995.
Bakhtin, Mikhail. "Discourse in the Novel." *The Critical Tradition*. Ed. David Richter. New York: St. Martin's, 1989. 781-91.
—. *Rabelais and His World*. Cambridge: MIT P, 1968.
Benedetti, Paul, and Nancy DeHart. *Forward Through the Rearview Mirror*. Cambridge: MIT P, 1996.
Cook, Guy. *The Discourse of Advertising*. New York: Routledge, 1992.
Cross, Mary. "Reading Television Texts: The Postmodern Language of Advertising." *Advertising and Culture: Theoretical Perspectives*. Ed. Mary Cross. Westport, CT: Praeger, 1996. 1-10.
Fox, Stephen. *The Mirror Makers: A History of American Advertising and Its Creators*. New York: William Morrow, 1984.
Grierson, Bruce. "Shock's Next Wave." *Adbusters* Winter 1998: 20.
Hauser, Gerard A. *Introduction to Rhetorical Theory*. Prospect Heights, IL: Waveland, 1991.
Ogilvy, David. *On Advertising*. New York: Vintage, 1985.
Riney, Hal. "Taste and Style in Advertising." Ogilvy & Mather 6th International Management Meeting. Stanford Court Hotel, San Francisco. 4 Apr. 1984.
Twitchell, James. *Adcult USA: The Triumph of Advertising in American Culture*. New York: Columbia UP, 1996.
Vagnoni, Anthony. "They Might Be Giants: These Creatives Set the Standards." *Advertising Age* 27 Apr. 1998: 1+.
Williamson, Judith. *Decoding Advertisements: Ideology and Meaning in Advertising*. London and New York: Marion Boyars, 1978.
Wolf, Naomi. *The Beauty Myth: How Images of Beauty Are Used Against Women*. New York: William Morrow, 1991.

ED CUTLER
Brigham Young University

Dialectic of Technology: Critical Affinities between Kenneth Burke and the Frankfurt School

Axiomatic to any critical inquiry into mass communication is the question of how the enabling technologies and methods of social discourse may themselves condition, even determine, social life. Before the somewhat utopian discourses of an emergent global village in the 1960s, and before the liberatory discourses surrounding the Internet today, social criticism of mass society in the twentieth century was almost uniformly wary of the political power of mass media to condition the social body for political domination. For Frankfurt School critics like Theodor Adorno and Max Horkheimer, the rise of German fascism provided a case study in the power of mass media to "instrumentalize" culture and to "produce" public opinion. Horkheimer and Adorno's landmark study of the "culture industry" in the United States, *Dialectic of Enlightenment*, argued that conditions for an incipient fascism were becoming manifest throughout the forms of U.S. mass culture. Whereas Kenneth Burke appears to have been unaware of this study and of other work by the Frankfurt School, his appraisal of the prospects for meaningful public discourse in the media age was similarly bleak; moreover, Burke often extended his social criticism to the same discursive sites that Frankfurt School critics addressed. Both *Dialectic of Enlightenment* and Burke's *A Grammar of Motives* provided a series of "dialectical" readings of twentieth-century culture and both found midcentury, mass discourses on democracy, technological progress, and the triumph of rational man to offer more social containment than expressions of social promise and possibility. Within this irony one finds the dialectical method of social critique common to both Burke's and the Frankfurt School's criticism at work: the very instruments that appear to liberate society from nature, from history, even from time-space constraints, in fact turn to deliver that society up, most brutally, to the very world it is thought to have transcended. For Burke and for the Frankfurt School critics, totalitarian fascism and Stalinism were the inevitable outcome of the ongoing perfection of enlightenment ideology. In an age of technological progress, the perpetuation of such "anachronisms" as war, alienation, class division, racism, violence, and the will to political domination had come less and less to appear as holdovers from a benighted age, showing themselves, rather, to be inevitable, dialectical symptoms of a social machinery that extended domination of nature into all spheres of social experience. As our century draws to a close and the political totalitarianism that impelled this criticism appears to have faded into history, postmodern social criticisms have, of course, called into question the types of "monolithic" social critique common to Burke and the Frankfurt School critics. Yet, in an era of seemingly unchallenged global capitalization and unprecedented ecological destruction, in a world where "media" and "culture" have become nearly synonymous terms, in an era, moreover, that just witnessed the birth of two new "nuclear" powers in India and Pakistan, the dialectical method of social criticism and the cultural prognoses of Burke, Adorno, Horkheimer and Marcuse seem well worth revisiting at a conference addressing "Rhetoric, the Polis, and the Global Village."

Influences and Methods: Dialectic and Totality

A comic book version of the history of philosophy opens its entry on the Frankfurt School showing a cartoon of Freud and Marx standing before the altar (Freud in the wedding dress) with a shotgun-toting hillbilly standing by to ensure that the marriage proceeds. A critical synthesis of Freudian symbology and Marxist materialism is the distinguishing feature of Frankfurt School criticism, notwithstanding the cartoon's suggestion that the union requires some degree of coercion. In the 1930s, attempts at bringing Marxism and psychoanalysis together in a single methodology certainly troubled the orthodox left. For Adorno and Horkheimer, as for Kenneth Burke in America, this fusion was greeted with resistance. Although Burke appears to have been unaware of the 1930s criticism coming out of the Frankfurt School, he had written Malcolm Cowley in 1936 that "potential synthesis" of Freud and Marx was a "burning issue," which he had broached in his recently published *Permanence and Change* (Jay, *Correspondences* 210). As a literary critic in the twenties, Burke had espoused a theory of art as "self-expression," but turned to Marx following the Depression, when economic realities seemed to call for a "new orientation" (Jay, "Kenneth Burke" 536).

His turn to Marx, however, never took a "party-line" form. He outraged Granville Hicks, Joseph Freeman, and other members of the intellectual left at the 1935 American Writers Congress in New York, where he presented an infamous paper titled "Revolutionary Symbolism in America." Following the delivery of the paper, Freeman is said to have declared to the group, "'We have a traitor among us!'" (Lentricchia 22). Frank Lentricchia notes that, for the official left, a consideration of "revolutionary *symbolism*" had the "discomforting feel of ideological deviance," such that it confused mere superstructural effect with the economic, directive forces of the base (22). Yet Burke had opened the essay by reminding the audience that "principles of collectivity, whatever their genetic relation to a society's mode of production, do not themselves possess primary reality from a strictly materialist point of view" (qtd. in Lentricchia 22). According to Lentricchia, Burke here was elaborating on Marx's first thesis on Feuerbach, in which Marx argues, dialectically, that the overriding defect of all previous philosophical materialism is that "the object, reality, what we apprehend through our senses, is understood only in the form of *object* or *contemplation*; but not as *sensuous human activity*, as *practice*; not subjectively" (Marx 135; emphasis in original). Following this lead, Burke, then, had rejected the materialism/idealism polarization and had begun the first of many elaborations on the symbolic as a form of "sensuous human activity," a kind of social dialectic at once material and symbolic.

In his 1937 elaboration of the method behind the Frankfurt School's "critical theory," Max Horkheimer offers a similar injunction against Marxist reductionism. He argues that the subject of "critical thinking," must be considered in the "web of relationships with the social totality and nature." For Horkheimer, "the subject is no mathematical point like the ego of bourgeois philosophy; his activity is the construction of the social present" (211). Because the subject is integrated with this social network, the social totality both reflects and emanates from the subject. Consequently, Horkheimer argues that "critical theory has never been reducible to specialized economic science," but that critical theory engages economic analysis "more fully and along the lines indicated by history" (250-51). The social body conceived as a totality of cultural development, in other words, cannot be reduced to mere economic cause and superstructural effect. Indeed, such an overt materialism reinforces political tendencies toward fascism and monopolistic capitalism, according to Horkheimer, because "the economic dynamism which has been set in motion and *in relation to which most individuals have been reduced to simple means*," only makes easier the explanation of social phenomena in terms of capital and state necessity (237; emphasis added).

Burke's *Permanence and Change* calls for a similar approach to social criticism, a method reflected in the dialectical proposition of the title. Both symbolic and historical considerations must inform theory, not as autonomous categories but as mutually reinforcing aspects of social existence. A shift in one category invariably alters the other. Burke thus notes that symbols of integration and cooperation necessarily arise out of cooperative enterprises, and a breakdown in the system ultimately leads to a shift in the symbolic order of rationality itself:

> [T]he mind, so largely a linguistic product, is constructed of the combined cooperative and communicative materials. Let the system of cooperation become impaired, and the communicative equipment is correspondingly impaired, while this impairment of the communicative medium in turn threatens the structure of rationality itself. (163)

Burke's argument here is not without drawbacks; indeed, one might argue that a fascist "system of cooperation" is the very embodiment of "the structure of rationality." The specific conditions Burke addresses, however, are the antagonistic conditions of competitive capitalism, where cooperation and self-interest collide. Symbolic appeals to unity, the basis of "rationality" in the sense that people share enough in common to communicate with one another, gives way when the economic system breaks down. Burke's interest in the revolutionary potential of "symbolic action" is thus both historically based and historically urgent—the power of the symbolic to provide a basis for collective action erodes in the wake of divisive economic trends. The symbolic, however, is not itself entirely determined by the economic—it can "act" in language and art to shift directions, inventions, applications, and procedures in the productive base. Burke would later come to identify "rhetoric" as the multivalent source of this capacity, albeit with the qualifications that preserve the modern theoretical categories already outlined.

The communicative possibilities of the symbolic in art preoccupied the early work of Max Horkheimer as well as that of Kenneth Burke. In "Art and Mass Culture," Horkheimer cites John Dewey's assertion that "today art is no longer communicative," but adds ironically that the official forms of mass communication have led to a condition where "men as they are today understand each other" (279). To the extent that the last works of art still communicate, Horkheimer argues dialectically that "they denounce the prevailing forms of communication as instruments of destruction, and harmony as a delusion of decay" (279). *Counter-Statement*, Burke's treatise on art in the modern age, had called for a similar form of political resistance grounded in the symbolic resources of the aesthetic. To counter the growth of fascist centralization and efficiency as the prevailing modern test of value, Burke imagined a "dis-integrating" art that would keep "the practical from becoming too hopelessly itself" (112). The gesture is again one of preserving a certain dialectical perspective. Art needs remain an "impractical, inefficient, vacillating, experimental and skeptical" social discourse, Burke contends, in order to impair "the Fascists, the hopeful, the propounders of business culture, [who] believe that the future lies in perfecting the means of control" (115).

Their shared concerns notwithstanding, Burke's and Horkheimer's work exhibit certain methodological differences. Horkheimer's concept of a "social totality" does not figure as rigidly in Burke, who would turn to a Nietzschean kind of "perspectivism" in his *A Grammar of Motives*. The analytical method of "dramatism" he sets forth in *Grammar* is an elaborate, perhaps overambitious, attempt to provide a formula for analyzing human motives, political, psychological, and otherwise. His method might be termed "penta-lectical," following on his varied dialectical pairings of five basic categories of motivation: "act," "scene," "agent," "agency," "purpose." *Grammar of Motives* does not systematically carry out all analysis within the specific categories of the pentad and its possible ratios; Burke, in fact, even offers alternate figures, or "master tropes," as an appendix to *Grammar*. The value of the categories and their combinations, rather, is to alert the critic to the various possible structures of argument itself, and to provide the resources for *perspective*, following Burke's concern that most arguments tend to reduce human motives to a single, total category of motivation, in keeping with the totalitarian tendencies of the age. Dramatism, therefore, was Burke's attempt to undermine the particular totalizing aura of scientific, positivistic, and behaviorist reductions of the human subject, more than it was an effort to provide the "last word" about human motives. Burke's *Grammar* and his follow-up volume, *The Rhetoric of Motives*, read as interesting companion volumes to the contemporary work of Theodor Adorno and Max Horkheimer, whose landmark work of social criticism, *Dialectic of Enlightenment*, appeared in 1944. Both criticisms arise from remarkably similar theoretical genealogies, and both examine the prevailing forms of modern thought and social behavior at midcentury with particular attention to the fear that the "perfection" of the enlightenment led to ecological destruction and political domination.

Science, Animal Experiments, and Fascism

Dialectic of Enlightenment identifies enlightenment rationality as the unlikely source of twentieth-century totalitarianism and global economic exploitation. Enlightenment, in Adorno's and Horkheimer's reading of it, set into motion the wholesale liquidation of nature and the will to totalitarian domination because enlightenment tends to convert all phenomena into the imagery of its own methodology and to rationalize anything outside or opposed to it, eventually even the very ideals of freedom and humanism out of which it emerged (11). The process by which enlightenment reduces the world to system and control is historically located in the extension of the positive sciences on the one hand and in the accelerating capitalist system of exchange on the other. Science "reduces" the world to what can be "known," thereby reducing thought itself to the protocols of method alone. The power to classify and abstract the known universe to general principles inscribes a logic of equivalence over the system of knowledge as a whole. That is, dissimilar phenomena are, by means of abstraction, reconciled at some "higher point" in "the system from which all and everything follows." Thus, the "multiplicity of [natural] forms is reduced to position and arrangement," and the "supernatural, spirits and demons" and "the many mythic figures can all be brought to a common denominator, and reduced to the human subject [whose subjective mind once projected them on the world]" (6-7). Insofar as materials or products can also be reduced to the universalizing idiom of money, they too are recast within the logic of the numerical system and reduced to an ultimately equivalent role as "use-values" or "exchange values" (7).

Grammar of Motives similarly examines the social consequences of the enlightenment from the standpoint of epistemological "reduction." Burke begins with a critique of behaviorist psychology and works backward to the origins of enlightenment logic:

> When the behaviorist experiments with animals to discover, under "controlled laboratory conditions," the springs of conduct that also operate in human beings, we consider his experiment as important as he does, though for a totally different reason. For we take it to indicate . . . the terministic relationship between the circumscription and the circumscribed. For no matter how much a matter of purely empirical observation it may seem to be, it is actually a very distinct choice of circumference. (78)

In choosing to consider "human motives in terms of an animal circumference," the scientist demonstrates only that the "study of conduct in so mechanistic a scene [i.e., the laboratory] led to a correspondingly mechanistic interpretation of the act." The scientist, in other words, begins with a series of reductions—studying the animal in the laboratory, sending it through mazes—that set a mechanistic and already rationalized scope within which behavior is to be considered. Any "discovery," therefore, is bound to be tautological. Animal experimentation, Burke goes on to observe, may teach a good deal more about human motives, insofar as the experiment places the animals in a "human" circumference, for "nothing is more distinctly human than a scientific laboratory" (78). Adorno and Horkheimer cite the same issue and draw almost identical conclusions in *Dialectic of Enlightenment*, where they propose that the formulas and findings behaviorists "force from defenseless animals in their nauseating physiological laboratories" applies "not to animals in the free state but to man as he is today," because "he and he alone in all creation voluntarily functions as mechanically, as blindly and as automatically as the twitching limbs of the victim which the specialist knows how to turn to account" (244).

Burke's *Grammar* and *Dialectic of Enlightenment* both delineate a similar historical trajectory of the reductions in conceptual scope that each see as culminating in twentieth-century attempts to ground behavior in mechanistic and dominating "scenes." Adorno and Horkheimer note that "science managed without [metaphysical] categories" (5) and Burke makes a similar observation, noting that, dialectically, the metaphysical concept of a monotheistic god "contained its dissolution as its ultimate destiny"; a concept of the supernatural in which god's center is everywhere and his circumference nowhere opens the way for "nature . . . to be[come] a perfect embodiment of God's will," a move that allows conceptual circumference to be narrowed "to omit 'God' as a necessary term" in the study of "creation" (80). Enlightenment thus begins here for Burke, in "the almost imperceptible terministic logic that takes one from supernaturalism to 'chemism'" (82).

As do Adorno and Horkheimer, Burke frequently notes the implicit dialectical reversals that "embarrass" the logic of science and economics—enlightenment turns back toward its origins in myth, and its dominant social forms (i.e., technology and monetary symbolism) harbor metaphysical and supernatural assumptions that enlightenment rationality proper would dismiss. Indeed, Burke notes that capitalism relies on implicit supernatural associations along the following lines:

> Since the religious circumference traditionally provides the basic terms for the tribal or collective motives of a culture ("God" being felt to be "real" insofar as these unifying motives really do make up the most extensive and intensive aspects of men's consciousness) the spread of secularization and rationalistic individualism is "normally" a sure sign of cultural disintegration. But the combination of technological and monetary rationalism transformed these "signs of decay" into trends wholly "progressive." For the fact is that the monetary motive . . . could provide an effective technical substitute for the religious motive, as a "symbolic" or "spiritual" ground of social cohesion, a means of "keeping body and soul together." (94)

He goes on to suggest that "the technological motive is protected in other quarters where it is granted immunity in the name of 'science' as an absolute good," and that "our very aversion to 'talking about money matters' has done much to conceal our understanding of it as a motive, though . . . this aversion itself indicates the godhead of money, since formal religions men fear to behold or name lightly their God, or motivational center" (116).

A final correspondence between Burke and Adorno and Horkheimer is their shared view of the "specialist" in modern society. *Dialectic of Enlightenment* draws a portrait of the "family man," who in his "occupation" manufactures gas crystals for the extermination camps (206). In his *A Rhetoric of Motives*, Burke would comment on the fascist implications of specialization in postwar America, noting how "a specialty at the service of sinister interests" becomes rationalized as a redemptive social endeavor:

> If the technical expert, as such, is assigned the task of perfecting new powers of chemical, bacteriological or atomic destruction, his morality *as technical expert* requires only that he applies himself to his task as effectively as possible. . . . [W]hat this new force might mean [when] released into a social texture emotionally and intellectually unfit to control it, or [when] surrendered to men whose

specialty is *professional killing*—well, that is simply "none of his business" as specialist, however great may be his misgivings as father of a family, or as citizen of his nation or of the world. (30)

Like Adorno and Horkheimer, Burke also connects this kind of specialization to an emergent fascist condition in the United States. He observes that the same people who, with reference to the "scientific horrors of Hitlerism, admonish against the ingredients of Hitlerite thinking in our own society, will be outraged if you follow out the implications of their own premises and look for similar temptations among our specialists" (30).

Conclusions

One cannot help but read these midcentury critiques of mass society without the occasional raised eyebrow. If the substance of the critique still holds true, then concern with totalitarian fascism has certainly dwindled with the ongoing decline of the modernist nation-state. Technology and mass media do not appear as overtly controlled or controllable by authoritative central administration within our supposed postmodern condition. From a contemporary perspective, Frankfurt School and Burkean social criticism may indeed appear anachronistic. But to dismiss their grounding concerns and critical methodology would certainly be a mistake. For if anything, Burke, Adorno, and Horkheimer may have been guilty of underselling their concerns. The globalization of capitalism moves forward at unprecedented pace and scale, seemingly without any substantive, "dis-integrating" forms of resistance such as Burke had called for in the 1930s. If mass communication technology is no longer an overt agency of political manipulation, Kenneth Burke would no doubt have appreciated the irony of the utopian discourse surrounding the Internet, which enthusiasts proclaim to be politically autonomous because it "can never be turned off." He surely would have seen this as another step toward the "perfection" of technological culture and its ongoing displacement of the natural world. Whether nature itself can stay "on" in the coming century is still an open question. Monetary symbolism likewise has become increasingly "natural," as electronic money and recent attempts at forming a "universal currency" make clear, as does the often heard lament that it "costs too much" to preserve the environment. The sites of domination and the modes may have changed, but surely the conversion of nature into culture and subjectivity into technology continues at an accelerated pace.

If this new conditionality is cause for celebration and liberatory manifestoes, so too should be the historical amnesia that pervades such ecstatic proclamations, given the political and ecological devastation this century has already witnessed under similar technological and discursive forms. It may well be a function of the triumph of an omnipresent technology of mediation that this history can at once be increasingly known and increasingly inconsequential—experienced merely as so much media. Writing at a watershed moment of this unfolding conditionality, Burke and the Frankfurt School offered a necessarily complex and multivalent view of the discursive and historical genesis of our contemporary problems, a critique that should continue to promote committed critical inquiry into the most urgent and difficult question of our time: how to keep humankind from becoming altogether too much itself.

Works Cited

Burke, Kenneth. *Counter-Statement*. Los Altos: Hermes, 1931.
—. *A Grammar of Motives*. Berkeley: U of California P, 1945.
—. *Permanence and Change: An Anatomy of Purpose*. Los Angeles: U of California P, 1984.
—. *A Rhetoric of Motives*. Berkeley: U of California P, 1969.
Horkheimer, M. *Critical Theory: Selected Essays*. Trans. M. J. O'Connell. New York: Continuum, 1992.
Horkheimer, M., and T. Adorno. *Dialectic of Enlightenment*. Trans. J. Cumming. New York: Continuum, 1993.
Jay, Paul. "Kenneth Burke and the Motives of Rhetoric." *American Literary History* 1 (1989): 535-53.
—. *The Selected Correspondences of Kenneth Burke and Malcolm Cowley, 1915-1981*. New York: Viking, 1988.
Lentricchia, F. *Criticism and Social Change*. Chicago: U of Chicago P, 1984.
Marx, Karl. "Theses on Feuerbach." 1845. *The Portable Karl Marx*. New York: Penguin, 1984.

Part IV
Rhetorics of Ethics and Agency

ALAN BILANSKY
Pennsylvania State University

Rhetoric, Democracy, and the Deliberative Horizon

Rhetorical theory enters into dialogue with political theory when it reinforces or extends the deliberative horizon of a given politics—that is, what is expected and what is possible. Two statements about democracy—one about the Peloponnesian War and one about the Vietnam War—can clearly show this connection.

Pericles' funeral oration (or at least Thucydides' representation of it) gives us an early statement of democratic principles. His role in speaking is to praise the war dead, and he does this by praising the Athenian democratic way of life and defining it as the coupling of public deliberation and public action, "words" and "deeds": "We Athenians, in our own persons, take our decisions on policy or submit them to proper discussions" (147).

The war dead of Athens are that much braver than, say, the Spartans, because it is their obligation not just to fight in the war, but also to understand the consequences, both "taking risks and estimating them beforehand" (147). Rather than voting or possessing certain rights, the practice that defines democracy here is deliberation, or "proper discussions." Pericles' goal is to shore up his fellow citizens' commitment to the war. He does this by reminding them that they are responsible for it, because under a regime of *demokratía*, public actions reflect public deliberation. I do not intend this description of Pericles' Athens as nostalgia. Rather, by referring to classical democracy, or to New England town meetings, or to the direct democracy on a pirate ship (as in Marcus Rediker's account) or the Paris Commune (as in Marx's account in "The Civil War in France"), I am simply arguing that there are possibilities for democracy radically different from current practice. Against this backdrop, the current practice of welfare-state, liberal democracy no longer looks inevitable.

The second statement of democracy I want to consider is Michael Crozier's report prepared for the Trilateral Commission, *A Crisis for Democracy*. In discussing media coverage of the Vietnam War, he relies on an understanding of democracy starkly reduced in scope compared to the Athenian model. Crozier argues that the media lost the war. By showing the public too much of the violence of the conflict, by being too critical of U.S. foreign policy and the U.S. military, and by not being critical enough toward the enemy, the media collaborated to make the public lose its nerve. Stricter state control of the press might in the future be called for. Crozier's critique relies tacitly on both a rhetorical theory and a democratic theory. He sees himself as able to reflect on the war coverage in a way that we must assume "the people" cannot. He can determine that the coverage is slanted, often immaterial or even inaccurate, and inflammatory. The mass of the American people, presumably members of a class of people distinct from Crozier and his audience, cannot respond to the media's arguments in the same way. Crozier relies, then, on a tacit rhetorical theory similar to that of Richard Whately and George Campbell, distinguishing between convincing intellectually and persuading emotionally. Also, Crozier assumes a particular representation of democracy that allows him to equate public deliberations with the mass media. Intervention in public deliberations is most directly accomplished through intervening in the mass media.

Pericles expects deliberations from all participants in his audience, not just himself. Although we associate great men speaking well with classical rhetorical culture, this sort of rhetorical leadership is much more a necessity in liberal representative democracy than in direct democracy. In the case drawn from the Vietnam War, we see a rhetorical culture that is hierarchical and centralized. This would seem a fact of life of large modern states. But we must recall also that James Madison argued for large units of sovereignty expressly because they make direct participation impossible, and drive a wedge between public deliberations and public action.

The purpose of this chapter is not to argue for linking democratic and rhetorical theory, or for linking the practices of rhetoric and democracy. As I hope these two examples suggest, rhetoric and democracy are already linked. My goal is to argue that we cannot understand them independently of each other. Every democratic theory implicitly or explicitly relies on a theory of argumentation and deliberation. Likewise, every rhetorical theory implies a theory of political action. As both Pericles and Crozier demonstrate, the quality of democracy can be described in terms of the quality of public deliberations and whether public policy reflects those deliberations. The purpose of this chapter, then, is to explicate the rhetorical culture corresponding to liberal politics and then the rhetorical culture suggested by participatory democratic theory.

But first, to establish our terms, look briefly at the well-known story of the classical polis. Classical Athens holds a special place for historians of rhetoric that cannot be overstated. The historiography of rhetoric strongly shows that the practice and study of rhetoric have never known a more friendly environment.[1] It was here that lack of unitary authority required resort to consensus, and hence democracy was born. Rhetoric thrived because it was needed to make the democratic regime work. This led to a regime with a remarkably flat organizational structure. The preferred form of decision making was not majority rule, but consensus, or *homonia*. This called for imaginative, active deliberation, as the final agreement would often be something no one had in mind from the start. The practice of assembly democracy placed heavy demands on its participants. Also crucial, conflict between tribes to defend honor was replaced by argumentative competition in the law courts. And here, in the context in which Aristotle wrote, it is easier to see that rhetorical practices are inseparable from political practices, and the necessities and opportunities of time and place.

And so when Aristotle lectured on rhetoric through a sort of community extension course in Plato's Academy, this became his intervention into Athenian democracy. The *Rhetoric* is a treatise on how to do three kinds of rhetoric in three specific contexts, really three places. Aristotle is showing citizens how their polis governs itself. He says that the persuasive "is persuasive in reference to someone" and thus rhetoric considers "that which seems probable to this or that class of persons" (I.II.ii). To engage in rhetoric, one needs to know the lines of reasoning used by that community. These topoi are the substance of deliberations in the Ecclesia and the Boule and in the law court, and are reproduced and perhaps altered in civic ceremonies. Our translations of the terms for the "deliberative" and "forensic" genres do not sound like place names, but Aristotle's own terms did. The deliberative is called *symbouleutic* or *demagoric*, referring to the Boule or the agora, and the forensic is called *dikanic*, suggesting a *dikasterion* (literally, place of justice). *Dikanic* topoi are the ways that juries deliberate in the *dikasterion*. A topos is a "place" where you find lines of argument, no?

The three rhetorical genres that Aristotle isolates can be said to comprise a major portion of the rhetorical culture in which he wrote. Aristotle is identifying a set of rhetorical *habits*. People do rhetoric because they can and because they have to. The rhetorical habits that Aristotle sees have a strong sense of place. This is because rhetorical culture develops as a response to rhetorical geography, material conditions, and relations among people, pressures, opportunities, and necessities that both constrain and enable.

If rhetoricians are not satisfied with the current state of rhetorical culture, then it is not enough to look to the discursive plane. We need to look at the terrain in which rhetoric moves, and ask what the possibilities are for alternative geography. Thus I want to look at liberal politics and the alternative of participatory politics.

* * *

A democratic form of government combined in the classical polis with a lively deliberative culture and a strong sense of civic duty and dedication to political community. In that context they were seen as mutually reinforcing each other, a face-to-face democracy and the communion of face-to-face deliberation. Aristotle (in his *Politics*) does not even distinguish political institutions from political culture; they are both subsumed under *politeia*, a public way of life. After the Middle Ages, both democracy and a form of communion reemerge, but they are now independent of each other. First, a virtual deliberative community, a "public sphere," develops.[2] At first this community is apolitical, as it develops in the context of absolute monarchy. Just the same, a critical discourse thrives in this new environment, a rhetorical practice clearly distinct from classical patterns of cultural action. The public sphere was a venue where members of the bourgeois found empowerment leading to a sort of political participation.[3] Eventually this discourse came to question the legitimacy of government, and to construct a notion of legitimacy that was grounded in this discursive sphere. This led to speculation about government, the retheorizing of democracy. As economic power shifted and power became more dispersed, absolute power gave way to mixed government. Republican government, sometimes called democracy (although as often as not democracy was a bad word), was the result of bourgeois revolutions and took forms requiring little participation and curiously circumscribing rhetorical practice. The Enlightenment is marked by constitutions that can function without a polis, and a virtual polis that can function without a strong politics.

Liberal political theory developed as part of the public sphere that I have been describing. These writers moved in what could be called a polis without geography. The bourgeois public sphere has no true location, and the members of the community it constitutes have no persons. And this is precisely its defining character. A pre-print culture community is incarnated in a material relation between persons, and is a public at its most real when it is concretized in a form such as a church service or town meeting. This new Enlightenment form of community, a public, is by definition never realized as a localizable relation between persons. The power that print took on in the eighteenth century came from its impersonality, which came to represent universality. Persons in print become abstractions and interact with other abstractions, and it is this impersonality that opens the possibility for political interaction in terms of universality.[4]

The Internet is a perfect metaphor for the rhetorical geography of liberalism. That is, it is not subject to any of the constraints of place, the necessities of inequality and tradition (at least on the ideological plane). This decenteredness, or independence from situated existence, allows for critique (Habermas, *Communicative Action* 1: 216). This discursive space without place enabled the liberal critique of monarchy that made possible the reinvention of democracy, but it was also responsible for a blind spot when it came to the possibilities of face-to-face community. Thus we find John Stuart Mill calling the press his day's "equivalent . . . of the Pnyx and Forum" (176), and Madison warning about the excesses of ancient direct democracies while seemingly unaware of an already established tradition of New England town meetings.

We find in the Federalist papers one of the most concrete expressions of liberal democracy, or republicanism. Among canonical writers of democratic theory, Madison is probably the most antidemocratic, for, as David Held observes, "[H]is judgment is similar to Plato's . . . and sometimes more severe, underpinned as it is by Hobbesian assumptions about human nature" (89). Conflict, Madison asserts, is intrinsic to human nature, and we are inherently selfish and contentious. The central cause for potentially destructive conflicts, Madison observes sixty years before Marx, is class.[5] Elimination of those inequalities, he says, is impractical. And even if we could establish economic equality, we would find something else to quarrel about. The cure for factions, Madison argues in Federalist 10, is to make the republic as large as possible, with democratic action diluted and the state itself stymied by a division of powers.

In addition to being prone to conflict, according to Madison we are not very good at deliberating. Throughout the Federalist papers there is not much representation of deliberation and argumentation as a positive force, even in discussing the work of the Constitutional Convention. In Federalist 37, Madison argues for excusing the Constitution as naturally imperfect ("The most the Convention could do . . . was to avoid the errors suggested by . . . past experience" [267]). He does this by way of an elaborate and far-reaching exposition of the limits of human deliberation. First, he makes an argument reminiscent of the older sophist Gorgias of Leontini, who argued that "nothing exists; . . . even if it exists it is inapprehensible to man; . . . even if it is apprehensible . . . it is . . . incapable of being expressed or explained to the next man" (42). Madison argues that the proper dividing line between the executive and the legislature, for example, cannot be determined with accuracy, as neither can the line separating the animal from the vegetable kingdom. He argues that "indistinctness of the object, imperfection of the organ of conception, inadequateness of the vehicle of ideas . . . [t]he convention . . . experienced the full effect of them all" (270). Given the imperfection of our capacity to deliberate, Madison admits that the delegates then turned to the method of compromise, but then quickly dismisses this as an explanation of the Constitution, because one compromise leads to another, leading to interminable complexity. No, the Constitution is the result of "a finger of that Almighty hand which has been so frequently and signally extended to our relief in the critical stages of the revolution" (Madison 271). Human agency and collective self-determination could not have produced anything so good.

We have looked at a figure of the American Revolution who is typically read as the most cautious of democrats. Now I want to turn to Rousseau, typically read as the most radical democrat to come out of the Enlightenment.

Although Rousseau does present the strongest argument for direct democracy, he also shares the central liberal belief in the autonomy of individuals held by Madison and the other liberals. In fact, Rousseau's distinction between public opinion and the General Will, according to cultural historian Dena Goodman, flows from his identifying public opinion with salon culture, specifically with women. This misogynist view leads Rousseau to have no patience for deliberative culture itself. The General Will, Goodman argues, is men's will. It is produced by otherwise individual men who come together to somehow deliberate in manly fashion, considering only the common interest. They just do it:

> When, among the happiest people in the world, bands of peasants are seen regulating their affairs of state under an oak tree, and always acting wisely, can one help scorning the refinements of other nations, which make themselves illustrious and miserable with so much art and mystery? (Rousseau 203)

Rousseau's citizenry, to use a metaphor that Marx uses to describe French peasantry, "is formed by simple addition of homologous magnitudes, much as potatoes in a sack form a sack of potatoes" ("Eighteenth Brumaire" 608). It is perhaps this aversion to deliberative culture that is responsible for the lack of any methodological discussion of how the General Will comes into being. The Madisonian state functions not so much through deliberation as through calculation, a simple counting of votes. Deliberation is not asked for, and so is easily forgotten and underestimated.

* * *

So far we have looked at two sorts of democratic politics: the classical (a well-known ideal) and the liberal (a paradigm so dominant today that it looks inevitable). A third politics is observed in practice and theorized by a school of contemporary political theory, one that recovers much of the classical paradigm and is realized locally within a broader liberal landscape. The school of democratic theory called "participatory" has recently attempted to bring back together the two halves of a *politeia*: civic culture and constitution. Carole Pateman, Benjamin Barber, Jane Mansbridge, and Kathleen Iannello, among others, have accomplished this by turning liberal theory on its head. I think rhetoricians would benefit from reading these democrats, just as I am sure democratic theorists could learn from reading rhetoricians.

Democrats start from the simple claim that consensus, the preferred form of participatory democracy, is difficult. It requires time, commitment, deliberative skill, and face-to-face contact. It was Pateman's innovation to argue that the very difficulty of self-government has a transformative effect. People who deliberate get better at deliberating through an enhanced willingness to engage issues, improved rhetorical skills, and a feeling of agency. Barber extends this by arguing that a deliberating community is a strong community. Close, efficacious collaboration with fellow citizens and engaging in "creative argumentation" to transform conflict through a politics of distinctive inventiveness and discovery will produce a stronger community, because this deliberation requires the use of a "public language" (119). Face-to-face deliberative communities do not have to be revolutionary to produce participatory rhetorical culture: the defining characteristic of their geography is that they create direct avenues for collective self-determination. Democrats cite examples like democratized work places, town meeting government, activist groups, and community organizations.

Iannello contrasts *power*[6] (control over others) with *empowerment* (control over ourselves). Empowerment is the ability of people to act collectively and achieve things that they could not otherwise do. This collective action is organized not through bureaucracy and hierarchy but through consensus. A politics of empowerment requires participants to invest heavily in deliberation, to maintain consensus of ends and means. This requires a rich, complex rhetorical culture, much like the needs Aristotle perceived for the Greek polis. In a liberal polity, the people are governed by a state with power to represent them. In a polity of empowerment, the people collectively augment each other's agency, mediated by consensus. The realm of consensus, as distinct from the realm of power, corresponds to the realm of rhetoric. Empowerment operates in a sphere distinct from power and coercion. It requires efforts of all around to establish communion. It allows people to discover and realize common ends. "Empowerment" might be another word for "rhetoric."

Notes

1. This discussion of classical rhetoric depends on Grimaldi, Kennedy, Cole, Garver, Poulakos, and Cohen. For classical democracy I relied on Hansen, Barker, Held, Sabine, and Finely.

2. I am relying on Habermas's historical paradigm for its explanatory force. Cultural historians of the Enlightenment have extended Habermas's analysis to relate the public sphere to more radical eighteenth-century political changes, notably the French and American revolutions. Dena Goodman analyzes the French Enlightenment, and Michael Warner looks at the American.

3. An example of this can be seen in one of Hugh Blair's recommendations for developing writing style. He recommends "translating" a respected English writer:

> What I mean is, to take, for instance, some page of one of Mr. Addison's Spectators, and read it carefully over two or three times, till we have got a firm hold of the thoughts contained in it; then to lay aside the book; to attempt to write out the passage from memory, in the best way we can; and having done so, next to open the book, and compare what we have written with the style of the author. (85-86)

Intriguingly, this advice is nearly identical to Benjamin Franklin's description of how he learned to write, after his father had critiqued his writing style. The self-taught Franklin did not mention receiving any advice to this effect; he claimed that he had run across a stray volume of the Spectator, and was so impressed with the writing that he wanted to imitate it. Following a procedure very similar to that described by Blair, when he was done Franklin said he "discover'd many faults and amended them" but, even more, on some occasions he "had the pleasure of fancying that in certain particulars of small import, I had been lucky enough to improve the method or the language and this encourag'd me to think I might possibly in time come to be a tolerable English writer." Thus easily, it would seem, reading could become writing, a consumer could become an actor. Despite its exclusions, to some the discourse of the public sphere seems to have indicated an invitation to participate.

4. In his history of American print culture, Michael Warner argues that the mediation of print

culture mirrors the forms of representative government:

> The meaning of public utterance ... is established by the very fact that their exchange can be read and participated in by any number of unknown and *in principle unknowable* others.... The resulting form of mediated relation ... was to become the paradigmatic political relation of republican America. (40)

5. Madison says,

> The most common and durable source of factions, has been the various and unequal distribution of property. Those who hold, and those who are without property, have ever formed distinct interests in society. Those who are creditors, and those who are debtors, fall under a like discrimination. (58-59)

6. We can take "power" here to mean either legitimate, hierarchical coercion, or in the Foucauldian sense.

Works Cited

Aristotle. *The "Art" of Rhetoric*. Trans. John Henry Freese. Cambridge: Harvard UP, 1982.
—. *Politics*. Trans. H. Rackham. Cambridge: Harvard UP, 1932.
—. *Rhetoric*. Trans. W. Rhys Roberts. New York: Random House, 1954.
Barber, Benjamin. *Strong Democracy: Participatory Politics for a New Age*. Berkeley: U of California P, 1984.
Barker, Ernest. Introduction. *The Politics of Aristotle*. New York: Oxford UP, 1969.
Blair, Hugh. *Lectures on Rhetoric and Belles Lettres. The Rhetoric of Blair, Campbell, and Whateley*. Ed. James L. Golden and Edward P. J. Corbett. Southern Illinois UP, 1990.
Campbell, George. *The Philosophy of Rhetoric. The Rhetoric of Blair, Campbell, and Whately*. Ed. James L. Golden and Edward P. J. Corbett. Southern Illinois UP, 1990.
Cohen, David. *Law, Violence, and Community in Classical Athens*. New York: Cambridge UP, 1995.
Cole, Thomas. *The Origins of Rhetoric in Ancient Greece*. Baltimore: Johns Hopkins UP, 1991.
Crozier, Michael. *The Crisis of Democracy: Report on the Governability of Democracies to the Trilateral Commission*. New York: New York UP, 1975.
Finely, M. I. *Politics in the Ancient World*. Cambridge: Cambridge UP, 1983.
Franklin, Benjamin. *Autobiography*. New York: Library of America, 1990.
Garver, Eugene. *Aristotle's Rhetoric: An Art of Character*. Chicago: U of Chicago P, 1994.
Goodman, Dena. *The Republic of Letters: A Cultural History of the French Enlightenment*. Ithaca, NY: Cornell UP, 1994.
Grimaldi, William M. A. *Studies in the Philosophy of Aristotle's Rhetoric*. Wiesbaden: Franz Steiner, 1972.
Habermas, Jürgen. *The Structural Transformation of the Public Sphere: An Inquiry into a Category of Bourgeois Society*. Trans. Thomas Burger. Cambridge: MIT P, 1989.
—. *The Theory of Communicative Action*. Trans. Thomas McCarthy. 2 vols. Boston: Beacon, 1984.
Hansen, Mogens Herman. *The Athenian Democracy in the Age of Demosthenes*. Oxford: Blackwell, 1991.
Held, David. *Models of Democracy*. 2nd ed. Stanford UP, 1996.
Iannello, Kathleen P. *Decisions without Hierarchy: Feminist Interventions in Organization Theory and Practice*. New York: Routledge, 1992.
Kennedy, George A. *Classical Rhetoric and Its Christian and Secular Tradition from Ancient to*

Modern Times. Chapel Hill: U of North Carolina P, 1980.
Madison, James, Alexander Hamilton, and John Jay. *The Federalist.* Ed. Benjamin Fletcher Wright. Cambridge: Harvard UP, 1961.
Mansbridge, Jane. *Beyond Adversary Democracy.* New York: Basic, 1980.
Marx, Karl. "The Civil War in France." *The Marx-Engels Reader.* Ed. Robert C. Tucker. New York: Norton, 1978. 618-52.
—. "The Eighteenth Brumaire of Louis Bonaparte." *The Marx-Engels Reader.* Ed. Robert C. Tucker. New York: Norton, 1978. 594-617.
Mill, John Stuart. *Considerations on Representative Government. Utilitarianism, Liberty, and Representative Government.* Ed. H. B. Acton. London: Dent, 1951.
Pateman, Carole. *Participation and Democratic Theory.* Cambridge: Cambridge UP, 1970.
Poulakos, John. *Sophistical Rhetoric in Classical Greece.* U of South Carolina P, 1995.
Rediker, Marcus. *Between the Devil and the Deep Blue Sea: Merchant Seamen, Pirates, and the Anglo-American Maritime World, 1700-1750.* Cambridge: Cambridge UP, 1987.
Rousseau, Jean-Jacques. *On the Social Contract.* Indianapolis: Hackett, 1987.
Sabine, G. H. *A History of Political Theory.* London: George G. Harrap, 1963.
Thucydides. *History of the Peloponnesian War.* Harmondsworth: Penguin, 1972.
Warner, Michael. *The Letters of the Republic: Publication and the Public Sphere in Eighteenth-Century America.* Cambridge: Harvard UP, 1990.
Whately, Richard. *Elements of Rhetoric. The Rhetoric of Blair, Campbell, and Whately.* Ed. James L. Golden and Edward P. J. Corbett. Southern Illinois UP, 1990.

DOUG SWEET
Santa Clara University

When Language Is Just Another Commodity: Enlightenment Theories, Erasure of Agency, and the End of the Political

> **FOX NEWS**
>
> We Report. You Decide
>
> "Fair and Balanced."
>
> Consistently Unbiased.

I have begun with this rendering of Fox News Network's logo and pitch because I doubt that I could have found a better example of Enlightenment epistemology alive and well and ubiquitously present.

"We Report. You Decide."

It sounds a bit liberating, even empowering—"You decide." Of course, the inherent claim here is that "reporting" is a matter of simple observation. Fox News goes to great pains to stress that their reporters only present what "really" happened, that is, they appeal thus to feckless, naïve empiricism. As viewers, or in this case as consumers, we need only "see" what wares are being displayed before we choose which we would like. Adding "Fair and Balanced" to the mix seems to be meant to define both the content of said "news" and the motivation that presents it—"Consistently unbiased." These are some claims, indeed.

And although many of us might just shrug or shake our heads dismissively at the blatant disregard for the complexities and nuances of linguistic interaction these claims evidence, I would like to suggest that, as we gather up our collective regalia hems to step into the next century, we are continuing to face what Peter McLaren has called a "'crisis of representation' . . . a steady and sometimes vehement erosion of confidence in prevailing conceptualizations of what constitutes knowledge and truth and their pedagogical means of attainment" (145). Surely the evidence for this "crisis" is all around. Any of us could recite a litany of positions, of critical approaches contending for the academic upperhand. What the Fox News Network wants us to believe—a fair mind that balances itself unbiasedly is the way to useful knowledge—is echoed in current critical thinking curricula, much of which claims to measure "student learning outcomes" while simultaneously claiming to prepare those students to be active, intellectual agents. What I am going to try to trace here is a method of teaching argument that relies on a blend of Ramist "place logic" and Enlightenment epistemologies, and I would also like to examine what I consider to be the suspicious timing of Critical Thinking pedagogy's elevation in the academy.

To begin with then, here is an example from the "Consensus Statement Regarding Critical Thinking and the Ideal Thinker," prepared for the American Philosophical Association in 1990:

> While not synonymous with good thinking, Critical Thinking is a pervasive and self-rectifying human phenomenon. The *ideal* critical thinker is habitually inquisitive, well-informed, *trustful of reason*, *open-minded*, flexible, *fair-minded* in evaluation, *honest* in facing personal biases, *prudent* in making judgments, willing to reconsider, *clear* about issues, *orderly* in complex matters, *diligent* in seeking relevant information, *reasonable* in the selection of criteria, focused in inquiry, and persistent in seeking results which are as *precise* as the subject and the circumstances of inquiry permit. (emphasis added)

Notice that the italicized terms could have been lifted from Locke, perhaps, or Kant. The critical thinking described here rests, as does the Fox News Network, on notions of argument as reasonableness made clear, and on the idea that reason itself is essentially ahistorically transparent. And these notions, I am going to claim, are deeply rooted in a Ramist theory of knowledge that actually "sees" truth as inert, static and clear, derived from orderly taxonomical progression through a bipolar world—a theory that presupposes what bell hooks calls "the false assumption that education is neutral, that there is some 'even' emotional ground we stand on that enables us to treat everyone dispassionately" (117). What Ramist theory and Critical Thinking theory and Fox News Network have in common here is the presupposition that "fairness" is an attribute of the search for truth just as objectivity is its form, that the "political" is always somehow distorted by motivation; that logic (in the Western tradition) ought to be inherently privileged over rhetoric; that language is transparent at its best, but can nevertheless be seen as commodity to be possessed and exchanged; most importantly, these attitudes presuppose Western metaphysical dualism—a view that meaning is always an either/or proposition in a binarily coded world.

The traits of thinking I have just enumerated teach some strong lessons: that to think "critically" is to be "objective," to see "both sides of something"; that if a decision is to be reached in this rhetorical context, then it will be after the fact (We Report. *Then* You Decide); that the best decisions will be based on the impartiality of the evidence, as though argument, by nature, relies on a leveling, an equilibrium, an even-handedness. "A good argument is one that can address both the 'pro' and the 'con' of the issue," we read in text after text. Or, as students in one college Critical Thinking class were told: "A case involves two parts. It involves presenting arguments for the conclusion you're trying to persuade someone of. But it also involves responding to the negative arguments, the arguments that are on the *other sides* of the question" (Swanson-Owens 10; emphasis added). How clear it all seems. This adjudication, the forensic rhetorical form, seems to have become "the" master narrative for persuasion, both on the airwaves and in classroom. And, as Jim Berlin has noted, "dominant groups will always attempt to make sense of history, at the very least to account for the justice of their access to power. These histories will, of course, deny the ideological commitments of their master narratives, usually in the name of an innocent empiricism, an insistence that the facts of the matter, not any ruling narrative codes, make the case" (Berlin 73). Call this master rational narrative in action what you will: "Fair and Balanced News. A Comparison and Contrast Essay. Critical Thinking Skills."

I have not just arbitrarily stumbled into this particular inquiry. I have been driven to pursue my rhetorical research by the way I see my students commodifying language, day in and day out. "The values I *hold* are important to me," I read. "The belief *that I carry* was given to me by my parents. . . . The attitudes *I possess* help make me the person I am today." These are brief, though telling examples of students thinking about concepts as reified commodities, as "things" that can be possessed, as spatial entities being understood visually, as objects, as commodities to be displayed for consumption.

Let me see if I can trace, quickly, how I see rhetorical *praxis* as having fallen victim to, first, a Ramist separation of rhetoric and dialectic, and second, to an intellectual attitude that separates object from subject, knowledge from power, rationality from ideology—solidifying a worldview that worships the former as "proof," while denigrating the latter as "contamination."

Walter Ong devotes a considerable portion of his Ramus study to tracing the development, by way of Agricola, of "place logic"—a rephrasing (and reconceptualizing) of Aristotelian *topoi* (for a detailed examination of "Class Logic in Space" see Ong, bk. 3, chap. 9). Ramus's appeal to the "real" in argument was, according to Ong,

> an appeal to consider the bits of knowledge derived from common experience as though they themselves were items to be observed and manipulated. . . . In a parallel maneuver Ramus organizes in an observational field not the external world but the "contents" of consciousness. (195)

What I find interesting about this account of Ramus's thinking is not just how it looks, but how "familiar" it looks: minds as vats, invention as recalling preformed arguments, division/taxonomy, "structuring" one's thinking by "building" arguments. Or, as the college critical thinking class I referred to earlier was told, "the task is to differentiate the argument. That's what we're really working on now. How to separate arguments into, mentally, into separate compartments and deal with them one at a time" (Swanson-Owens 21).

It may not be news that Ramus's great gesture was to sever invention and arrangement from the five canons, leaving only elocution and delivery (memory being part of reason itself), but I would like to emphasize that not only has *logos* been severed from *ethos* and *pathos*, but the very concept of *logos* has been reified into a taxonomic, binary schedule of oppositions that can be plotted, charted, recalled, and followed to perfection. What Ramus conceives of as "rationality" in this way is demonstrably visible; he *holds* the idea because it is a clear and distinct "thing." The topics, then, in this system, are indeed "sites" of argument, places, spaces containing items: bits of reason, data, empirical evidence, thought—they are all the same. Thoughts take up space. Concepts are rational units that have a particular form.

According to Grimaldi's reading of Aristotle, Ramus's "method" had been presaged "from Cicero on" by adaptations of the topics into "mere mechanics of invention." What gets lost in this translation, according to Grimaldi, is the very concept of invention that subsequently comes to mean collecting "mere static, stock 'commonplaces,' stylized sources for discussion on all kinds of subject-matter." The topics, says Grimaldi, have "lost the vital, dynamic character given to them by Aristotle, a character extremely fruitful for intelligent, mature discussion of the innumerable significant problems which face man" (116).

And this is where I would like to tighten the noose, a little bit. My concern with my students' commodification of language is not just that I dislike the passive voice or prefer detail to generality. My concern is that the epistemology that underwrites such language use has two other, important extensions: the agent must disappear as material being in the name of "fairness," and the political cannot be discussed at all. These together represent a drastic disfiguring of Aristotelian rhetoric, which was concerned with "matters within our power and of consequence to us." According to Grimaldi, when Aristotle conceived of invention as a way of deriving proofs, he thought that "*pathos, ethos* and reason [were] intimately united in *praxis*. In rhetoric which prepares for *praxis* we should expect to find them closely united" (148). In other words, reason alone would hardly be sufficient for persuasion.

In a reified world of commodity exchange, however, *ethos* and *pathos* can only exist as weaknesses in argument; they allow for bias, agenda, and motivation. In short, you cannot get to the "there" of persuasion from the "here" of desire. Any quick turn around the grounds of Enlightenment thinkers will confirm my point. In an often quoted passage, Locke "confesses" that "besides order and clearness" rhetoric has nothing to offer but to "insinuate wrong ideas, move the passions, and thereby mislead the judgment" (3.10.34). Certainly, Locke's view of the world is a divided one: truth exists in one place—language describes it, if possible, somewhere else. His essentially dualistic concept of language itself tells us much of the Enlightenment story. "Civil" language concerns communication of "thoughts and ideas by words, as may serve for the upholding of common conversation and commerce." And contrarily, "philosophical use of words may serve to convey the *precise* notion of things, and to express, in general proposition, *certain and undoubted truths*, which the mind may rest on" (Locke 3.9.3; emphasis added). This is Fox News in a nutshell: "fair and unbiased" taking the place of "certain and undoubted." And, if you want to see how this sleight of hand was achieved, then we only have to look to Kant's "purely rational will . . . which cannot be called 'good' because by definition it cannot err" (Coleman 41). Rationality, in this rarefied air, will become the foundation for morality, for fairness. In Kant, even taste is "universalizable," hooked as it is into an epistemology that equates "nature" with "the harmony of reason," another balancing act. In fact, as Jim Berlin also noted, "Kant's insertion of the aesthetic in place of the rhetorical was quite self-conscious on his part, since Kant, never guilty of democratic sympathies, was extremely distrustful of public discourse as a means for resolving political questions" (55).

We should not be surprised at all to see that rhetoric's fault—for Locke, Descartes, Kant, and others—is that it relies on "artificial" language, language not "clear and distinct," language in which tropes and figures can turn one's head from the truth that reason dictates. To follow Enlightenment theories, then, is to fall back on the transparent word: reasonable language is such because its referent is clearly obvious, observable, "there." Reason is accessible "by nature" as long as we do not use language that smacks in any way of personal contamination, of attitude, of prior interest, or of ideology. I see the same epistemology when Fox claims to be "consistently unbiased" and when critical thinking is described as "clear," "orderly," or "fair-minded."

Now comes the "so what" question. What indeed is wrong with this picture?

If I have learned anything about rhetorics, it is that specific rhetorical theories appear to hold sway in response to particular circumstances, and are designed to achieve particular, specific intellectual ends. So what ends does a critical thinking pedagogy rooted in Enlightenment epistemology serve? What historical moment have these ways of thinking about argument and proof and reason and truth been conjured to meet? It seems to me that Critical Thinking courses really began to blossom, to become instrumental pieces of "core" curricula, to be taught in high schools as preparation for college entrance—it seems to me that all of this really began to occur at roughly the same time our colleges and universities were swelling with what we fondly refer to as a more "multicultural" student population. This is a subject I have not seen seriously examined before, one that seems to beg for attention. But, if my initial investigations prove reliable, then there is an interesting story here.

Imagine, if you cannot remember, the near-panic that visited most all higher education when faculty were seemingly "all of a sudden" being asked to "explain" how their curricula met new institutional standards for "diversity" or "pluralism." In the department where I worked at that time, I was sent a revolving letter onto which I was asked to add my particular contributions to this end. "I've begun teaching more non-Western writers," I remember one of my literature colleagues having scribbled. "I'm certainly doing 'Letter from a Birmingham Jail'" one compositionist wrote, "but I'm also including something from Nancy Mairs this term." There was quite a bit more, mostly in the same vein. I passed the list on without adding anything. I could not really out-ante anyone. What could I say? "I'll see your gay Asian writer and raise you a South American and a recently revitalized Hungarian?"

But perhaps, and this really is supposition at this point, these proliferating "learning to learn" courses really did appear to meet these new and different student populations. "Welcome to the university," this curriculum would then seem to say. "We're happy you're here; we value your unique contributions to our community. But first you need to learn a couple quick lessons about how we do our business here in academia, starting with what counts as knowledge, what counts as evidence, what constitutes a valid argument. You must be fair and balanced in these matters, consistently unbiased, because that's what knowledge is."

Fifteen years ago, Henry Giroux, among many others, complained about what he called a "culture of positivism" that based all claims to knowledge on a "technical rationality." "By rationality," Giroux explained, "I mean a specific set of assumptions and social practices that mediate how an individual or group relates to the wider society. Underlying any one mode of rationality is a set of interests that define and qualify how one reflects on the world" (Giroux 324).

I am wondering whose interests are being served by theories of argument whose initiating gesture is to efface, neutralize, and depoliticize those who use them? When I was an undergraduate, I was amused by my school's constant, pleading admonition not to "politicize" the university. Administrators said such things with a straight face, even though we were all at the same "state-subsidized" institution, governed by a "state" system of higher education. I see the same thinking bouncing off the airwaves all around me today. I see the same thinking when my students complain that the writer I have asked them to read is "biased," because she "didn't give the other side." When they do not like the writer's conclusions, they say, "well, statistics can show anything. And if we take away all the statistics, we're only left with the author's opinion, and we don't have to pay attention to opinion because it's one-sided." I find these attitudes pervasive and disheartening, but it is really not their fault.

My contention is that the Enlightenment model of language they have been taught to use is woefully simplistic, assuming, as it must, that language is essentially "identified," or "found," in the world (if only the world of the mind)—an effect of the severed subject "seeing"—ideologically neutral. I am reminded here of Voloshinov's comment that "[a]n experience of which an individual is conscious is already ideological and, therefore, from a scientific point of view, can in no way be a primary and irreducible datum: rather, it is an entity that has already undergone ideological processing of some specific kind" (87).

In this way of thinking, there are not any neutral subjects. So identifying oneself as subject implies a cathexis of context. Or, as Vygotsky says,

> Thought development is determined by language, i.e., by the linguistic tools of thought and by the sociocultural experience of the child. The development of logic in the child, as Piaget's studies have shown, is a direct function of his socializing speech. The child's intellectual growth is contingent on his mastering the social means of thought, that is language. (51)

If language is the "social means" of thought, and "thought development" is determined by language, then what thought is not social? I stress these points because I believe that to truly offer students experience in critically negotiating their experience, we ought to dispense with notions of "un-ideological" people, of "un-situated" consciousness, of the privileging that tells one and all that being "critical" means concentrating on finding objective arguments.

I like the way Ernesto Grassi positions this discussion:

> The defects of rationalistic, critical philosophy are much more important than they appear at first sight. By failing to take into account political faculties and the art of eloquence, this philosophy disregards two of the most important branches of human activity. The one-sided concern about truth misses the preparation for recognizing individual cases, and it ignores the necessity for political education. (40)

I would argue, along with Grassi, that preparing for individual cases and recognizing the necessity of political education are essential, inseparable elements of a rhetoric that concerns itself with human interaction. And I would further maintain that such a rhetoric is indeed vital to any conceptualization of argument that views individuals as an active force in their world. What I have wanted to do here was to suggest how the best intentioned of teachers often reinforce epistemologies they would be hard pressed to accept at face value—how the messages we give our students about argument are often predicated on a Western metaphysical dualism that implicitly proscribes and delimits the kinds of thinking we accredit or accept as valid. From such positions, students effect their own erasure of the "political" from their thinking under the guise of being "critically" aware. They have, then, no access to matter "of consequence" to them except in a judging capacity, after the fact. From such a position, we could hardly expect our students to take us seriously when we utter platitudes about empowering their thinking.

Works Cited

Berlin, James. *Rhetorics, Poetics, and Cultures: Refiguring College English*. Urbana, IL: NCTE, 1996.

Coleman, Francis X. J. *The Harmony of Reason: A Study in Kant's Aesthetics*. Pittsburgh, PA: U of Pittsburgh P, 1974.

Giroux, Henry. "Critical Theory and Rationality in Citizenship Education." *The Hidden Curriculum and Moral Education*. Ed. Henry Giroux and David Purpel. Berkeley: McCutchan, 1983.

Grassi, Ernesto. *Rhetoric as Philosophy*. University Park, PA: Pennsylvania State UP, 1980.

Grimaldi, William M. A., S.J. *Aristotle, Rhetoric I: A Commentary*. New York: Fordham UP, 1980

hooks, bell. "Eros, Eroticism, and the Pedagogical Process." *Beyond Borders: Pedagogy and the Politics of Cultural Studies*. Ed. Henry A. Giroux and Peter McLaren. New York: Routledge, 1994.

Locke, John. *An Essay Concerning Human Understanding*. Ed. Alexander Fraser. Vol. 2. Oxford: Clarendon, 1984.

McLaren, Peter. "Schooling the Postmodern Body: Critical Pedagogy and the Politics of Enfleshment." *Postmodernism, Feminism, and Cultural Politics*. Ed. Henry A. Giroux. Albany: State U of New York P, 1991.

Ong, Walter J. *Ramus: Method, and the Decay of Dialogue*. Cambridge: Harvard UP, 1958.

Swanson-Owens, Deborah. "Learning to 'Invent the University': A Case Study of Students Acquiring Discourse Structure Knowledge in Two Freshman Composition Classes." Diss. Stanford U, 1993. *DAI* 54 (1994): 1662A.

Voloshinov, V. N. *Freudianism: A Critical Sketch*. Trans. I. R. Titunik. Ed. Neal H. Bruss. Bloomington: Indiana UP, 1976.

Vygotsky, Lev. *Thought and Language*. Ed. and trans. Eugenia Hanfmann and Gertrude Vakar. Cambridge: MIT P, 1962.

DAVID C. PLOTKIN
University of California, Irvine

Nourishing Equality, Converting Difference: Matthew Arnold and the Rhetoric of Popular Education

This chapter will discuss the rhetorical context out of which Matthew Arnold's notion of "culture" developed, in particular the cultural rhetoric of popular education in nineteenth-century Britain, including Arnold's adaptation of the idea of education as a "civilizing mission" and its link to the evangelical drive to convert. However, because this chapter is part of a larger work-in-process, I want to start by tracing two points of departure for that larger project.

First, the rhetoric of popular education in the nineteenth century has a genealogical relation to current debates about culture, literacy, and community. Current discussions concerning the need in a democracy for a common culture, envisioned by many on the cultural right as a shared body of knowledge, are indebted in particular to Arnold's definitions of culture. This perceived need for a common American culture has been, and still is, translated into the educational goals of transmitting core elements of Western civilization, focusing on the "traditional" information of "our" culture. Thus William Bennett, in his 1984 National Endowment for the Humanities report *To Reclaim a Legacy*, uses Arnold's phrase "the best which has been thought and said in the world" to define a conservative vision of education in the humanities (3). Arnold is a natural reference in debates about the need for a common culture. His arguments that his version of culture will address "the beginnings of confusion" in a divided British society through some "sound order and authority" (*Culture* 144) are analogous to arguments that see a traditional core curriculum as the necessary response to the supposed balkanization or "cultural fragmentation" of American society (Hirsch 21). However, references to Arnold in current debates, both from the cultural left and the right, tend to forget the conflicted nature of Arnold's yearnings, and more importantly, the historical and rhetorical context out of which Arnold wrote. Current anxieties about cultural fragmentation and objections to multiculturalism are responses to the legacies of imperialism, including globalization and the hybrid nature of American culture and identity. In turn, Arnold, in both his advocacy of popular education as Her Majesty's Inspector of Schools and his criticisms of middle-class philistinism, adopted the vocabulary of Britain's imperial mission to justify the need for culture. Thus, Arnold's nineteenth-century anxieties and the current anxieties of the cultural right are not simply analogous, but they are reactions to the effects of imperialism, an historical process that postcolonial critics such as Edward Said have demonstrated continues even after "decolonization ha[s] set in motion the dismantling of the classical empires" (Said 280).

This brings me to the second consideration informing my work on Arnold: the tropes, narratives, and arguments used to represent the need for popular education (i.e., the cultural rhetoric of popular education) must be seen in relation to the larger frame of an imperialist ideology. One component of that ideology contrasts English or European superiority with the inferiority of colonized peoples (e.g., through the opposition of civilization vs. savagery), justifying British expansion and control. This ideology assumes a homogeneous "home" culture, and one key contradiction in it that became a source of anxiety and debate, at least for middle-class writers and readers considering the topic of education and the poor, is the presence of a large working-class and pauper population inside England. This population was often represented with the same vocabulary used to describe colonial peoples outside England. For instance, Thomas Macaulay, arguing in favor of popular education in an 1847 speech in the House of Commons, claimed that it is the "duty of the State to provide means of education for the common people." Without this education, anarchy will ensue, caused by "the ignorance of a population which [has] been suffered, in the neighbourhood of palaces, theatres, temples, to grow up as rude and stupid as any tribe of tattooed cannibals in New Zealand" (302, 304). Arnold's ideal of culture, derived in part from debates concerning popular education, is intended to provide a kind of homogeneity, of perfectly integrated and harmonious individuals as reflections of an integrated and harmonious society. This ideal is a response to anxieties about radical heterogeneity in British society, figured by many middle-class rhetors as savage otherness.

I will discuss two key examples of Arnold's indebtedness to debates over popular education that show his concerns about converting difference: (1) the view that popular education was a necessary civilizing process; and (2) Arnold's secular use of "conversion," with conversion being a significant idea in British evangelical Christianity and a common topic in nineteenth-century discussions both of the working classes and of colonial subjects. In both these examples, Arnold views heterogeneous elements in British society as a threat to social harmony and he represents these elements in terms that implicitly and explicitly allude to concerns about the savage poor.

In 1852, Matthew Arnold, in his role as an inspector for the Education Department, wrote that there was "an utter disproportion between the great amount of positive information and the low degree of mental culture" exhibited by the pupil-teachers, or apprenticed teachers, he examined and that "too little attention has hitherto been paid to this side of education; the side through which it chiefly forms the character" (*Reports* 19-20). This report was written fifteen years before he published "Culture and Its Enemies," the first in the series of articles that would eventually form *Culture and Anarchy*. Already, though, Arnold was formulating his notion of culture, an inward mental attribute contributing to the character of the individual, but cultivated through the State—in this case provided by a state-supported school. The formation of character that Arnold advocated in this report involved developing working-class and lower middle-class pupil-teachers in order to "cultivate" and "humanize" them, implying their lack of culture or even humanity. Education has the great effect, as Arnold wrote to his wife early in his career as an inspector, of "civilizing the next generation of the lower classes, who as things are going, will have most of the political power of the country in their hands" (*Letters* 20). Early on, Arnold considered the role that popular education could play in a growing democracy: the masses needed to be civilized, even made human, in order to enable social and political order.

The strength of Arnold's beliefs about popular education are best exemplified by his role in the controversy surrounding the Revised Code of 1862. His contribution to this debate shows his indebtedness to an established educational discourse that provided a paradigm within which he worked. The Revised Code was first introduced in July 1861 by Robert Lowe, the vice president of the Committee of Council for Education. It was intended to answer criticisms of elementary schooling raised by the Newcastle Commission, first convened in 1858, regarding a perceived lack in the basic skills of younger children. Lowe proposed sweeping changes in the way funds were allocated to schools; rather than depend on attendance records and an inspector's report on the general quality of a school, payment would depend on the examination of every student by the inspector in very basic skills. To Arnold and other opponents of Lowe's changes, the Revised Code would encourage "cramming" for the exam, would impose an impossible burden on inspectors, and most significantly would damage the "vital connexion" of the government to teachers and pupils, making that connection wholly mechanical (*Complete Prose* 234).

Arnold criticized the Revised Code in letters-to-the-editor and articles, the most important being "The Twice-Revised Code," published in March 1862. He draws his readers' attention to the fact—despite Lowe's protestations in parliament that religion and moral instruction would not be ignored—that the very act of overemphasizing basic skills leads away from religious and moral instruction and their civilizing effect. Arnold turns the tables on the claim for basic skills, because it is exactly the laboring classes' lack of "civilization" and discipline that impedes literacy.

Poor children are not able to read with intelligence, but not because teachers do not pay enough attention to basics. Arnold wrote that children do not attain literacy because of "the general want of civilization in themselves and in those among whom they pass their lives" (*Complete Prose* 223). According to Arnold, the State "has an interest in [schools] so far as they keep children out of the streets, so far as they teach them—the dull as well as the clever—an orderly, decent, and human behaviour; so far as they civilize the neighbourhood where they are placed" (*Complete Prose* 228). Education, as far as the state is concerned, is responsible for the general character of the student, particularly in promoting "orderly" and "human" behavior and "civilizing" slums. We see already Arnold's decision to pit "culture" against "anarchy" in these arguments marshaled against the Revised Code.

Arnold's notion of the civilizing function of education was in dialogue with an ongoing rhetoric of popular education. Arnold circulated his arguments about the Revised Code to members of parliament, who used the civilizing function of education to attack the Revised Code. However, it is clear in reading the parliamentary debates and indeed the history of education since the British state began funding schools, that this argument was familiar to politicians and educational reformers. As Arnold himself tells us, his article on the Revised Code is truly a revision of an argument already presented in an open letter by Sir James Kay-Shuttleworth to one of the framers of the code. Kay-Shuttleworth's letter itself depends on his long-standing advocacy of education as a means for civilizing the savage poor. As J. Dover Wilson claims, Kay-Shuttleworth "regarded elementary education as missionary work on behalf of civilization, and the inspectors he sent out as apostles of culture" (xii).

This evangelical notion that education will have a civilizing effect on the lower orders permeated much of the discourse of popular education. "Civilizing" stands in for a range of ideological representations of the poor, including rhetoric that could easily come from the colonial missionary. Certainly in Kay-Shuttleworth's "Letter" on which Arnold based his attack on the Revised Code, we read of the "wild, untamed barbarism" of children who resist the "graft[ing] on [of] civilization." Education must get rid of the "brutish incapacity to learn, gross habits, heathenism and barbarism," as well as the "semi-barbarism of children from coarse, sensual homes" (Kay-Shuttleworth 585). The rationale that education functioned to "civilize" heathens, and that this was especially necessary for an imperial nation, animated much of Kay-Shuttleworth's thought on education and certainly influenced his development of policy as the first administrative head of the Education Department.

It is important to note that Kay-Shuttleworth was not a marginal figure in English education. Arnold himself claimed that state funding of education in England was due "almost entirely to the zeal and perseverance of one man, Sir James Shuttleworth," and Kay-Shuttleworth was invoked repeatedly in the parliamentary debates as an authority (*Complete Prose* 233). Although Kay-Shuttleworth was a crucial figure in educational discourse, the idea that the poor needed to be converted was a common one: thus, missions for the poor became more widespread in urban England in the 1840s and 1850s. When Arnold talks in his "Twice-revised Code" about civilizing neighborhoods, or in *Culture and Anarchy* about class equality encouraged by "apostles of culture," we hear the echo of an anxiety about heterogeneity and radical difference; about the fear of wild, untamed barbarism; about heathenism; and about brutish ignorance in need of conversion (*Culture* 70).

Conversion does indeed figure importantly, though ironically, in Arnold's *Culture and Anarchy*. It is not the lower orders who are in need of conversion in that work, but rather the middle class, which was comprised mainly of Dissenting Protestants or evangelical Anglicans. Thus, Arnold adopted the language of evangelical Christianity as a double strategy: it is the currency of those he hopes to persuade, a recognizable discourse to all of his readers, including middle-class Philistines. In that sense, culture is legitimated as religion and by religion, for in its aims "religion comes to a conclusion identical with that which culture . . . likewise reaches" (*Culture* 47). Arnold's talk of culture as a means to convert middle-class Philistines appropriates the very rhetoric of conversion that many from the middle classes aimed at the poor as colonial other. Arnold then uses a shared point of reference as a means of persuasion and provocation: culture, like popular education, is a kind of missionary work that should ideally mold and shape the soul. At the same time, adapting the rhetoric of religion and conversion also serves to deflate the self-satisfaction of the English middle class, using their own strategies against them.

The dissemination of culture through the state connects individual and community in a harmonious relation that, for Arnold, is almost mystical at times. Arnold's concern with the individual's development is expressed in eschatological terms. In critiquing the middle-class tendency toward a rigidly earnest focus on moral rectitude, he claimed that they "fail to follow the true way of salvation" (*Culture* 11). True, in this passage, Arnold is mimicking the language of those he takes to task, but he is only partly ironic in this usage. For bringing the narrow-minded and one-sided philistine to harmonious perfection is a matter of "conversion" in which culture will "work on them inwardly and cure their spirit. Ousted they will not be, but transformed" (*Culture* 37).

To sum up Arnold's claims about conversion in *Culture and Anarchy*: the middle-class Philistine needs to be converted from a narrow provincial view to one that is more balanced and integrated into the life of the nation. This conversion can take place through the power and authority of the state. The idea of personal liberty that characterizes British liberal thought must be constrained by a common "principle of authority," one that rises above class and faction. This principle is embodied in the state as bearer of culture and of the best self (*Culture* 82). This integration through the best self will promote social harmony because dissent will be erased through sweetness, or beauty, and light, or reason. The need to convert the middle classes is based, at least in part, on anxieties about portions of society that resist integration, which are so different, or are thought to be so different, that they make harmony impossible. Arnold thus appeals to middle-class fears of the lower classes and their supposed savagery to convince them that they themselves are in need of conversion. Arnold focuses on the middle classes because he believes that they must provide a model of balanced thought and behavior for the lower classes. However, he also justifies the need to educate the middle classes because he worries about their inner character and its vulnerability to contagion.

Arnold felt that, in a vital and harmonious society, an educated and cultured middle class would be a model for the lower classes. Thus, if the lower orders had contact with, or the opportunity to emulate, the middle classes, then this would be salutary. Arnold wrote in the preface to *The Popular Education of France* that the principal danger of a middle class without culture is not simply their narrow, provincial, and factious views, but rather that the middle class will fail "to mould or assimilate the masses below them." The working class's "natural educators and initiators are those immediately above them, the middle classes. If these classes cannot win their sympathy or give them their direction society is in danger of falling into anarchy" (*Complete Prose* 26). The failure of the middle classes to "assimilate the masses below them" results from their "narrow, harsh, unintelligent and unattractive spirit and culture" (*Complete Prose* 26), which also prevents the nation as a whole community from embracing an expansive equality and a noble and grand style that characterizes a great, democratic nation. The lower classes need to be educated and molded by the middle class, but only a middle class that itself is properly cultivated and refined.

The contact between classes that Arnold believes will lead to the assimilation of the lower orders works in two ways. If culture can spread, then so can anarchy. The danger to the middle classes, which requires them to embrace culture, comes not only from their failure to shape the lower classes. They themselves are in danger from the "populace" (as Arnold names the lower classes) within them, within their character. He claims that under all class divisions there "is a common basis of human nature, therefore, in every one of us . . . there exists, sometimes only in germ and potentially, sometimes more or less developed, the same tendencies and passions which have made our fellow-citizens of other classes what they are" (*Culture* 106). Whereas this may lead to tolerance and sympathy between classes, it also means that we all have the tendencies of other classes in us and if the middle classes are not careful they may grow into the populace. Arnold describes in detail the temptations of this part of "our" character:

> Every time that we snatch up a vehement opinion in ignorance and passion, every time that we long to crush an adversary by sheer violence, every time that we are envious, every time that we are brutal, every time that we adore mere power or success, every time that we add our voice to swell a blind clamour against some unpopular per-

sonage, every time that we trample *savagely* on the fallen—he has found in his bosom the eternal spirit of the Populace, and that there needs only a little help from circumstances to make it triumph in him *untameably.*" (*Culture* 107; emphasis added)

The brutal, violent, ignorant, savage, and untameable populace resides within us, Arnold told his readers, and we must reject that evil part of ourselves. The middle classes feared the possibility that the poor constituted a colonized population in the heart of the nation. The perceived need for a homogeneous and harmonious society, a cohesive center, became more pressing in the nineteenth century, as travel, commerce, and contact with the periphery of the empire became more common. Arnold takes this anxiety further: not only must his audience worry about social heterogeneity and divisiveness, but without an internal conversion through culture, individual subjects risk carrying that social heterogeneity within them as a kind of spiritual failing. Arnold's notion of culture is thus framed on the one hand by the civilizing mission of popular education and on the other by the spiritual mission of evangelical religion, both adopting and contributing to the vocabulary of England's imperial mission.

Ultimately, Arnoldian culture is animated as much by the consequences of its failure as it is by the hope of its achievement. Although Arnold yearned for an ideal of social harmony (which he recognized as an ideal), one senses that he feared much more a cultural apostasy that would lead to a fractured national identity. He expressed, as many of his contemporaries expressed, what Homi Bhabha calls the "*unheimlich* terror of the space or race of the Other" within the nation (2). This terror is constitutive of the imperial experience and continues to plague current debates over the role of education in the conservation, on the right hand, or the re-creation, on the left, of community. Hence William Bennett's overwrought fear in *To Reclaim a Legacy* that students will become "aliens in their own culture, strangers in their own land" if they are not "shareholders" in "civilization" (30, 4) is a legacy of "our" tradition it were best we not reclaim.

Works Cited

Arnold, Matthew. *The Complete Prose Works of Matthew Arnold*. Ed. R. H. Super. Vol. 2. Ann Arbor: U of Michigan P, 1962.

—. *Culture and Anarchy*. Ed. J. Dover Wilson. Cambridge: Cambridge UP, 1960.

—. *Letters of Matthew Arnold*. Ed. George W. E. Russell. 2 vols. London: Macmillan, 1896.

—. *Reports on Elementary Schools, 1852-1882*. Ed. Sir Francis Sandford. London: Macmillan, 1889.

Bennett, William J. *To Reclaim a Legacy*. Washington: National Endowment for the Humanities, 1984.

Bhaba, Homi K. "Introduction: Narrating the Nation." *Nation and Narration*. Ed. Homi K. Bhaba. London: Routledge, 1990.

Hirsch, E. D., Jr. *Cultural Literacy: What Every American Needs to Know*. New York: Vintage-Random, 1988.
Kay-Shuttleworth, Sir James. *Four Periods of Education*. London: Longman, 1862.
Macaulay, Thomas Babington. *Speeches by Lord Macaulay, with his Minute on Indian Education*. Ed. G. M. Young. London: Oxford UP, 1952.
Said, Edward W. *Culture and Imperialism*. New York: Vintage-Random, 1994.
Wilson, J. Dover. Introduction. *Culture and Anarchy*. By Matthew Arnold. Cambridge: Cambridge UP, 1960. xi-xl.

ROLF NORGAARD
University of Colorado, Boulder

The Rhetoric of Civility and the Fate of Argument

On this much the pundits agree: today's social and political discourse has deteriorated to levels of discord that extend beyond rudeness to acts of intolerance and disrespect. Deborah Tannen speaks of the pervasive antagonistic atmosphere that infects public discourse. Likewise, Yale University law professor Stephen Carter argues that civility is disintegrating because we have forgotten the obligations we owe to each other, and are awash instead in a sea of self-indulgence. Clearly, the sin of incivility has risen to the top of our national consciousness, even if our behavior does not bear that out.

Universities, among them my own, are themselves calling for civility. Little wonder, for the *Chronicle of Higher Education* reports that "insubordination and intimidation signal the end of decorum in many classrooms" (Schneider). Mean-spirited faculty meetings add fuel to appeals that we replace debate with dialogue, rancor with civility.

Who among us would argue against civility? Yet I submit we must argue with civility, in the multiple senses of that phrase. We need to question the term, the conceptual schemes in which we place it, and the rhetoric by which we deploy it. Absent that self-reflection, I maintain that well-meaning appeals to civility will remain ineffectual—or worse, become counterproductive—because the ways in which we talk about civility bear all the traces of our misunderstandings of argument.

This problem has been brought home to me at my own institution, the University of Colorado, Boulder, where in spring 1996 the chancellor appointed a Task Force on Civility and Campus Community. The task force was asked to respond to and heal a climate of incivility brought on by a divisive faculty insurrection against our university president that led to her resignation in 1995, and by racially charged incidents involving students. Linking civil conduct to what it saw as the fundamental mission of the university, inquiry, the task force released a statement (Byyny) that can serve as a springboard for exploring various dimensions of the rhetoric of civility. Like the new rhetoric of civility we witness in the media, that campus statement reenacts the very tensions and misunderstandings it seeks to cure.

To make good on my claim, I will be examining how we situate or frame civility in our conceptual schemes. I will also consider how civility bears on central concerns of the university: argument and inquiry. Throughout, I will be exploring both how the "evils of argument" have, ironically, found a new home in civility, and how the new rhetoric of civility might therefore shape the fate of argument by perpetuating precisely the misunderstandings civility is meant to cure. I will close by briefly exploring what a rhetorical approach to civility might hold for our teaching.

Books by Tannen and Carter, whatever their other virtues, are only the most recent to ignore the rhetorical dimensions of civility. If and when discussion of the concept extends beyond decorum, manners, and etiquette (Carter's focus), or beyond a critique of pugnacious cultural attitudes (Tannen's focus), it generally takes off in the direction of political philosophy. And yet, civility—and especially the rhetoric of civility—touches on the core concerns of our field.

The very term reminds us of rhetoric's roots in the *polis* and the role of the citizen. But even as technology and mass communication make possible a global village that forces us to reconsider the notion of a *polis*, the powerful and troubled connection between rhetoric and civility, for all its permutations, endures. Indeed, given those new technologies, and our now multiple arenas of citizenship and action, the rhetoric of civility requires of us all a heightened level of self-reflection—one that is missing in today's appeals.

As rhetoricians, we recognize that instances of civility and incivility are closely related to epideictic discourse, the language of praise or blame. In turn, when civility becomes itself the subject of discourse, as is so prevalent in the new rhetoric of civility, we have what we might call epideictic about epideictic. Rarely tame or innocuous in its own right, "epideictic squared" forces us to take special note of the veiled arguments that are always at work in this genre.

Not only does the epideictic rhetoric of civility carry argumentative force, that rhetoric also alerts us to the many ways civility regulates discourse. As Donovan Ochs has observed, "Community values, ideologies, networks of interpretation, criteria for admission and exclusion, unquestioned ethical yardsticks against which one's behavior is measured—all these are now in play when epideictic is deployed" (2). As a social—and socializing—network of symbolic action and interpretation, civility delimits and shapes rhetoric, even as rhetoric constructs civility.

Given that incivility is now the latest sin du jour, I would like to offer, herewith, the seven sins of unexamined civility. In each instance, the sin can be traced to, and thus perpetuates, a common misunderstanding of argument. (I will ignore, for now, where in the various circles of hell we might place these transgressions.)

Sin 1: Ignoring Context

Reading the campus statement as a barometer of larger rhetorical practice, we find that the concept of civility has been largely decontextualized.

The statement offers no mention of a range of possible contexts, from the private to the public, from the student dorm to the professor's classroom, to the far more contentious fountain area near our student union. Nor do we find much awareness of how those contexts might overlap or compete. A similar disregard for rhetorical context pervades media homilies on civility, and even the books by Tannen and Carter, who mingle examples from a variety of contexts. Sensitivity to context is crucial because most instances of incivility occur at "thresholds" between contexts or forums, or when audiences "frame" discourse in competing ways, given their various interpretations of one context.

In decontextualizing its project, the new rhetoric of civility trades on equally decontextualized—and impoverished—notions of inquiry and argument. Inquiry is reified to a debate about ideas as abstract propositions (where real people and real communication do not get in the way). Likewise, argument is reduced to a crossfire of opposing views unmoored from matters of audience and exigence. Even as we try to reclaim argument from these misunderstandings (Crosswhite), the appeal to civility merely perpetuates them in a different guise.

Sin 2: Ignoring How Publics Form and Issues Coalesce

In an effort to redress the wrongs done to specific groups, the campus statement, like much of the new rhetoric of civility, elevates "community" to an ideal, often pairing it with "civility." And so, our rhetoric about civility vacillates between two extremes: "community" becomes at once a homogeneous, static, abstract ideal, and an amalgam of distinct groups with special interests. Our rhetoric thus ignores how both civility and community take on different forms for different issues and for different publics. More generally, the new rhetoric of civility fails to account for how "communities" overlap, form, change, divide, and experience internal inconsistencies. Consider a case in point: trading immediate exigence and impact for an inconsequential bureaucratic permanence, the University of Colorado pronouncement ignores the very genesis of the civility issue on campus (specific acts against students, the presidential affair). Instead, the document, like the media's coverage of civility, trades on nostalgia. It offers a Jeremiad, with its narrative logic of decline and redemption.

And so, today's appeal to civility runs the risk of ignoring how publics form and issues coalesce. Misconceptions of argument and inquiry sprout from the same seed. Obsessed with competing claims, we often fail to reflect on how we formulate questions at issue, and on whom we are talking to, and why. The new rhetoric of civility can ill afford to repeat those errors.

Sin 3: Confusing Representations of Self

The new rhetoric of civility easily confuses different ways of representing ourselves to others. For example, the campus statement speaks of the roles or personae we adopt in an inherently public environment even as it asserts we are "neighbors" and "friends," with the campus community existing largely as a collection of private selves. As a result, the new rhetoric of civility muddles distinctions between public and private, the masked and the unmasked. And yet, the very incivility the document means to cure often arises out of precisely such muddles between public and private.

The same muddle between public and private plagues our sense of argument and our conceptions of inquiry. How many times have we found our own students retreating into private assertion ("It's just my opinion") precisely when they need to give a more public accounting of their views. Likewise, we muddle our conception of inquiry when we fail to distinguish between—and, in so doing, bridge—private discovery and public justification (Crosswhite). The new rhetoric of civility thus runs the risk of repeating the confusions to which civility is meant to be a cure.

Sin 4: Reducing Discursive Interaction to Monologue

To whom do we refer when we speak of incivility? The offender. And where do we locate that sin? In the rude, disrespectful person. Two problems follow. We reduce civility to behavior, decorum, and good manners—the need to be "nice." Moreover, we reduce civility to the "person," ignoring the complex social and discursive interactions in which we find ourselves. How do we get out of the "niceness" trap and the "person" trap? By questioning precisely what the new rhetoric of civility takes to be transparent: the offender and the offense.

In so doing, we begin to uncover the complex social and rhetorical dimensions of civility. Incivility involves complex ethical interactions between the offender and the offended. How do we come to occupy those roles? Who gets to name "incivility"? (There are complex speech acts and strategic purposes having to do with that naming.) What are the cultural assumptions that help regulate our interactions? And what are the complex issues of power and standing that constrain those interactions? Who is the outsider, and who is the insider? Who is disenfranchised, and who is enfranchised? Who is the novice, and who is the expert?

The new rhetoric of civility tends to paint argument and disagreement as merely agonistic and aggressive. In turn, appeals to "dialogue" as the cure (Tannen) easily reinforce those misunderstandings. In the process, the new rhetoric of civility offers, ironically, a new home to misunderstandings about argument. For example, the campus document focuses almost exclusively on acts of speakers, and has little to say about listeners and the ethics of listening.

The practice of deliberation and discernment (listening) is not seen to bear on the practice of forwarding beliefs in argument (speaking), despite the admonition offered by Heraclitus: "Not knowing how to listen, neither can they speak." And so, although the document rues the loss of conversation and dialogue, the document characterizes civility in largely monologic and narcissistic terms.

Sin 5: Confusing the Aims of Civility

The new rhetoric of civility too easily assumes that we know why we have adopted the aim of civility and what the nature of our commitment is. There is actually a good deal of confusion on this score. The campus document simultaneously offers a negative definition, with civility as the absence or avoidance of "disrespectful behavior," and a positive, teleological definition, with civility as a means to "community" and "inquiry." Likewise, the document vacillates between two kinds of commitments: a minimal, negative commitment to civility, as to refrain from doing harm or offering offense; and an expansive, positive commitment to "embrace" or "share" diverse values and thoughts. The statement's mantra—"share" and "embrace"—ignores not just these confusions about aims, but the potentially coercive dimension of the project. "Sharing" and "embracing" can become problematic goals fraught with ideological agendas.

Replicated here are all the confusions about the aims of argument and the degree and nature of our commitment to it—problems addressed by James Crosswhite. Is argument merely instrumental, that is, a dubious means of persuasion and a questionable device to carry on conflict without coming to blows? Or, does argument constitute an opportunity for personal and intellectual growth and for the development of community? Misunderstandings and false binaries abound. Today's appeal to civility will remain ineffectual, even counterproductive, unless it reflects on the manner in which it positions and portrays argument.

Sin 6: Defining Civility in Normative Terms

Like the new rhetoric of civility, the campus document defines the virtue of civility in normative terms. Civility is "X," and we know what that "X" is either because the nature of the virtue is self-evident (to those who are "civilized"), or because we can identify the "X" of civility as being the opposite of some baneful, unwelcome "Y" (most often the villain is some debased notion of argument). By offering civility as a normative virtue, the campus document runs three risks. In its attempt to cure disrespectful behavior, it ignores the dangers of having civility slide into the other extreme: mousy compliance, often to what is politically correct. Moreover, the dyad civility/argument, into which most discussions of civility slide, makes the term susceptible to the very misconceptions of argument that it means to cure. Finally, a naive appeal to civility as a normative virtue leaves precious little room for judgment or practical wisdom (*phronesis*).

We may be far better off defining civility, in Aristotelian fashion, as a contextual virtue. Here, civility functions as a means between extremes. Just as courage is a means between cowardice and foolhardiness, so too can civility become a means between mousy compliance and disrespectful confrontation.

Why is this approach so rarely invoked? It robs university administrators, media pundits, and cultural critics of their most prized commodity: moral certitude. As a means between extremes, civility remains inherently unstable and contextual, and thus requires of us, above all, judgment. Discussions that ignore the role of *phronesis* not only impoverish our sense of civility but can also strip argument of its own most compelling virtue—its reliance on and cultivation of judgment, discernment, practical wisdom (Farrell). With respect to judgment, civility and its supposed evil twin, argument, ought to be fundamentally allies.

Sin 7: Ignoring Civility as a Process

The campus document seeks to establish a "norm" for civility and to set "boundaries" for behavior. The document even goes so far as to speak of "rules" and "sanctions." Yet this approach neglects the subtle, often invisible process of socialization and negotiation so essential to the development of norms in an ongoing system. It ignores, if you will, the hidden life of civility in the fabric of our daily interactions with others.

This failing is perhaps the most grievous of the seven sins. The new rhetoric of civility misunderstands the role of argument as a social and socializing process. In so doing, it dissuades the public from embracing and refining argument as a means to achieve civility. In seeking a cure to incivility, today's discussions have characterized argument as a disease, when its cultivation might actually offer the most efficacious cure.

Repentance

These seven sins of unexamined civility all point to an unrhetorical framing of the civility discussion. The problem to which the campus document is the answer does not lie at the level of abstract principle. Rather, the problem lies in the nitty-gritty of human, discursive interaction. And it is with rhetorical awareness and reflection at that level that we can best foster civility as we struggle to gain our bearings in what is now a global village.

We can repent for these sins by taking a more rhetorical, contextually sensitive, and interactional approach to civility. I am not suggesting that we teach civility directly. Nevertheless, bearing in mind the connection between civic education and language education (Stotsky), we might reflect on the ethical dimensions of argument and, in so doing, develop a more rhetorical and robust sense of civility. In turn, a more rhetorical approach to civility might help us get at and revise misleading popular notions of argument—notions that persist despite our current efforts in the classroom.

If we fail to redeem ourselves through rhetoric, we condemn ourselves to recycling platitudes about civility. And through those platitudes, the new rhetoric of civility will continue to perpetuate the very stereotypes about argument that, ironically, have led to today's call for civility.

Acknowledgments

This work was supported in part by the Center for the Humanities and the Arts at the University of Colorado, Boulder, and has been enriched by conversations in a seminar on civility with my colleagues James Nickel, Karen Tracy, Andrew Calabrese, Lumen Mulligen, Zala Volcic, John Petrovic, and Peter Hester.

Works Cited

Byyny, R. "Civility in the UCB Campus." [University of Colorado at Boulder] *Silver and Gold Record* 10 Apr. 1997: 2.

Carter, S. L. *Civility: Manners, Morals, and the Etiquette of Democracy*. New York: Basic, 1998.

Crosswhite, J. *The Rhetoric of Reason: Writing and the Attractions of Argument*. Madison: U of Wisconsin P, 1996.

Farrell, T. B. *Norms of Rhetorical Culture*. New Haven: Yale UP, 1993.

Ochs, D. J. "Epideictic, Ethos, and Educators." *Rhetoric, Cultural Studies, and Literacy*. Ed. J. F. Reynolds. Hillsdale, NJ: Lawrence Erlbaum, 1995. 1-9.

Schneider, A. "Insubordination and Intimidation Signal the End of Decorum in Many Classrooms." *Chronicle of Higher Education* 27 Mar. 1998: A12-A14.

Stotsky, S. *Connecting Civic Education and Language Education: The Contemporary Challenge*. New York: Teacher's College Press, 1991.

Tannen, Deborah. *The Argument Culture: Moving from Debate to Dialogue*. New York: Random, 1998.

Index

abolitionist 45, 157
Adorno, Theodor 200, 212
advertising 7, 103, 199
aesthetics 85
African American 9, 11, 12, 39, 41, 46
agency 97, 212, 231
agon, agonistic 88
American
    landscapes 183
    national identity 5, 42, 187, 239
    postwar overspecialization 215
American Indian Movement 148
American Missionary Association 42
Amistad 12, 39, 45
Anaxarchus 78
aoidoi 87
argument 32, 55, 233, 247, 249
Aristotle 55, 58, 67, 191, 223, 226
Arnold, Matthew 239
Asian American 9
Aspasia 155
assimilation 79, 122, 129, 136, 147
audience 10, 55, 86, 139, 189, 194, 204, 212, 249
    "suits" 201
author 57
autobiography 122
Bain, Alexander 130
Bakhtin, Mikhail 204
barbarians, barbarism 90, 175, 177
Bateson, Gregory 193

belles lettres 115
Bhaba, Homi 245
bilingual 7, 4, 9, 16
Blair, Hugh 117
boundary, boundaries 9, 16, 49
Burke, Kenneth 7, 58, 105, 183, 209
Chicano/a 9, 15
China, Chinese 10, 55, 155
cinema, film 57, 58
civic, civility 91, 183, 247
civil rights 8, 12
class 157, 240
classical Greece 56, 222, 226
colloquial 58
community 4, 10, 23, 178, 211, 248
    virtual 180, 183
compassion 65, 71
computer 9, 19, 23, 57
    in education 23, 30
    technologies 29, 57, 75
conduct manuals 161
confession 124
conversation 156, 160
conversion 42, 121, 240, 243
Corax 77
critical thinking 231, 236
cruelty 65, 71
culture, cultural 4, 88, 150, 222, 239
Currier and Ives 186
cybernetic, cyberspace 20, 24, 191
declamation 94, 99
deliberation 222, 226
delivery 57

democracy 24, 60, 221, 226
Democritus 78
demos 65
DeQuincey, Thomas 113
Descartes, René 176
dialectic 56, 209, 212
dialogue 88
discourse/discursive 10, 55, 101, 145, 194, 224
dissoi logoi 78
diversity 5, 7, 20
Douglass, Frederick 5, 32, 169
education 5, 84, 129, 158, 176, 239, 242
electronic media 20, 58, 83, 181
eleos (pity) 65
e-mail 58, 129
empowerment 15, 227
enthymeme 104
epic 67
epideictic 55, 103, 105, 248
essentialist 77, 101
ethics 59, 66
ethnography 7, 39, 46, 48, 147, 207
ethos 47, 55, 117, 165, 178, 191, 199, 201, 234
   cyberethos 191
   of scriptures 166
Ewok, utopian global village 6, 77, 129
face 58, 139
face-to-face/viva voce communication 58, 226
fascist 91
feminine 10
feminist 9, 31, 55, 163
figures 59
film 58
Frankfurt School 209
freedom 42
Fuller, Buckminster 7
Fuller, Margaret 163, 169

gender 10
genre 27, 145
global, global village 6, 8, 9, 17, 19, 48, 55, 75, 78, 103, 199, 207, 209
gossip 159
grammar 131, 156
Grimké, Sarah 32, 163
Habermas, Jurgen 224
Havelock, Eric 83
hegemony, hegemonic 65, 78, 86, 89
hermeneutics 27, 166
heuristic 76
Hispanic 5, 15
historical examples 56
history, historiography 4, 11, 39, 47, 222
Horkheimer, Max 200, 211
Hudson River School 184
Hume, David 65
imagination 113, 181
Indian/Native American 12, 147, 195
individualism 149, 178
information, information age 180, 193
Internet 6, 19, 24, 57, 129, 209, 224
intertextuality 87, 87
intuition 114
invention 113
Isocrates 83, 89
   logos politikos 84
judgment 67, 87, 113, 131
justice 42
kairos 77
katharsis 65
Kennedy, George 12, 27
Kinneavy, James 27, 31
Latino/a 5, 15
letter writing 160
listening 156, 160

Index

literacy, literate 12, 15, 56, 83, 130, 193, 241
logic, logical 55, 232
logography 86
logos 55, 234
Machiavelli 70
McLuhan, Marshall 7, 23, 204
media 190, 193
memory 56, 104
Mencius 55
message 76
metis/mixed blood 147
mimesis 68, 88
minorities 4, 9, 12, 28, 32
moral value 184
More, Hannah 155
motherhood 93, 157
multicultural 4, 9, 10, 78, 79, 130
myth, *mythos*, mythopoieic 86, 87
narrative 67, 184, 249
    epic 67
    logic 249
Nazi 90
oikos 104
oiktos 65
Ong, Walter 83, 139, 233
opinion 114
orality 5, 83, 117
oratory 12
Packard, Vance 201
Pan Chao 155
pathos 234
performance 89
Pericles 155, 221
persuasion 9, 10, 31, 55
    pity as 66
peyote religion 151, 195
phronesis 5
pistis, pisteis 31, 56, 165
pity 65
    in political rhetoric 69
    oratorical context of 67
    rhetoric of 67, 70
    theater of 67
polis 3, 49, 66, 106, 227, 248
    sacred 7, 28
politics 6, 31, 58, 121, 231
    and pity 66
power 76, 142, 157, 227
    vs. empowerment 227
presocratic 78
private 104
probable 114
proof, *pisteis* 56, 165
prose 86
public speaking 31, 56, 235
public sphere 48, 104, 122, 156, 163, 250
Pudentilla 93
puns 156
Quintilian 59, 65, 69
    Q Question 59
race, racism 12, 41, 150, 247
Ramus, Peter 59, 232, 233
reading 56, 160
receiver 76
religion 6, 8, 27, 31, 44, 55, 106, 132, 163, 189
    Anglicanism, Episcopalianism 165, 243
    evangelical Christianity 240
    Methodism 165
    Protestantism 163, 243
    Society of Friends 165
    transcendentalism 163, 168
    Unitarianism 165, 168
religious rhetoric 7, 27, 31, 165, 189
remedial 6, 16
Renaissance 12, 57, 175, 181, 204
rhetor 55, 194, 201
    "creatives" 201
rhetoric
    adversarial/nonadversarial 10
    aesthetics of 85
    Aztec 12

British 117
Chinese 141
Christian 27, 31
classical 7, 55, 104
deceptive 69, 200
epistemic 60
forensic 66, 233
inclusive 5, 33, 10
Native American 147
of human sciences 60
philosophy 27
political 32
public, social function 32, 113, 211, 225
race 9, 11, 15, 247
religion 8, 27, 31, 165
Roman 31, 68, 93
Scots 130
and technology 6, 27, 29, 55-61
women's and girls' 159
rhetorical
act 194, 212
culture 9, 12, 211, 222
education 68, 83, 89, 113, 129, 175, 239, 247
event 200, 211
knowledge 49, 210
theory 27, 56, 221
traditions 49
rights, human rights, civil rights 8, 12, 93, 41, 80, 170, 221
Rome, Roman 31, 93
Royal Society 114
salon culture 155, 157, 225
sender 76
separate spheres, cult of True Womanhood 157, 164, 170
Shakespeare 71

signs, semiotics 68, 103
silence 12, 101
Sinon 70
slavery 4, 12, 39, 41
Smith, Adam 65, 117
sophist, sophistic 77
Spanish 5, 12, 15
Sprat, Thomas 114
style 10, 115
subject, subjectivity 101
teaching 157
technology 19, 57, 178, 191, 216
television 57
temperance 125
tropes 59
   cultural 17
universals, universality 77, 79, 88
values
   ethical 66
   social 56
Vergil 71
vernacular 130
Vico, Giambattista 175, 181
virtual 19, 24, 206, 212
   communities 24
   landscapes 183
visual rhetoric 183
   lithography 186
   prints 186
   steel engraving 184
voice 10, 93
Washington Temperance Society 121
women 10, 32, 39, 46, 50, 93, 155, 163
   women's clubs 159
World Wide Web 19, 23, 58
writing 84

For Product Safety Concerns and Information please contact our EU
representative GPSR@taylorandfrancis.com
Taylor & Francis Verlag GmbH, Kaufingerstraße 24, 80331 München, Germany

www.ingramcontent.com/pod-product-compliance
Lightning Source LLC
Chambersburg PA
CBHW051518230426
43668CB00012B/1658